EXAMINING RELIGIONS

Contemporary Moral Issues

Joe Jenkins

HEINEMANN
EDUCATIONAL

Heinemann Educational
a division of Heinemann Educational Books Ltd
Halley Court, Jordan Hill, Oxford OX2 8EJ

OXFORD LONDON EDINBURGH
MADRID ATHENS BOLOGNA PARIS
MELBOURNE SYDNEY AUCKLAND
SINGAPORE TOKYO IBADAN NAIROBI
HARARE GABORONE PORTSMOUTH NH (USA)

© Joe Jenkins 1987, 1992
First published 1987
This edition published 1992

92 93 94 95 96 10 9 8 7 6 5 4 3 2

British Library Cataloguing in Publication Data

A catalogue record for this book is available from the
British Library.
ISBN 0 435 30317 1

The publishers would like to thank the following for permission to
reproduce photographs, which are listed below by section numbers:
Amnesty International 65 (torture victim), 66; Animal Aid Society 69, 70;
Anti-Slavery Society 67 (child enslaved); Aspect Picture Library/Mike
Wells 41; Associated Press/Topham 65 (Vietnamese boat people in Hong
Kong); Barnaby's Picture Library 18; Barnaby's Picture Library/Jane
Skinner 2, 25; Camera Press Ltd 36; Camera Press Ltd/Benoit Gysembergh
67 (a boy being abducted in Thailand); Camera Press Ltd/David Hoffmann
11, 60 (urban poverty, showing flats), 76 (anti-Cruse demonstration);
Camera Press Ltd/Claude Sauvageot 83; Ebenezer Pictures/Susanna
Burton 43; Ebenezer Pictures/C & J Pemberton 68; Ebenezer
Pictures/Christopher Phillips 12 (a modern nuclear family), 44, 73;
Format/Maggie Murray 48 (pro-abortion rally), 52; Format/Val Wilmer
24, 34 (road sweeper); Glasgow Museums and Art Galleries 55; Sally and
Richard Greenhill 40; Greenpeace/Gleizes 76 (spraying a seal pup); Health
Education Authority 20; Impact Photos/Penny Tweedie 90 (Aborigine
girls); Magnum Photos/Rio Branco 91; Magnum Photos/Donald McCullin
67 (African boy abducted into army); Magnum Photos/Steve McCurry 84;
Magnum Photos/Wayne Miller 45; Magnum Photos/Ian Perry 78; Mansell
Collection 54 (Panopticon); Mary Evans Picture Library 12 (a Victorian
family), 34 (slave train in Zanzibar, a slave auction, a West African
shooting party), 54 (an execution by hanging, a public execution);
Network/Doran 60 (The Derby); Network/Mike Goldwater 63;
Network/Jordan 72; Network/Lowe 29; Lennart Nilsson 48 (Life poster);
Real London/Neill Menneer 17; Retna Pictures/Neal Preston 93; Rex
Features 71; Rex Features/Frilet 79 (a handful of grain); Rex
Features/Today 56; Royal Observatory Edinburgh/Anglo-Austrian
Telescope Board 3; Shelter 58; Frank Spooner Pictures/Gamma 75; Frank
Spooner Pictures/Bartholemew—Liaison 77; Still Pictures/Mark Edwards
79 (Haiti), 88; Survival International/Victor Engelbert 90 (Yandmani
family); Syndication International/Aldus Archive/Zydowski
Instytut/History Czny, Warsaw 38 (Isabella and her family being rounded
up); Syndication International/Weiner Library 38 (Jews digging their own
graves at Auschwitz); Tate Gallery Publications 16; Terence Higgins Trust
21 (It's that condom moment); Tibet Information Network 92 (Chinese
convoys, lighting candles to Buddha); Topham 86; Topham/Press
Association 85; Topham/UPPA 21 (Freddie Mercury); Wendy Wallace 5;
Zefa 87,89; Zefa Stockmarket 15.

Cover photographs by: Magnum Photos/James Nachtwey (small boy in
Lebanon with gun); Magnum Photos/Peter Marlow (homeless man in
Britain). The Publishers have been unable to trace the copyright holders of
the picture of the two children in a burned-out forest. Due
acknowledgement will, of course, be given in any future edition of this
book, should the holders contact the Publishers.

The author would like to thank the following individuals and
organizations for their help, guidance and inspiration in the writing of this
new edition:
Angela Mitchell; the New Internationalist; Amnesty International; CAAT;
Christian Aid; Oxfam; the Corrymeela Community; the estate of Kahlil
Gibran; Ellen Jenkins; the Brothers at Belmont; Beat the Border; Survival
International; Sting; Gaia Books Ltd; Aileen Milne; the Campaign Against
Pornography; the estate of Martin Luther King; Daniel Leech; Joanne
Egerton, Rachel Houghton, Anne Priestley and Sue Walton at Heinemann
Educational; and all Religious Studies teachers everywhere.

This book is dedicated to the memory of George Jeffery a man of
immense wisdom, courage and humour.

The Publishers would also like to thank the following for their kind
permission to reproduce copyright material:
Age Concern England, for the article by Pamela Martin adapted from the
booklet I Shall Wear Purple on pp. 88–9; Amnesty International, for the
extract on p. 112; British Humanist Association for the extracts and
adaptations of articles appearing in the Humanist Dipper on pp. 8, 15, 34–5,
51, 53, 97, 99 and 115; for extracts from the Humanist Manifesto for the Future
of Humankind on pp. 67, 122, 146 and 150; and for the article adapted from
The Humanist on pp. 128–9; Cambridge University Press for the extracts
from the Book of Common Prayer on p. 52; Catholic Truth Society for the
extracts on pp. 46, 51, 69, 78–9, 94 and 99; Century Hutchinson for the
extract from The Making of the Modern Homosexual by K. Plummer on p. 51;
Church House Publishing for the extracts on pp. 59, 91, 95, 99, 118, 120–1
and 126; Darton, Longman and Todd Ltd for the extracts from The Capacity
to Love by Jack Dominion on pp. 36 and 37; EXIT for the extracts on pp. 96
and 97; Dr. M. Fitzgerald and J. Sim for the extract on p.114 from their book
British Prisons; Gaia Books Ltd for the extract from the Gaia Atlas of Planet
Management by Lewis Thomas on p. 81; Guardian News Service for the
article by Chris Mihill on p. 45; Robert Hale Ltd for extracts from the
Modern Catholic Dictionary by John Hardon on pp. 93 and 123; Health
Education Authority for the material on pp. 42 and 43; HarperCollins
Publishers Ltd for the extract from Desmond Tutu's sermon 'Divine
Intervention' quoted in his book Hope and Suffering on pp. 174 and 175;
William Heinemann Ltd for the extract from The Prophet by Kahlil Gibran
on pp. 33 and 55; Controller of Her Majesty's Stationery Office for the
extract adapted from Working Together; A guide to arrangements for
interagency co-operation for the protection of children from abuse (DSS) on p.
126; the Independent for the article by Celia Hall on p. 58; LIFE for the
extract from Save the Unborn Child on p. 99; Longman Group UK for the
extract from Longman's Dictionary of Contemporary English on p. 120;
Methodist Publishing House for the extracts from the Methodist
Conference on pp. 51, 53, 57, 61, 63, 97, 121, 123; National Abortion
Campaign for the extract on o. 98; National Union of Students, Women's
Unit for the extract on p. 138; New Internationalist for the extracts on pp. 40,
107, 108, 124 and 159, and the articles on pp. 70–71, 92, 106, 111 and 142–3;
Oxfam for the material adapted from Seven Myths about World Hunger on
pp. 164–5; Pan Books for the extract and adapted material from
North–South: A Programme for Survival, the report of the Independent
Commission on International Development Issues, on pp. 156/7; Penguin
Books Ltd for the extract from Camillo Torres: Revolutionary Priest, edited by
John Geriffi, on p. 173; Quaker Home Service for the extract from Towards a
Quaker View of Sex on p. 51; Queen Anne Press for the quote by Vladimir
Shatalov in The Home Planet (edited by Kevin W. Kelly) on p. 180; Radius
for the extracts from Dear Clare: this is what women feel about Page 3 by Clare
Short (edited by Kiri Tunks and Diane Hutchinson) on pp. 41 and 103;
Religious Society of Friends for the extracts from The Marriage Relationship
on p. 57 and from A Declaration from the Harmless and Innocent People of God,
called Quakers on p. 147; Saint Andrew Press for extracts from Biting the
Bullet by Dr Chris Arthur on pp. 83 and 85; Socialist Worker for the article on
p. 73; Survival International for the extracts on p. 186; Chris Tchaikovsky of
Women in Prison for the article on pp. 116–17; Tibet Support Group UK for
the extract from their Newsletter on p. 133; Times Newspapers Ltd for the
articles by Libby Jukes and Richard Duce on p. 127; Turnstone Books for
the quote by J.G. Bennett in Gurdjieff: Making a New World on p. 180; United
Nations for the material quoted on pp. 130, 132, 133, 136, 145 and 160;
Ward Lock Educational for the extract from Humanism by B. Smoker on p.
65. Extracts from The Church of England and Racism – and Beyond (Board for
Social Responsibility 1982), General Synod Report of Proceedings, Vol. 14
(General Synod 1983), Human Fertilisation and Embryology (Board for Social
Responsibility 1984), pp. 95, 99; The Local Church and Mentally Handicapped
People by Michael Bayley (Board for Social Responsibility: CIO Publishing
1984), p. 91; Faith in the City: Report of the Archbishop of Canterbury's
Commission on Urban Priority Areas (Church House Publishing 1985), p. 118;
and Child Abuse and Neglect, GS Misc 297 (General Synod 1988), p. 126 are
reproduced by permission of the Central Board of Finance of the Church of
England.

The Publishers have made every effort to trace copyright holders.
However, if any material has been incorrectly acknowledged we would be
pleased to correct this at the earliest opportunity.

Design, typesetting and artwork by Gecko Limited, Bicester, Oxon
Printed in Great Britain by Scotprint Ltd., Musselburgh

CONTENTS

We all have different views about what is right and what is wrong. People often disagree with each other about what is right and what is wrong. People have different beliefs and views. Often a person's own particular beliefs will affect his or her view of what is right and what is wrong.

This book aims to do **four** things:

1   to give you some relevant **facts** about some of the important issues and problems facing human beings today,
2   to help you to **understand** these issues and problems,
3   to help you to understand that people have **different views** on these issues and problems and to explain what these views are,
4   to enable you to begin to understand, develop and express **your own views** on these issues and problems.

It can all be rather confusing. How can we ever know that other people's views are the right ones? How can we ever know whether our own views and opinions are the right ones?

One of the best ways of beginning to understand other people's views and our own views on something is to look at the **reasons** they or we give for believing in something.

OFFERING REASONS

We can hold any view we want about something without offering reasons for that view. However, if we refuse to give reasons for our beliefs and views, people are not going to listen to us. Likewise, if somebody else fails to give reasons for their beliefs we are not really likely to take that much notice of them.

To give reasons for our beliefs and opinions is the **key** to greater understanding of ourselves, of others and of the problem or issue under discussion.

It is important to be able to provide and offer reasons for our opinions if we want others to consider them. It is important to be able to offer reasons if we are to persuade ourselves that we hold opinions worth having.

If others are unable to understand why we hold the views we do, they may not listen to us. If we do not understand why **we** hold certain opinions, we are likely to feel rather unsure about **our** opinions.

So we need

a   to offer good reasons for our beliefs and opinions,
b   to decide whether others are offering good reasons for their beliefs and opinions.

So what are good reasons?
Generally, good reasons

1   should whenever possible be based on facts,
2   should be relevant,
3   should provide understanding and explain an opinion,
4   should be believable to the listener.

EXERCISE I

When is a reason a good reason?

Look at each of the statements below. For each one decide whether it is

a   a good reason,
b   a reason but not a good one,
c   not a reason.

1   'Gary's homework is written in blue ink. He must have copied mine 'cos I use blue ink.'

2   'I suspect Gary didn't copy my homework. He told me so.'

3   'I suspect Gary didn't copy my homework 'cos his is different from mine.'

4   'Gary must have copied my homework, he can't do the subject anyway.'

5   'I believe in pixies . . . I once saw a photograph of one.'

6   'I believe in pixies . . . when I was young my gran told me they existed.'

7   'I believe in pixies.'

It is important that during your GCSE Religious Studies course you learn how to form your own opinions on the issues and problems of today. You will get more out of the course if you are able to argue your point of view using good reasons. You will begin to understand other people's points of view if you can look closely and carefully at their reasons.

You must also beware of 'jumping to conclusions', and be alert to other people jumping to conclusions. People jump to conclusions when they fail to use reasons to arrive at a conclusion or an opinion.

EXERCISE II

Jumping to conclusions

Here are some examples of reasoning. Decide whether you would classify them as

a   good reasoning,
b   not so good but possibly all right,
c   seems good but possibly unsound,
d   poor reasoning.

Explain your choice for each situation below.

1   'My father's been reading in the paper that smoking causes cancer, so he says he's going to give up reading.'

2   'I've been reading that one child out of every five that's born in the world is Chinese. I have three brothers and so I think the next baby in our family will probably look pretty Oriental.'

3   'Whenever I see Jason I ask him what he thinks of Sharon, and he gets really embarrassed. Cor, he hasn't half got a crush on me.'

4   'I once met a French boy who was a brilliant dancer. I'll bet all those Frenchmen are brilliant dancers.'

! Whenever you see this symbol in this book think about **good reasons**. It will mean either that you must examine the reasons given or that you must examine your own reasons.

NOTE

The views recorded in this book are not all of the same authority. Official statements, declarations and resolutions of the governing bodies of the Churches have more authority than 'reports' — which may or may not have been accepted by the bodies to which they were presented.

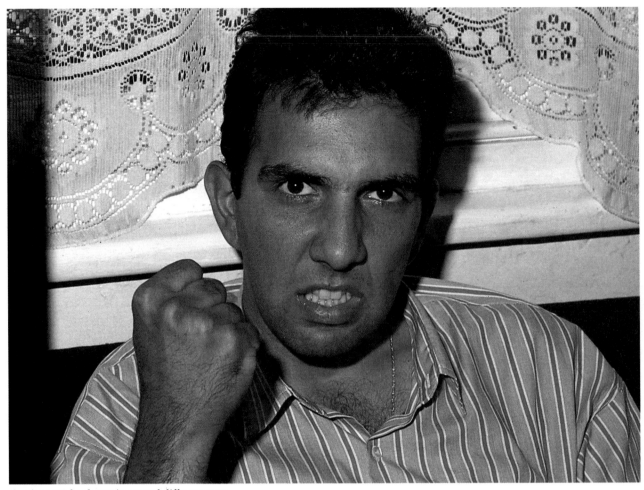

Anxiety can be shown in several different ways

As human beings we are aware of our own existence. We *know* that we exist, we know that there is something about us that relates to the world. We are aware of certain things about ourselves – our personality, our thinking, our movement and our emotions. We know that we are involved in the world; we also know, although perhaps don't think about it very often, that our involvement with the world will one day end and that we will die. Nobody gets out of life alive.

As far as we humans know, there are certain qualities we possess that make us different from the rest of the animal kingdom. We are aware of ourselves as seemingly separate beings. We have the ability to remember our past, to imagine the future, to recognize objects and understand the meaning of symbols. We are able to reason and we attempt to understand the world. We have imagination. As self-conscious beings we can sense ourselves in the here and now and we know where we have been and can imagine where we might be.

When we talk about the human condition we are not talking about other human beings, we are talking about ourselves. One aspect of ourselves that we can only glimpse at is the amount of time and mental energy that we spend daydreaming. Most of us spend a huge percentage of our time daydreaming. We wish that things could be different from the way that they are: 'One day I'm going to do this . . .', 'Oh, if only . . .', 'What will happen if . . .?'

Because things aren't often as we want them, because we imagine they could be different, we attempt to make our lives different. We are always building new worlds for ourselves. Motivated by this desire for a better life, people go to work and create artificial worlds where there are television commercials, rapid transport, central heating and CD players. All human enterprises, such as science and religion, come about through human need, in our awareness of the inadequacies in ourselves and in our world. We try to reform the world with science. We try to make it more reasonable and less frightening with religion.

TALKING POINTS

'To truly know and accept that this body dies and that this is the only time that we have is the most powerful weapon we can ever have. With this understanding, we can begin to live passionately, not wasting a moment of precious time that is allocated to us, plunging gratefully into the immediacy of living. We work now, for the future of humanity and, as we know we are loved, time will be on our side.'

(Reshad Feild, *The Invisible Way*, 1959)

'To be alone in an office – dozens of telephones all ringing at the same time – these anxieties should make us one. But we let them isolate us, as if the citizens of a country would defend it by each barricading themselves in their houses.'

(John Fowles)

FOR DISCUSSION

As we grow up we become more aware of our anxiety about things. Break up into groups of two, preferably with a close friend, read through the following list and discuss each item.

!▶ THE ANXIETY OF: sex; money; health; ambition; not being loved; being unable to love; responsibility; otherness; choosing right; death; knowing the future; the ignorance of the meaning of life; problems facing the human race.

Since the dawn of history human beings have felt and experienced another world, a world that is not visible, but a world that is invisible. Some of the questions and ideas that you have discussed above, have been discussed and thought about by millions of people before you. People are always looking for some sort of truth in life. People look for meaning in this enormous universe and this world which has been called a 'pain factory'. This search for meaning is at the root of all religions and all philosophies. Today in our culture we see only a small aspect of religion, whether it be the local church, the local mosque, Songs of Praise on television, or a priest. However, these are external forms and we all know that within us is a whole universe. We all have sides to ourselves that we do not understand – invisible sides – our dreams, the continual murmuring of our minds, the strong feelings of our emotions.

In ancient Greece there was a very sacred place at Delphi where people would go for inspiration. Above the door were the words: 'KNOW THYSELF AND THY WILL KNOW THE UNIVERSE'. The journey towards knowing oneself is the most important journey that we can go on.

PATHOS

Pathos is a Greek word meaning 'suffering'. It also includes the idea of being the passive recipient, not the initiator of one's experience.

If you think about your life can you think of examples of times when life seems out of control? Times when you are passive and life seems to be acting upon you? Try and imagine what it would be like to be in control of your life and how this might reduce the amount of anxiety and suffering that you experience.

Planet Earth lies in the galaxy called the Milky Way. It is estimated that there are 100 billion galaxies each containing some 10 billion trillion stars and planets (10,000,000,000,000,000,000,000).

> *'We had the sky up there all speckled with stars and we used to lay on our backs and look up at them and discuss whether they was made or only just happened.'*
>
> (Huckleberry Finn)

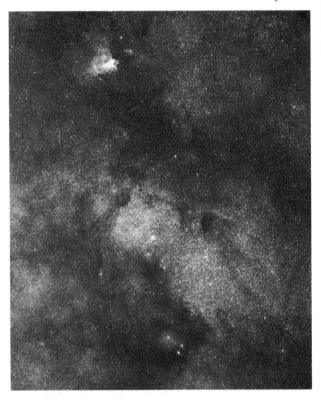

The Milky Way

The question whether everything was made or 'just happened' is a very important one. Some people believe that the universe exists as it does because of pure accident, others believe that it was made by God. The way we answer the question 'How did we get here?' will affect the way we answer the question 'Why are we here?'

The Bible states that 'In the beginning God created the heavens and the earth' *(Genesis 1: 1).* It also states that God 'made man in his own image' *(Genesis 1: 27).* This means that human beings have a special place in creation and have a responsibility to God and to the world.

Some people believe that God does not exist (atheists) and that we are here by pure accident.

> *'I think the universe is all spots and jumps without unity, without continuity, without coherence or orderliness.'*
>
> (Bertrand Russell, philosopher)

However, many people who do not believe in God still think that life has a meaning and purpose. In reply to the question 'What is the purpose of life?' a Humanist would answer:

> *'We choose our own purposes in life; we choose our own activities. For some people creating a happy family life may be more important than anything else. For others it may be music, playing football, or racing pigeons, sewing or knitting, or swimming or climbing. Humanists hope for fairer societies throughout the world so that more people may choose satisfying ways of life. At present, political oppression and the lack of the basic necessities mean that many people in the world have little freedom of choice.'*
>
> (Humanist Dipper)

Human beings have a lot in common with other forms of life on Earth, especially animals. Sometimes humans are called animals – for instance, here are six statements about human animals.

Human beings are:

- social animals
- thinking animals
- creative animals
- moral animals
- responsible animals
- spiritual animals.

IN GROUPS

Look at these **key questions**, discuss them in groups of three to four, write some notes on your ideas and report back to the class.

▶ How can life be important in such an enormous universe?

▶ Are we merely 'born to die'?

▶ Are we no more than just mixtures of chemicals and gases?

THINKING POINTS

'People travel to wonder
at the height of mountains,
at the huge waves of the sea,
at the long courses of rivers,
at the vast compass of the ocean,
at the circular motion of the stars,
and they pass themselves by
without wondering.'

(St Augustine 354–430 CE)

'Some people see things as they are and say, why? I dream things that never were and say, why not?'

(John F. Kennedy)

'Most people suppose that truth can be acquired like some commodity, in the markets of the world, from libraries, laboratories or encyclopaedias, when all the time we contain it within ourselves. It is the last resort, a Self-Finding.'

(Hugh L'Anson Fausset, *The Lost Dimension*, 1966)

'Know thyself and thy will know the universe.'

(Ancient Greek saying)

'You are led
through your lifetime
by the inner learning creature,
the playful spiritual being
that is your real self.'

(Richard Bach)

'When someone finds no Meaning in anything he has at the same time no feeling of God. Meaninglessness is a terrible illness. It has to be got over. It is the same as godlessness, because if you say there is not God, you are saying that there is no Meaning in things. But if you think there is Meaning, you believe in God. Meaning is God. You cannot say that you do not believe in God but believe there is Meaning in things. The two are the same, in that one cannot be without the other. God is Meaning. If you dislike the word God, then say Meaning instead. The word God shuts some people's minds. The word Meaning cannot. It opens the mind.'

(Maurice Nicoll, *The Mark*, 1954)

FOR DISCUSSION

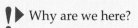 Why are we here?

'May the force be with you.'

(Star Wars)

'My God, my God, why hast thou forsaken me?'

(Jesus)

'In the beginning God made Heaven and Earth.'

(Genesis 1:1)

'When you see something big, something infinite, then you are seeing God.'

(Vincent van Gogh)

'Father of day, Father of night, Father of black and Father of white. Father who moveth the rivers and streams.'

(Bob Dylan)

'God is dead.'

(Friedrich Nietzsche)

'When I see the glories of the cosmos I can't help but believe that there is a Divine Hand behind it all.'

(Albert Einstein)

'If God did not exist, it would be necessary to invent him.'

(Voltaire)

Most world religions believe in a God. However, gone are the days when the word 'God' conjures up ideas of an old man with a white beard and kind eyes sitting on some golden throne watching us humans carrying on our business. 'God' means different things to different people.

BASIC CHRISTIAN IDEAS ABOUT GOD

God is:
- perfect
- personal
- creator of the universe
- loving
- the only God
- all-powerful
- unchanging
- infinite
- sustainer of the universe
- holy
- all-knowing
- ever-present.

Some people argue that if there is no God then there is no meaning in life, and life itself is futile. Humanists, however, argue that there is still meaning in life without God and that humans have for too long blamed God for the world's problems rather than facing up to them and being responsible for them themselves.

People who believe in God are called **theists.**

People who do not believe in a God are called **atheists.**

People who are not sure whether God exists are called **agnostics**.

People who believe in more than one God are called **polytheists.**

DOES GOD EXIST?

Here are some ideas which might help you.

Reasons why God might exist	Reasons why God might not exist
1 There is so much order, design, beauty and purpose in the world, it must have come from some designer. Look at the complexity of life, of nature. It must have been designed.	1 If there is a God why is there so much suffering in the world? Wars, poverty, disease, floods, earthquakes, the threat of nuclear destruction, etc.
2 Everything has a cause. The world, the universe, must have begun from something. God was this creator.	2 I need proof. I need to see God. Where is God? What is the point of believing in something which I can't see and others can't see either?
3 Throughout history, so many have experienced God – felt God – that they can't all be talking nonsense.	3 People made God. They invented God to give them some comfort and security in a harsh huge universe and in a world full of death, darkness and disease.
4 We will never prove God exists (or evil does not exist), but everything in the world points to the possibility of Design and Purpose.	4 The universe was not created, it has always been. It had no beginning.
5 Humans are different from all other animals – they have art, music, culture, morality. This is all the result of some Divine Purpose for them.	5 If there is a God, then why doesn't God help us? God never answers my prayers or stops wars and things.
6 There are many things that as humans we can't see . . . atoms, love, electricity, hope, dreams, time, etc . . . yet we know they exist. So to say I don't believe in a God because I don't see God is foolish.	6 Science has proved the Bible to be wrong about many things. The role of God in our world has been reduced stage by stage with the advance of science.

TO DEBATE

▶ The motion is 'This house believes that God does not exist.' Using the arguments in the table, organize a class debate and take a vote before and after.

▶ Today more and more people believe that God is neither male nor female, but rather is a universal spirit. The motion is 'This house believes that God has no gender'.

FOR YOUR FOLDERS

▶ Without using the arguments listed, make a list of
a why some people believe in God,
b why some people don't believe in God.

▶ Look at the quotes. Write a sentence explaining what each one is trying to say.

FOR DISCUSSION

▶ Does it really matter if God exists or not?

Humans and animals not only die but sometimes they suffer the most terrible pain. In the Nazi Holocaust during the Second World War at least six million Jewish people died as well as millions of others. They died in mental, physical and spiritual agony. We cannot imagine the scale of the suffering. It was a period of history when the human potential for creating a hell on earth reached one of its most terrible points. Where was God at Auschwitz, Belsen, Treblinka and all the other death camps?

Today, around the world millions of people are going through terrible suffering. In many cases this suffering is caused by other human beings. As well as the physical suffering that is going on everyone suffers in other ways – psychological ways. Suffering, it seems, is part of human and animal existence. We live in what has been called a 'pain factory' in the universe.

> 'Someone tells us that God loves us as a father loves his children. We are reassured. But then we see a child dying of inoperable cancer of the throat. His earthly father is driven frantic in his efforts to help, but his heavenly father reveals no obvious sign of concern.'

(Anthony Flew, *New Essays in Philosophical Theology*, 1955)

The amount of suffering in the world at any moment is staggering. It is a problem for us all. It is also a special kind of problem for those who believe the world is ruled by a God of power and love. The problem is this:

> Either God wills to remove evil and is not able to do so, or God does not will to remove it. If God does not will to remove it then he is not a God of love. If God is not able to remove it then he is not all powerful.

The question for people who believe in an all-knowing (omniscient), all-loving (benevolent), and all-powerful (omnipotent) God, is how can this evil exist in a world that he supposedly created? This problem has been called the problem of evil or the problem of suffering. It raises serious questions about the nature and existence of the traditional God of Christianity. Dealing with this problem has been a major concern of Western thinkers and ordinary Christians for hundreds of years. Some thinkers have tried to answer the problem of evil. Here are seven of their ideas.

Famine in Sudan caught the attention of the world's media in 1985

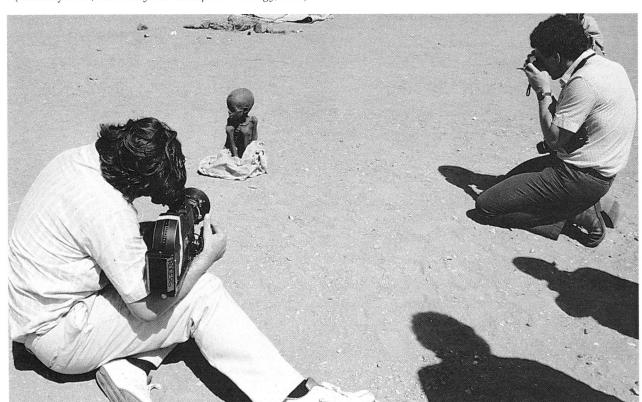

1 **It is not a question to be asked. God works in mysterious ways.**

This is not a very satisfactory answer and we might ask why did God give human beings minds capable of asking questions?

2 **Suffering is the result of sin.**

We might accept this idea that an individual or a nation suffers because of past wrongs. But what about children who are supposedly innocent, or animals?

3 **Some Christians talk about 'the Satan answer'. There is a constant cosmic battle going on between the forces of good and evil.**

This answer raises many questions. What is Satan? Did God create Satan? If God created everything, he must have created Satan and if God is all-knowing he must have known what Satan would do. Could God not stop Satan once Satan got started?

4 **Evil is not a thing of God. It is not a thing at all. It is an illusion or simply the absence of good.** (This illusion hypothesis is represented in the ideas of Christian Science.)

Again, this is begging the question because for humans and animals suffering is a reality.

5 **Evil is useful. If there was no evil in the world there could be no good.** We would have nothing to measure good against. Because evil exists we are given situations and choices to help us develop as human beings. One who experiences the pain of a toothache can surely appreciate more fully the pleasure of not having toothache.

But why does it have to be such bad toothache? Why so much evil? Could not growth and perfection exist without the horrors of Auschwitz or Hiroshima or the Gulf War?

6 **Perhaps God is not unlimited in power.** He was the creator but once he created the world he let the forces of evolution take their course. God wanted to build up a perfect world but matter resisted.

This is one of the stronger arguments for it accepts that, in order to grow, everything has to go through the struggle of opposites.

7 **God can do anything that can be done but God cannot do what cannot be done.** For example, we cannot have water that will quench thirst yet not drown people, fire which will warm homes and not scorch flesh.

This goes against the idea of God being all-powerful. Because if he was all-powerful and all-loving, would he not have created a perfect planet? Some people, however, argue that the world could be perfect if human beings were not so ignorant.

FOR DISCUSSION

!▶ After reading this section divide into pairs. Go through all the arguments again. Discuss them and report back to the rest of the class about your conclusions.

FOR YOUR FOLDERS

▶ Make a list of all the types of: (a) physical suffering and (b) psychological suffering that go on in the human and animal world.

!▶ Write a short article entitled 'The Problem of Suffering'. Use your article to describe and explain what your views are.

Humanists believe that:

- if human problems are to be solved at all, they will only be solved by human beings

- life should be as satisfying as possible for every individual

- human beings have evolved from simpler forms of life through natural processes taking millions of years

- people can more than ever today influence, for better or worse, the future of life on this planet

- because human beings have evolved together, all have equal rights without discrimination by race, sex or age.

Humanists do not believe:

- in a God or gods. Many describe themselves as agnostic (*a-gnostic* = 'not knowing', i.e. a person who does not claim to know). They say nobody can really know whether there is a supernatural power or not. All live their lives as atheists (*atheist* = 'without God')

- in life after death. But they *do* believe that the effect of a person's life can be felt long after she or he has died

- that there is a supernatural power to guide us or help us.

Humanists would agree with these statements which are sometimes referred to as the *golden rule* of human behaviour:

Confucius	The treatment which you would not have for yourself do not mete out to other people.
Buddha	Hurt not others with that which pains yourself.
Jain scriptures	The essence of right conduct is not to injure anyone.
Jewish Talmud	What is harmful to yourself do not do to your fellow men. That is the whole of the law and the remainder is but commentary.
Jesus	Always treat others as you would like them to treat you.

HUMANIST MORALITY

Humanists do not believe in a God-given code of behaviour.

Morality is about how people should treat one another. Humanists believe that human experience of life and of one another is an adequate guide as to how we behave.

They use their own reason, and try to think out all the possible consequences of their actions. The main questions they ask themselves are: 'Will it make someone feel better (happier, more loved)?' and 'Will it hurt anyone?'

Humanists have a great regard for sincerity, fairness and compassion. They try to behave responsibly and thoughtfully, rejecting the temptation to exploit or cheat anyone.

They respect and care for older people – whether parents, neighbours, the homeless and disabled or others. But they reserve the right to criticize dishonesty, unkindness and unreasonableness.

Humanists think that moral decisions involving sex should not be put in a separate category. The same principles should apply as in all other matters – not hurting anyone, being responsible, thoughtful and sincere.

WHAT ARE HUMANIST VALUES AND PRINCIPLES?

Humanists value **people** and their **happiness**. They value our human powers of **reasoning** and **imagining,** and they value **love.** These qualities are fundamental because they make us distinctively human.

Humanists try always to give reasons for the values they live by, such as

- **fairness** and **justice**, because they regard each person as valuable and entitled to a happy and satisfying life

- **tolerance**, because they accept people's right to hold differing views and opinions, so long as they do not make others suffer

- **sincerity** and **talking** and **listening**, because understanding of one another is important. Only if feelings are expressed sincerely can people learn how to help each other and to appreciate points of view different from their own

- **curiosity** and **creativity**, because they lead us to extend our understanding and enjoyment of the world

- **courage**, because in order to live fully, we need the heart to face difficulties, and to stand up for what we believe to be right
- **feeling**, because it is not only having the right ideas but also the capacity to feel with sensitivity and passion that makes life rich for ourselves and others
- **independence**, because they believe that there is no Infallible Authority. We have to work things out for ourselves as intelligent human beings
- **freedom** – as much as possible for each, so long as it does not interfere with other people's freedom, happiness and security
- **confidence**, based on the development of our own powers, so that we can set about making the world a better place
- **cooperation**, because it is by participating together to achieve things that human progress is made
- **concern for the world and for the future** because we are united with all life through evolution so that we must accept responsibility for the future of Planet Earth, its life and its peoples.

WHAT DO HUMANISTS ACTUALLY DO?

Some **play an active part in local humanist groups** which hold discussions, social events and conferences. Many are active in their local areas in such things as getting more attractive Registry Offices for people who don't want to marry in church; trying to get better nursery school provision; making surveys of parents' attitudes to religion in schools; giving practical help in providing hostels for young people in difficulties, and raising money for projects in developing countries overseas.

Some of them **work in campaigns**. For example, to ensure a humane and responsible approach to abortion; for a free Family Planning service; for people not to be punished because they are homosexuals; for civil liberties and freedom of expression, especially in books, films, plays and TV programmes.

Some **work for bodies** such as:

- The Independent Adoption Society – for people who do not practise a religion who wish to adopt children;
- The Humanist Housing Association – housing for elderly people.

Humanists **support and join organizations** such as Shelter, Friends of the Earth, The Conservation Society, Oxfam, Age Concern, the National Council for Civil Liberties, Amnesty International, the British Pregnancy Advisory Service, the Howard League for Penal Reform, the World Disarmament Campaign and CND.

Some **work as individuals** in marriage guidance counselling; as prison and hospital visitors; as local councillors; as social workers, teachers, nurses and doctors; as magistrates; as officiants (the person in charge) at funerals where no hymns or prayers are included.

(Humanist Dipper)

FOR DISCUSSION

 Humanists think it unfair when a religious person assumes that 'the unbeliever has no moral standards'. Why might Humanists think this?

 It is easier to face life, and to make decisions throughout it, if you believe in God, or if you don't believe in a God?

FOR YOUR FOLDERS

▶ If you had a million pounds to support a team of research workers, describe what you would like them to investigate. Give reasons for your choice.

▶ Think back over your life. Pick out an incident in which you remember someone behaving with particular thoughtfulness and consideration. Write about it.

THE SEARCH

The modern Western world has often been called 'secular'. This basically means that this part of the world is no longer 'religious'. However, on a deeper level, because we are humans we still ask basic questions about our existence. Who am I? Where did I come from? Why am I here? Where am I going? How do I cope with life? What is right and what is wrong? Human beings are always searching for meaning in their lives. Whatever happens to the outer (external) world, we still feel a deep need to explore and understand our inner (internal) world. The questions that all religions ask and the answers they give are an attempt to help people to explore and understand both the external and internal worlds.

BASIC CHRISTIAN BELIEFS

Christianity is not the only religion in the world, but in the Western world it has played the dominant role in shaping many of the attitudes and ideas that influence society. There are many different Christian groups. Although they share some common beliefs, their expressions of these beliefs can seem very different. Also, their views on some issues are not always the same. We therefore need to be careful about saying 'Christians believe . . .' because one Christian might have very different views on something than another Christian.

At the centre of a Christian's faith is the person of Jesus of Nazareth who lived in Palestine (now called Israel) about 2000 years ago. Christians remember his life, his teachings and his death.

It is not easy to define exactly what ordinary Christians believe and think about their religion. In general, however, it is possible to say they hold the following beliefs:

- There is a God who created the world. Christians believe that God is perfect, loving, all-knowing, all-powerful, infinite, holy and ever-present.
- God gave the world his only son, Jesus Christ to show the world a new way of living. His son was crucified and Christians believe that he rose from the dead.
- God has made his will known to people in a holy book called the Bible.
- The spirit of God can help and guide people.
- The teachings of Jesus, as laid out in the New Testament, show human beings what God requires of them.
- God has given human beings the freedom to choose between good and evil.
- By dying on the cross and rising from the dead, Jesus brought humanity closer to an understanding of God.

THE TEN COMMANDMENTS

Jesus was born into a part of the world that was heavily influenced by the Jewish religion. The beliefs and teachings of Judaism can be found in the part of the Christian Bible known as the Old Testament. The Old Testament stresses that human beings have been given duties which they must follow. These duties became known as 'The Law' and are still very important to Jews today. Through the teachings of the Old Testament people learnt what God required of them. Here are ten of the most famous teachings, known as the Ten Commandments, or the Decalogue:

1 I am the Lord your God.
2 You shall have no other gods before me. You shall not make for yourself a graven image . . .
3 You shall not blaspheme.
4 Keep the sabbath holy.
5 Honour your parents.
6 You shall not kill.
7 You shall not commit adultery.
8 You shall not steal.
9 You shall not lie.
10 Do not desire what is not yours.

(*Deuteronomy 5: 6–21*)

THE NEW TESTAMENT

The central message of Christian ethics as taught by Jesus of Nazareth in the New Testament is the idea of concern for all people. Christians call this concern 'love'. Christian love is called 'agape'. It is not a sexual or romantic love but rather an attitude of caring for people no matter who they are or what they are like. It is the kind of love shown in the Parable of the Good Samaritan (see *Luke 10: 25ff*).

The Gospels are full of incidents showing Jesus' concern for other people. His teachings, too, illustrate this.

> 'Always treat others as you would like them to treat you.' (*Matthew 7: 12* – this is called the Golden Rule)

Jesus' teachings differ from the Old Testament in that they do not consist of a series of rules or laws to be followed. Instead Jesus was concerned that people try to change from within. They must try to be 'pure in heart' and change their inner thoughts and feelings. He taught that thoughts and feelings matter as much as actual conduct or action. An example of this was when he condemned not only murder but the anger that may be behind it . . .

> 'Everyone who is angry with his brother shall be brought to judgement.'
>
> (*Matthew 5: 22*)

> 'I give you a new commandment: love one another; as I have loved you, so you are to love one another.'
>
> (*John 13: 34*)

Some of his other teachings include:

> 'Do not judge and you will not be judged.'
>
> (*Matthew 7: 1*)

> 'A man can have no greater love than to lay down his life for his friends.'
>
> (*John 15: 13*)

> 'It is easier for a camel to pass through the eye of a needle than for a rich man to enter the Kingdom of God.'
>
> (*Mark 10: 25–26*)

BIBLICAL TEACHINGS AS A GUIDE

The teachings in the Bible can act as a guide for Christians in the modern world. Obviously some of the great problems and issues that face us today are specifically modern problems, and so no direct reference can be found to them in the Bible, e.g. pollution, medical ethics, drug abuse, pornography. However, the teachings are often **guidelines** and so can be **applied** to present-day problems. Many Christians believe that the teachings are **eternal** and are still relevant to human beings today.

FOR YOUR FOLDERS

▶ Explain in your own words what you think is meant by our 'internal' world.

▶ Write an article of about 250 words on the major beliefs of Christianity. At the end of the article write a paragraph on your own views.

! ▶ Read the Ten Commandments. Do you think they are relevant to our modern world? Give reasons.

! ▶ The teachings of the New Testament are **ideals**. Do you think that it is possible for human beings to reach the sort of understanding that will enable them to live up to these ideals?

▶ Write down three situations you have experienced (e.g. bullying, arguments, false accusations, stealing) and apply some of the teachings outlined in this section to them.

From the moment we are born we begin learning. At first we learn most things from our parent(s) but as we grow so do our influences. These are our major influences:

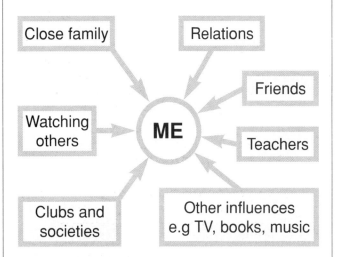

The way we learn about the correct way to behave in our own society, and the habits, customs, language and manners of our society is called **socialization**. We also slowly learn what is right and what is wrong, what is good and what is bad.

Some of the ways we begin to discover what is right and what is wrong are:

- by **consequence** – if you do this, such and such a thing will happen
- by **example** – watching how others behave
- by **experience** – if you do something yourself you find out what happens
- by **emotions** – e.g. do this to please your mother.
- by **following rules.**

Morality is concerned with what is right and wrong. As human beings we are able to think about what we do and say. Because we are able to think, we are also able to decide or choose what we think is the right way and what we think is the wrong way to behave.

- a **moral** act – an act considered to be right
- an **immoral** act – an act considered to be wrong
- an **amoral** act – an act that shows no understanding of right or wrong
- a **non-moral act** – an act not concerned with right or wrong
- a **non-moral** judgement – a view or opinion that is nothing to do with right or wrong.

Sometimes we get confused by language. Can you see the difference between Statements A and Statements B?

> ### Task A
> Write a sentence on the differences between these statements.
>
> | Statements A | Statements B |
> |---|---|
> | 'It is right to help the poor.' | 'He got ten out of ten right.' |
> | 'Martin Luther King was a good man.' | 'This apple is good.' |
> | | 'The school team are bad.' |
> | 'It is bad to tell lies.' | |
> | 'It is wrong to steal.' | 'You are wrong – they will win the cup.' |

JUDGEMENTS

Our sense of what is right and what is wrong depends upon many things – upbringing, parental attitudes, friends, what type of environment we have grown up in and live in now, and so on. Morality is therefore very complicated. What we consider to be right, somebody else might see as wrong. In the end we have to come to our own decisions about how we live and how we look at the way others live. We all have the ability to make moral judgements.

> ### Task B
> Look at the following situations. How would you judge them?
>
> ! Try to give reasons for your opinion of each situation.
>
> 1 killing animals for meat,
> 2 bombing an enemy's city during wartime,
> 3 making abortion illegal,
> 4 refusing to give a fully qualified black person a job,
> 5 bullying younger children.

IN GROUPS

▶ In groups of four to five discuss the following.

CONSEQUENCES

We are usually able to work out the consequences of our actions. As children we often learn about consequences by quite hard experience but as we grow up we are more able to see the possible results of our actions. Let us have a look at some consequences.

Consequences I

You have a Saturday morning job in a shop. A good friend asks if she can buy a magazine. As you get it for her, you notice her putting a bar of chocolate from the counter into her pocket.

Do you tell her to put it back?
Do you tell the owner of the shop?
Do you ignore her?
Do you tell her parents?

What are the consequences of all these?

Consequences II

There is a film on at the pictures that you want to see with your friends. However, you know your parents do not want you to see this particular film. You also have no money.

Do you ask your mother for the money?
Do you tell her what it's for?
Do you pretend it's for something else?
Do you tell your friends that your parents won't let you go or tell them you have no money?
Do you try and borrow the money from a friend?
Do you try and get the money another way?

What are the consequences of all these?

▶ Now report back your findings to the rest of the class.

Consequences I

Consequences II

Although it might seem easy to decide what is right and wrong in some situations, in others it is not so simple. Every situation is different and, as a result, the way you approach a situation and decide what is the right course of action may be different every time. Many of the problems we face as individuals or as a community are very complicated and it is not always easy to know the right way to react to them.

Thinkers have tried to solve this difficulty in two ways.

1 Morality as **a system of rules**. This is when people have a system of moral laws that they hold and then apply them to a given situation. (These people are called **deontologists.**)

2 Morality as a **set of goals**. This is when people do not apply rules to a situation, but rather decide on what end result they want and follow the actions that reach this result. (These people are called **consequentialists**.)

A CASE

You have two Jews hiding upstairs from the Nazis. The Gestapo ask you if you know of any Jews being hidden.

What would you do:

1 if you were a deontologist who has a rule 'I will never lie'?

2 if you were a deontologist who has a rule 'All people should be respected'?

3 if you were a consequentialist who believed that it is wrong to persecute people?

4 if you were a consequentialist who believed that Nazism was evil?

Over the ages certain theories have been developed about the best way to make ethical decisions in life. Ethics can be simply defined as the 'science of behaviour'.

HEDONISM

Epicurus was a Greek thinker born in 342 BC. He wrote over 300 works and believed that everybody strives after pleasure which is happiness, the main end of human life. He wrote: 'Pleasure is the beginning and end of living happily.' Epicurus did not just mean physical pleasure but pleasures of the mind and soul as well. Indeed, he believed that excessive physical pleasures lead to pain and become nothing like pleasures. He believed that true pleasure and happiness lie in 'freedom of the body from pain, and of the soul from confusion'.
A Hedonist believes that the 'good' is pleasant or whatever is pleasant is good.

ETHICAL EGOISM

This theory does not refer to 'big-heads' or selfish, egoistic people. It is a theory stating that a person's one and only basic duty is to obtain for themself the greatest possible balance of good over evil. Ideally, if everybody's own personal advantage did not hurt anyone else then the world would be a good place. However, often in practice when we do something to help ourselves we might hurt someone else.

UTILITARIANISM

This system was devised by two eighteenth-century British thinkers, Jeremy Bentham and John Stuart Mill. They were both actively involved in improving prisons and the law in Britain. The utilitarian slogan is 'the greatest good of the greatest number'. All our actions and rules are to be decided upon by finding out which of them produces the greatest amount of good for the greatest number of people.

SITUATION ETHICS

In 1966 an American professor called Joseph Fletcher wrote a very important book called *Situation Ethics*. Fletcher believed that when we are faced with a decision about what is the right thing to do then we should not apply any rules but act on the basis of love. There is no absolutely right or wrong way to decide what to do; rather we have to work each particular situation out and then respond in a loving way.

FOR DISCUSSION

A On the Wilderness trail in the pioneering days in America many people lost their lives to the Indians. On one occasion a woman had a crying baby which threatened to give her party's hiding position away. She strangled the baby with her two hands to stop its crying – and all twenty people escaped.

B Your house is burning down. Inside are two people: your aged father who is in a wheelchair and a doctor who has discovered a cure for one of the world's greatest diseases, and who still carries the formula in his head. There is only time to save one. Whom do you save?

!▶ Discuss these two situations.

▶ How would followers of the four theories you've looked at respond to these situations?

FOR YOUR FOLDERS

▶ Write a sentence on hedonism, utilitarianism, situation ethics and ethical egoism.

We all think we can judge fairness pretty well. We recognize at once what is not fair and can usually give a quick answer to the question 'Why not?'

Fair means honest and just, giving the same chances and treatment to everyone, according to the rules if there are any.

Life would be fair if we all had an equal chance; if everyone had enough to eat and clean water to drink; if everyone were treated equally regardless of their colour, sex, or religion; if everyone could say what they wanted; if everyone could vote freely.

These are some examples of things that are fair. They are **human rights** and are due to every single one of us just because we are human. Human rights should automatically belong to everybody.

But life isn't fair, and many people are denied these rights. In some countries children starve to death; only the wealthy can go to school; people are treated differently because of the colour of their skin; people are tortured and imprisoned for saying what they think; there are no elections.

There are many more examples of unfairness. Being fair is not always easy. It means more than fair-sharing, and sometimes what is fair to one person may not be fair for another. It becomes more complicated when we consider people's **freedoms** and their **rights**. Freedoms and rights are quite different from each other. Having a party and riding a bicycle are freedoms – they are things we are lucky enough to enjoy. They are not rights – things we should all have. But both freedoms and rights involve fair treatment and responsibility.

In the same way, having rights involves having **responsibilities**. We may say what we like, but we shouldn't insult people. Having rights means being fair to others. It is our responsibility.

Being fair to others is often difficult. It is made more difficult by the great **inequalities** that exist. It is becoming more and more urgent that we achieve greater fairness in the world. When unfairness and suffering get worse, so, often, does violence and even war. The world needs to try and find a balance between rights and responsibilities. If there is no such balance people and nations will not trust and tolerate each other. To **tolerate** someone means to accept and understand them. It is sometimes difficult to be tolerant when something seems unfair.

FOR YOUR FOLDERS

Look at the following list of human rights and responsibilities. The rights and responsibilities are muddled up.

- A name and identity of our own
- To show respect to other people of other countries
- A country to belong to
- Food, shelter, warmth
- To be educated and develop new skills
- To buy and own things
- To treat other people as individuals, not as things or just part of a group
- To have the protection of the law
- Not to steal people's things
- To share our things with needy people
- To meet together to share new ideas
- To be safe from violence and fear
- To be helped when we are old or ill
- To protect other people from unfair treatment
- To listen to others

- To always try and find out what the truth is
- To respect other people's religious beliefs
- To be able to vote
- To always be friendly and helpful to everyone
- To treat animals kindly

Divide your page into two columns headed 'Rights' and 'Responsibilities'. Put each of the above statements in its correct column. Use the drawings to help you.

- Make a list of fairness and unfairness that you can think of. You can include things in your life as well as about people in general.

- In two columns write down 'My needs' and 'My wants'.

- Write a sentence about each of the following: human rights, freedom, rights, responsibilities, inequalities, tolerance.

Some examples of fairness, freedom, rights and responsibilities

The message from government, media and law enforcers is quite clear. Our society is plagued by violence. It's a crazy world out there. 'Stranger-danger' is the catch-phrase. Bolts, steel doors, alarm systems and all manner of sophisticated locking devices are enjoying boom sales in our cities.

Set against this violent world outside is a powerful and cherished ideal: The Family – offering love and security against the cruel world outside. However, statistics show a different picture. More than half the murders in the West are the result of domestic disputes. Children are more likely to be abused by their own parents than by anybody else. Most women are raped by people they know – in the home. To quote American sociologist Norval Morris: 'You are safer on the streets than at home, safer with a stranger than with a friend or relative.'

WHAT IS PERSONAL VIOLENCE?

Personal violence can take many forms: physical, psychological, sexual, economic – even supernatural. There are, however, some things common to all types of personal violence. Personal violence usually involves the person inflicting the violence gaining power – or extra power – over the victim by causing them pain. It's easier to do this to a person if you 'own' them. They become an object, a commodity that you can treat as you please. The brutal

Gangs of fighting youths learn the hard way that violence breeds violence

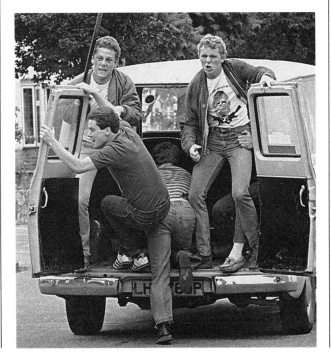

treatment of Africans sold into slavery is a shocking example of this. But the easiest thing of all has been for men to abuse women and adults to abuse children. In the past men have legally owned women and children but although this is not the case today, incest, rape and battering are on the increase.

Violence breeds violence. Parents who batter their children have often been battered themselves. These people are not simply sadistic. Often they are beating to make sense of their own confusing and painful childhood. Using violence against others they regain an element of control, even self respect.

Some people cannot express their anger and resentment to others in their home environment and so project their violence onto others. It is often the case that obedient children who never express anger towards their parents carry a psychological time-bomb in their heads. Many men find an escape for their anger in what sociologists call 'compulsive masculinity'. Some join the armed forces, some go into aggressive 'cut and thrust' business and some turn into street fighting machines on a Saturday afternoon or evening. The 'macho' way, continuously shown in Hollywood movies, presents the idea that action speaks louder than words. The hero bottles things up and then explodes in a display of violent power. But behind this bravado lies the fact that these men can't express their feelings and emotions until it is 'too late'.

One way this manifests itself is child sexual abuse. Men who can't express their emotions find it more desirable to have sexual relationships with children they easily dominate than with other adults with whom they feel emotionally inadequate.

Women, on the other hand, are more likely to 'internalize' aggression, become depressed and turn violence against themselves. Anorexia and tranquiliser dependency are typical symptoms of this self-destructive urge.

WHAT CAN BE DONE ABOUT PERSONAL VIOLENCE?

- At a personal level we should identify what or who is making us angry and express ourselves as directly and constructively as possible. We must try to look at our motives and be aware of the consequences of reacting violently and destructively. Violence breeds violence. This does not mean that we should just 'internalize' anger – this will lead to an explosion later, or to illness – but rather we should look to the root causes of our anger or frustration and try to change these causes.

- At a practical level this means:
  - providing more refuges to make it possible for women and children to leave violent men
  - making counselling readily available for people who are concerned about their own violence
  - creating conditions where children can reveal sexual abuse, be believed and receive professional help
  - respecting the rights of people who are the victims of violence – children, women, racial minorities, gays or any other group chosen as scapegoats.

THE MEDIA

Over the last 20 years the frequency, scale and explicitness of violence on film has increased. On television many kinds of violence are presented as 'entertainment': Tom and Jerry, the 'A' Team, a news item about Beirut, some drama about a psychotic killer, a documentary about torture, a car chase. The presenters, attractive and reasonable, maintain the same expression whether they are introducing news from the Ethiopian famine or about a footballer on a drink-driving charge.

Many Christians and humanists are concerned that people are becoming 'desensitized' by screen violence and unable to distinguish between fact and fiction.

FOOD

Reports by nutritionists and psychologists suggest that food affects our behaviour. For example, the food additive tartrazine (E120) can cause violent bouts of hyperactivity in some children; when the diets of a number of chronic juvenile offenders were analysed it was found that they were exceptionally high in sugar and low in nutrients.

A CHRISTIAN VIEW

'If any one strikes you on the right cheek turn to him the other also.'

(Matthew 5: 39)

In the Gospels Christ taught that people should look at their inner motives and learn not just to react blindly to situations. We need to try and develop our internal world so that we do not hit out and react violently. This does not mean that we shouldn't become angry – anger is part of the human experience – it means that we should try and learn to redirect our anger constructively and learn about other ways of responding.

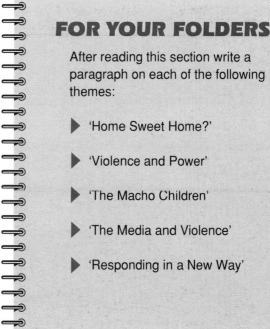

FOR YOUR FOLDERS

After reading this section write a paragraph on each of the following themes:

▶ 'Home Sweet Home?'

▶ 'Violence and Power'

▶ 'The Macho Children'

▶ 'The Media and Violence'

▶ 'Responding in a New Way'

WHAT IS THE 'FAMILY'?

- a husband and wife with children
- a biologically related group
- parents, children, etc., living in a household
- the group that someone grows up in.

The family is our basic social unit. It is the smallest and most common group in our society. It is found in every country and in every age through history.

Sociologists (people who study society and social behaviour) often distinguish between two types of family:

- the **nuclear family**, where husband and wife live alone with their children, and no close relatives live in the household or in the neighbourhood
- the **extended family**, which consists of several generations possibly living in the same house and having relatives living in the neighbourhood.

Every family is different. The picture of the 'ideal' family in advertising differs a great deal from most people's experiences of the family.

The organization and characteristics of the family may vary enormously.

- **monogamy** – in some countries the law states that a person may have only one partner in marriage
- **polyandry** – in some societies a woman can have more than one husband

- **polygamy** – where there are two or more husbands or wives
- **kibutzim** – communes where families and single people all choose to live together. Each person has a specific job, and babies and children are put into nurseries and communal homes. Most *kibbutzim* are in Israel
- **single parent families** – either a man or woman, for a variety of reasons, looks after the child or children
- **arranged marriages** – in some countries marriages are arranged by the parents
- **the elderly** – in some societies the old remain as the head of the family
- **reversed roles** – sometimes the woman goes out to work and the man brings up the children
- **step-parents** – children may be related not by blood but by a re-marriage.

WHAT DOES A FAMILY DO?

- it plays an important part in controlling sexual behaviour
- it is a responsible basis for having and rearing children
- it teaches us an acceptable way to behave, and the customs and traditions of our society (called socialization)
- it allows wealth and property to be passed on to a new generation
- it forms the group in which most humans spend most of their time
- it provides a base for the care of its dependants (e.g. the aged, the sick and the handicapped)
- it gives husband and wife certain economic rights and responsibilities.

A Victorian family

A modern nuclear family

FAMILY LIFE AND THE BIBLE

In the Old Testament there are specific references to family duty and loyalty:

'Honour your father and your mother.'

(Fifth Commandment, Exodus 20: 12)

'Listen to your father who gave you life, and do not despise your mother when she is old.'

(Proverbs 23: 22)

In the New Testament we read in Luke's gospel that Jesus was a dutiful son to his parents, although once they lost him when he went to the Temple (*Luke 2*). When he was older he was very concerned about his mother, Mary, a widow. At his death he asked his best friend to look after Mary when he was gone (*John 19*).

Jesus taught that human beings, as well as giving love, need to receive it. In terms of the family, it means that all the relationships (parent–child, brother–sister, etc.) should be loving, loyal, caring, and respectful – treating people as individuals in their own right.

A HUMANIST VIEWPOINT

'The loving and lively family nest is the basis of future mental and moral health within society.'

(James Hemming, *Individual Morality*)

Hemming outlines five important aspects of family life:

1. freedom of children from being made neurotic by their parents
2. a warm relationship between children and parents
3. a loving relationship between the parents
4. a closely knit and supportive family unit
5. understanding and consistency in discipline.

THE MODERN FAMILY

Although some families in our society are happy and closely knit, many are not. Indeed, even so-called 'happy families' have their problems. Today, there are even more pressures on family life, and tension in the family can be caused by such things as unemployment, changing roles, money worries and alcohol abuse.

FOR YOUR FOLDERS

▶ Make a list of some causes of tension in the family.

▶ Write down the names of members of your 'nuclear family' and 'extended family'.

▶ Write a paragraph about the way that the family has changed in our society over the last century.

❗▶ Explain why many people regard the family as being so important. What do you think?

THINGS TO DO

▶ At home, try to work out your family tree. (Your parents and your grandparents may be able to help you.)

FOR DISCUSSION

▶ 'If men and women are to live the same lives, the family must be abolished.'

(Plato, *c.* 300 BC)

IN GROUPS

▶ In pairs (do this with a friend), discuss the following:
1. arguments in my home,
2. my parents don't understand me,
3. I'll bring my kids up differently,
4. James Hemming's five points and my family.

In 1991 there were almost 200,000 children living with their fathers alone and about 900,000 with their mothers. Over 5% of all families in Britain in 1991 were single parent families. These figures have doubled since 1961. The single parent is usually without a partner for one of the following reasons:

- he or she has divorced or separated – the majority of single parents are in this group
- one of the spouses has died
- he or she has been deserted
- she has made a deliberate choice. Some mothers do not want to (or cannot) marry the father of their child.

In 1987 John was living with his daughter, Annie, who was nine. Here are John's thoughts on his family at that time.

'I've always got on with children. Having a younger brother by 13 years has helped me. One of the finest things I've noticed is the way that people, especially women, have encouraged and supported me. Strange really, because a lot of women do exactly the same thing and get no support or thanks at all. What they do is taken for granted. Women are expected to do it, but without support and encouragement they can find it quite devastating. Generally, most men don't fully appreciate what a demanding job it is bringing up children.

For many people the initial stages of becoming a single parent can be a difficult time. Often it is caused by the traumas of divorce or the grief of bereavement. This can be a tremendous strain. Sometimes, however, a child can feel a great sense of relief when he or she becomes part of a single parent family, after perhaps years of parental strife, arguments and marital breakdown.

Our society all too often stereotypes the abilities of men and women. I've had no problems with cooking, cleaning, washing and looking after our home. The only 'skill' I had to learn was how to iron. As for sewing, I still can't do it, and probably never will. Generally, however, supposedly 'feminine skills' are no problem to me.

Annie is a well-balanced and popular child. She's got lots of friends and is a very happy girl. I've given her a lot of room to express all her thoughts and feelings. Sometimes, quite naturally, she misses her mum. I let her cry and talk about what she's feeling. There's no point in hiding things from kids. I've always been honest and straightforward about our split-up and she sees her mum regularly.

There is something very wrong with the way our society is structured. Most people lead such private lives behind closed doors. Many people hardly ever come into contact with children and this is not good. It amazes me to think that often the first time a woman (or a man for that matter) holds a baby in her arms is in the maternity hospital – her own child.

Schools are at fault, too. All the students, not just the few young women who do child care, should learn about babies and young children. For goodness sake, it is often only a matter of months after leaving school that some young women start having children of their own. Yet we expect people to bring up a happy, well-balanced new generation.

Bringing a child up on your own is not always easy. Sometimes it'd be good to have another adult to share your experiences with.

However, it's got many advantages. You really get to know your child well. You can bring them up the way you want. You can give them all your love and all your time. The relationship can become very deep and loving. The child is not subject to a couple of warring parents. I'm lucky, it's been a joy bringing up Annie.'

Five years later, John had this to say:

'We're still living on our own and I can't ever remember life any other way. In these five years Annie's matured and 'grown-up' in so many ways; then she was a young child, now

she's a young woman with a strong and sensible mind of her own. It's brilliant that she's so independent and capable and basically dead honest – it's made my life a lot easier to get on with – but recently I've found the actual job of parenting more difficult than it's ever been.

We've always chosen to live a bit on our own, in our own rooms, doing things quietly, with our own friends – which worked much easier for me when I was the 'boss'; in times of dispute my decision carried more weight. Now it's a clash of two egos, one set through years of being that way, the other equally convinced it's right, 'cos it's 'my life', and 'things are different, all my mates do it'. Largely this has always been the pattern and I think I've probably learnt more from living with Annie than she has from living with me. The major difference, I feel, is that it's harder to make up, be friends and move on.

There's a simple reason for that . . . when Annie was younger there was no embarrassment about loving one another. We knew when and how to show our love, and how to make each other feel better. Now when we clash she's better able to make her point and more convinced she's right. If I upset her by disagreeing or going on at her, it's just not possible for us to hug and make up. She's fourteen and doesn't want to be cuddled, and to be honest I haven't found an alternative. If she sees me as the problem, it's hard for me to be the solution as well.

It's now that I (sometimes) wish there were two active parents, someone who could go to her and explain why I get so mad, or why I am saying no – and also someone who could help me to see things differently. Two egos clashing doesn't bring forth the most rational reasoning.

Also, after ten years of being a single parent, I long to be seen as a person who has needs, too. I would like to be treated as though I am special occasionally. But I feel guilty and selfish even having that thought.'

FOR DISCUSSION

▶ 'Generally, most men don't fully appreciate what a demanding job it is bringing up children.' What do you think are the advantages and disadvantages of being a single parent, after reading John's story?

▶ Boys should be taught child care and home economics at school.

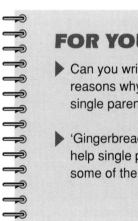

FOR YOUR FOLDERS

▶ Can you write down some of the reasons why there are more and more single parent families?

▶ 'Gingerbread' is a group that tries to help single parents. Can you think of some of the ways it can help?

TALKING POINT

'It amazes me to think that often the first time a woman (or a man for that matter) holds a baby in her arms is in the maternity hospital – her own child.'

Outside of our family, perhaps the most important influences on our lives are the friendships we make. Unlike our own families, we can pick and choose our own friends. They might influence the way we dress, think about life, the music we listen to, the interests we have and even the way we speak. Indeed, friends can greatly influence and even change our opinions, our attitudes and our beliefs about life.

In theory, any of the 55 million people living in Britain and indeed people living elsewhere could be our friends. In practice, most of our friends come from the area where we live and most of these will be around our age. We might meet and make friends in a variety of ways.

- our neighbours
- our church
- through introductions
- through work or school
- whilst on holiday
- through clubs or groups
- at discos/dances
- in clubs
- at evening classes.

WHAT ATTRACTS US TO SOME PEOPLE?

Some of the factors that go into making us friendly with people might include:

- appearance
- sense of humour
- common interests
- different interests
- somebody's nature (similar or opposite to ourselves)
- when we admire somebody
- characteristics
- being thrown together in a situation and getting to know somebody

'No man is an island' (John Donne). Human beings are generally sociable – we need other people's company. Friendships help us to share our experiences with others, learn from others, feel wanted, help our self-confidence, and so on. Our friends sometimes change as our interests and our situations change. Sometimes a friendship may be for a short time. Sometimes a friendship can be for life. Many of the friends you have now may no longer be your friends in, say, five years' time. Sometimes our best friends can be from the opposite sex. (This is called platonic love.)

It is possible to love our friends in the same way as we love members of our family. In the New Testament Jesus' close friends are his disciples, and in particular Peter. Jesus said to his disciples,

'This is my commandment, that you love one another as I have loved you. Greater love has no man than this, that a man lay down his life for his friends. You are my friends if you do what I command you.'

(John 15: 12–14)

This is the ultimate type of friendship – to be willing to sacrifice one's own life for a friend.

Jesus also said, 'You shall love your neighbour as yourself,' (*Mark 12: 31*). Christians believe that we should try to love and respect all people and not *just* people who are closest to us.

IN GROUPS

'One rotten fish plus one fresh fish equals two rotten fish.'

(Old Maori saying)

'The name of a friend is common, but faith in friendship is rare.'

(Phaedrus)

▶ What do these sayings mean?

❗▶ Do you agree with them?

FOR YOUR FOLDERS

▶ Make a list of the 10 qualities you consider to be most important in friendship.

▶ What did Jesus mean in *John 15*? Can you think of examples of people who have actually lived out this teaching?

QUIZ

HOW DO YOU RATE AS A FRIEND?

1 If you quarrel with a friend, are you the first to make it up?
   a Yes
   b No
   c Sometimes

2 If your friend bores you by continually going on about the same thing, do you politely try to change the subject?
   a Yes
   b No
   c No, tell them to shut up

3 Do you gossip to others about your friends?
   a Yes
   b No, never
   c Only sometimes

4 Do you sometimes tell your friend little white lies?
   a Yes
   b No
   c Sometimes

5 Do you keep the secrets that your friend tells you?
   a Yes
   b No
   c Not always

6 If you borrow an LP from your friend and accidentally scratch it would you
   a Tell your friend?
   b Keep quiet?
   c Offer to buy another one?

7 How much do you listen to your friend when they tell you their problems?
   a A lot
   b Not much
   c Occasionally

8 Your friend likes to show off in front of the opposite sex. You get embarrassed. Do you
   a Walk away?
   b Tell them to shut up?
   c Explain in private that you are embarrassed?

HOW TO SCORE

1 a 2	2 a 2	3 a 0	4 a 0
b 0	b 1	b 2	b 2
c 1	c 0	c 1	c 1
5 a 2	6 a 2	7 a 2	8 a 1
b 0	b 0	b 0	b 0
c 1	c 1	c 1	c 2

ADD UP YOUR TOTAL.

12–16 is excellent.
10–12 is very good.
8–10 is good.
6–8 is fair.
Below 6 is poor.

If we look at this week's Top Thirty we can be sure that many of the songs will be about love. Ever since men and women have written songs and poems, one of the most popular themes has been love. Hit songs often ask 'What is love?' and this question has been asked many times.

The word 'love' means many different things. Some of the main types of love are:

- warm affection or liking something, e.g. 'I love the Welsh mountains' (called *storge* by the Greeks)
- sexual affection, passion or desire (called *eros* by the Greeks)
- love of friends (called *philos* by the Greeks)
- love of family
- Christian love (called *agape* by the Greeks), which includes things like charity, tolerance and respect towards all people.

Love is a two-way process. We both receive love and give love. People who find it difficult to love have not always received love in the first place.

KEY IDEA

True happiness does not consist in just receiving love. Rather it is a balance of the receiving and the giving of love.

Young people sometimes get very confused by the emotions connected with love. Often at school relationships between boys and girls can cause problems. We can 'fall in love' with somebody who we 'fancy' and usually this means we are physically attracted to them. Sometimes we can fall in love with somebody and find out later that we don't even like them. Sometimes we can 'fall out of love' as quickly as we fall in love. Occasionally we find ourselves falling in love with somebody who we did not fancy or find attractive at first. Sometimes we fancy someone but are too shy to let them know – this is painful and is called 'unrequited love'.

Love is different from lust. Lust is defined as an 'animal desire for sex'. In conversation today the word 'sex' is usually taken to mean the physical act of sex relations between a couple. The word 'love' is usually taken to mean the whole personal relationship between a couple, including sex. Thus 'love' covers a far wider area than 'sex'.

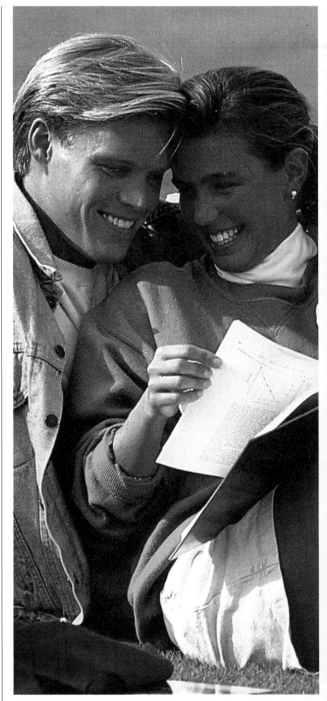

A young couple 'in love'

LOVE IS . . .

What is love? Is it just a sort of chemical reaction in the body when two people meet? Many people think it is more than this and one of the finest definitions of love was written nearly 2,000 years ago by St Paul:

'Love is patient; love is kind and envies no one. Love is never boastful nor conceited, nor rude; never selfish, not quick to take offence. Love keeps no score of wrongs; does not gloat over other men's sins, but delights in the truth. There is nothing love cannot face; there is no limit to its faith, its hope and endurance. Love will never come to an end.'

(I Corinthians 13: 4–8)

Humanists believe that love is very important and is one quality that makes us distinctively human.

THINGS TO FIND OUT

▶ Look at this week's Top Thirty. Make a list of all the songs that are about love.

▶ Are any of them about lust? (List them.)

FOR YOUR FOLDERS

▶ What do *eros* and *agape* mean?

▶ What is unrequited love?

▶ What is the difference between love and lust?

▶ List some of the qualities of love that St Paul mentions.

▶ Write a letter to a problem page about some problematic aspect of love. Try to think up a reply, offering advice.

TALKING POINT

'When love beckons to you, follow him,
Though his ways are hard and steep.
And when his wings unfold you yield to him,
Though the sword hidden among his pinions may wound you
And when he speaks to you believe in him,
Though his voice may shatter your dreams as the north wind lays waste the garden.
For even as love crowns you so shall he crucify you . . .
But if in your fear you would seek only love's peace and love's pleasure,
Then it is better for you that you cover your nakedness and pass out of love's threshing-floor, into the seasonless world where you shall laugh, but not all of your laughter, and weep, but not all of your tears.
Love gives naught but itself and takes naught but from itself.
Love possesses not nor would it be possessed; for love is sufficient unto love.
When you love you should not say "God is in my heart", but rather "I am in the heart of God".
And think not you can direct the course of love, for love, if it finds you worthy, directs your course.

(Kahlil Gibran, *The Prophet*, 1984)

FOR DISCUSSION

▶ 'Love is a fanclub with only two fans
Love is what happens when the music stops
Love is you and love is me
Love is a prison and love is free
Love's what's there when you're away from me
Love is . . .'

(from 'Love Is . . .' by Adrian Henri)

Most healthy human beings have the ability to reproduce. Unlike some other less complex forms of life, we do this sexually – involving the male and female of our species. Without this ability to reproduce there would be no biological survival. The sexual drive is one of the strongest drives known to us – at its biological level it is the desire to reproduce. However, human beings are different from other animals in that our sex drive is linked to our emotional and psychological needs as well.

We live in what is often called a 'permissive society'. This means that in general people are open-minded about sex. Often we like to think that sex, with all its problems, is a new thing and that our particular generation 'discovered' it.

ATTITUDES TO SEX

Often young people are under tremendous pressure about sex. Young boys feel pressurized to boast about their 'sexual conquests'. Girls are called names if it is believed that they have had sexual relationships. They are called different names if they have not. Society puts pressures on young people, through advertising and the media, with sexual images communicating ideas that sex is acceptable without the responsibilities of a whole and fulfilling relationship. Often young people find it difficult to talk openly and freely to their parents about their sexual feelings and this can lead to repression and misunderstandings about their emotions. Younger children often learn about sex through their peers and sex is seen as being something that is 'naughty' or 'dirty'. Unless young people are allowed to express and share their feelings with each other in a community free from the sorts of sexual conditioning that exist, then many people, when they grow older, find themselves with a whole bundle of sexual hang-ups.

In order for people to grow up experiencing happy and fulfilled sexual relationships they must learn the value of respecting other human beings not as objects of their own gratification but as other people with the same feelings, emotions and hopes as them.

It has been said that in earlier generations sex outside marriage was not as common as it is today because of three fears:

1 fear of detection
2 fear of infection
3 fear of conception.

Sex outside marriage, which means pre-marital (before marriage) and extra-marital (during marriage), has now become more common, possibly because of the following reasons:

● virginity is not considered to be so important
● contraceptive devices have improved
● education about contraception has improved
● abortions are easier to obtain
● sexual permissiveness is often encouraged in the media
● fewer people follow the teachings of the Church
● medical facilities have improved.

However, the results have been very serious:

● sexually transmitted diseases are increasing
● more children are being born out of wedlock
● emotionally immature young people are sexually active
● divorce rates have risen
● there is now a risk of contracting AIDS.

CHRISTIANITY AND SEX OUTSIDE MARRIAGE

Christians generally would say that sex outside marriage is wrong not just because it leads to the problems listed above but because Jesus spoke out against it. However, some Christians would agree that sexual intercourse between a couple who love one another and intend to create a life together is morally acceptable.

The New Testament frequently discusses sexual matters. Fornication and adultery are condemned over 30 times. Basically, Christianity teaches that:

● sex is a beautiful gift from God demanding responsibility, commitment and total love
● it is always wrong to use a person as a thing
● sexual intercourse is very special (it can create new life)
● sex is the most beautiful expression of a deep, loving, life-long union between two people.

HUMANISTS ANSWER SOME QUESTIONS ABOUT SEX

Do Humanists believe in sleeping around?
No they don't. Because casual sexual relationships all too often show lack of concern and lead to people getting hurt. Humanists believe that love is something we share with one another, sometimes with passion, but always with responsibility and caring. Love for one another and respect for one another go together.

If you don't think sex before marriage is wrong, what about illegitimate babies?

Happiness and love and security are especially vital, because babies will grow into unique, valuable individual people. Babies are created by their **parents**. This is why moral decisions involving sex may be difficult, in case an unplanned pregnancy should result. Efficient methods of contraception have made it possible for people to explore life deeply with another person without necessarily being tied to them forever. Babies should only be started when you are sure you can give them a loving and secure upbringing.

Is sex education important?

Indeed it is. Children's questions should be answered honestly all the time, and particularly those about sex, since it can be a very wonderful part of our lives. Nowadays biased ideas about sex are directed at school leavers from many sources – but decisions involving sex should be made (as should decisions not involving sex) from a standpoint of factual knowledge, and not in the darkness of ignorance. Therefore Humanists think you should learn about your own bodies and about sex, love, pregnancy, contraception, abortion, venereal disease and psychology.

(Humanist Dipper)

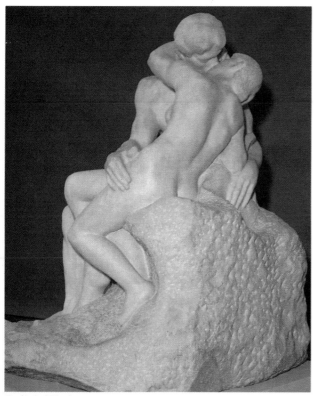

Rodin's 'Kiss'

FOR YOUR FOLDERS

▶ Write down what the following mean: permissive society, pre-marital sex, extra-marital sex, life-long union.

▶ Write a paragraph on each of the following: the Christian view of sex; the Humanist view of sex.

▶ What sort of pressures are young people put under as regards their sexual identities?

!▶ Write down what you think the 'three fears' are about.

FOR DISCUSSION

▶ 'If [the unmarried] cannot control themselves they should marry. Better be married than burn with vain desire'. (*I Corinthians 7: 9*). Discuss this statement of St Paul's.

▶ Discuss some of the reasons why sex outside marriage is apparently more common these days than for earlier generations.

IN GROUPS

In groups of two to three (be with your friends) do the following task.

▶ Imagine that you had to plan a sex education programme for people of your own age. There are 10 sessions of 45 minutes to organize. Discuss what topics you would like to be covered. Take 20 minutes to do this. Then write down on a piece of paper your suggestions and fold the paper before handing it to the teacher, who will arrange a class discussion.

Sexual relationships do not have to be within the framework of marriage

In this section we will be looking at the way Christians are beginning to change their attitudes towards sexual ethics. Traditionally, the Church has been negative towards pleasure and positive towards procreation. Sex was for creating children. The pleasure that went with it was nothing more than a suitable reward. Outside marriage sex was always forbidden.

Over the last 20 years, however, sexual pleasure has slowly been re-embraced by the Church. It is now more or less officially recognized as a precious gift from God.

The Roman Catholic Church has traditionally insisted that every time a man and woman have sex it should be possible for a new life to be created. This accounts for its strong teachings on contraception (see Section 22). But, even if everyone used methods of birth regulation approved by the Church, the fact still remains that nowadays 99 per cent of sexual intercourse is non-procreative. This raises some important questions.

1 Is pleasure the deepest reason for sex?

2 Should men and women have sex as and when they wish, either outside or inside marriage?

3 Has the time come to change attitudes and prohibitions on issues like sex before marriage, adultery and homosexuality?

For Christians, the Bible teaches fundamental truths about human behaviour. The problem is now that the Church finds itself in the situation where its teachings often seem old-fashioned and out of place in a world where sexual ethics are fast changing.

Jack Dominion is a Roman Catholic theologian and psychiatrist. In the following extract he argues that a case can be made for the traditional Christian view without rejecting modern experience and attitudes.

> *'The first step must be a fundamental reappraisal of the sex act itself. The act of intercourse has been traditionally regarded as a biological act; an act which first and foremost makes it possible for a sperm and an ovum to unite. In my view, this is a mistakenly narrow interpretation.*
>
> - *sexual intercourse is, first of all, a body language, through which couples talk to and do things for one another. When couples make love they rejoice in each other's presence and the pleasure they exchange. For this they want to give thanks. Thus sex is a recurrent act of thanksgiving.*
>
> - *Secondly, because people want to make love repeatedly, they trust that their partners will respond to them again. So sex is also a recurrent act of hope: the hope of being desired again.*
>
> - *Thirdly, in the course of the day couples hurt one another. Most of these hurts are forgiven and forgotten on the spot. But some are too painful to be forgiven so easily. Such hurts need a deeper level of love and communication to erase them. So sexual intercourse can also be an act of reconciliation.*
>
> - *Fourthly, sexual intercourse confirms the sexual identity of the partners.*

● *Finally, every time a couple makes love, they are saying to each other: "I recognize you, I want you, I appreciate you." In this way it is a recurrent act of personal affirmation.*

As a result, sexual intercourse has the capacity to give life in a more than biological sense. So sexual intercourse not only gives pleasure. It also has a powerful personal dimension in which the couple enrich one another's lives.

From this point of view marriage can be seen as providing the condition where the physical and personal can unite and transform the life of the couple. Marriage provides a continuous, reliable, and predictable relationship within which the rich potential of sex can thrive. In this sense, sex actually requires marriage for the realization of its potential.

This is the case for Christian morality: not that sex is dangerous and needs marriage and procreation to protect it; but rather that sex is so powerful and meaningful that justice can only be done to it in a continuous and enduring relationship.'

(from *The Capacity to Love*, 1985)

HOW DOES THIS VIEW DIFFER FROM THE TRADITIONAL CHRISTIAN TEACHING?

The first difference is in the understanding that sexual pleasure is a precious gift from God which needs to be appreciated and encouraged for itself. Sex is not just about procreation but is about nurturing a loving relationship.

At present some churches teach that all intercourse before marriage is wrong. However, there is a world of difference between a client and prostitute having intercourse and a young couple in love with one another having sex. In one there is a meeting only of bodies, in the other there is a continuing meeting of the union between bodies, minds, emotions and personalities.

These views also encourage us to think about homosexual and lesbian relationships. If the Church accepts that sex is not just for procreation, if its purpose is also to unite people in love, then one can perhaps see the day when permanent, loving relationships between homosexuals will be approved.

TALKING POINT

'"Should the Church move with the times?" The answer must be "Yes". Society has a lot to teach the Church about sex. But Christianity too embodies fundamental truths which – although in need of equally fundamental rethinking themselves – carry basic values which society ignores at its peril.'
(Jack Dominion)

FOR DISCUSSION

Read Jack Dominion's five comments on sexual intercourse. Do you feel that they are possible in today's world or do you think they are unrealistic?

FOR YOUR FOLDERS

▶ Try and explain in your own words how the traditional Christian view of sexuality needs to change to meet the needs of people today, according to Jack Dominion.

▶ Christians believe that the truths of their religion are eternal. In your view, has Christianity got anything to offer in terms of helping us understand sexual ethics?

We live in what has been called a 'patriachal society'. This basically means that men have the economic and social power to control the world as they see fit. From a very early age boys are conditioned into adopting and accepting certain values and attitudes about their roles in society. In this section you are encouraged to explore what these roles mean, what they imply and, hopefully, to begin to understand what it means to be a boy.

Over the last 30 years, women have begun to have more of a voice. The Women's Movement challenges many of the stereotypes concerning the role of men and women in our society.

For many men this has meant a reappraisal of their own values and attitudes about themselves and about women.

FOR DISCUSSION

It is not easy being a boy. Here are seven starting points for discussion concerning boyhood:

1   **Boys as babies.** The education of a boy starts as soon as he is born. Some examples of this sexual conditioning are notorious: pink and frilly for girls, blue and functional for boys; guns for boys and dolls for girls. But there are all kinds of more subtle influences which are probably more significant, e.g. boys are allowed to make more noise and cause more trouble ('boys will be boys'), while girls are expected to show more interest in talking to people. This kind of education prepares boys for power in the world but it restricts their options and the directions open to them.

2   **Boys under pressure.** A boy is supposed to be good at sport; a good fighter and capable of enduring pain without crying. These 'qualities' demand that he is sometimes hurtful to other children. Probably only a minority of boys are naturally all of these things. All boys are different and being good at cookery is just as valuable as being good at football. Boys, however, are supposed to be 'macho' and not 'wimps' and these images are strengthened by the media.

3   **Boys and boys.** Sometimes boys feel they have to put down girls to be cool. Often boys hide their more positive and tender feelings under a show of careless bravado. At some ages it is common for boys to band together and discuss people and things which are different. This means that some of their fun lies in sexist, racist or anti-gay jokes.

4   **Boys and love.** All boys are under enormous pressure to direct their sexual and romantic feelings towards girls. When sex comes up in conversation it is common for boys to bluster about their sexual prowess or else to lapse into giggly embarrassment. Romance is thought of as the province of girls, but many adolescent boys are incurable romantics.

5   **Boys and bullies.** Some boys encounter more violence as boys than they do in the whole of the rest of their lives. A boy's world is often a rough one in which the weak and the losers are picked on simply because they are physically weak. Bullies are the source of much violence in playground culture and knowing what to do about them can be a major problem for boys. It is a sad fact that bullies generally act the way they do because they have been bullied too – by a violent father for example. But it can help the bullies themselves to talk with other boys and teachers about how they have been mistreated, it helps them feel less isolated.

6   **Boys and girls.** Boys and girls are separated from each other and there are social pressures which send them in different directions. Sometimes they may even go to different schools. This means that to many boys girls are a world apart. It makes girls fascinating, but it can also make them a bit disturbing for a boy because they are out of his control. This means he is often eager to put them down out of self defence. Much of the contempt for women in adult male culture stems from this adolescent experience – in that sense sexist men just haven't grown up.

7   **Boys and the future.** Boys can be sensitive and brave, witty and sharp, agile and energetic. Much of what goes on in a boy's life dictates how he reacts to boys and girls when he is a man. If society could begin to reduce the pressure on boys to be macho then this might help them to grow into complete men. Boys need to be encouraged to be open to people, children and nature.

Boys are conditioned to accept certain roles and values at an early age

A HUMANIST VIEW

'The dominant form of masculinity in Western culture embodies men's social power over women. It emphasizes force, authority, aggressiveness. But to keep up this image the majority of men must be kept in their place. Some men fail to live up to this image: their legs are too thin, their chests not hairy enough, their glances insufficiently flinty. Others are actively suppressed, gay men and effeminate men most obviously. The prevailing school system, social indifference to youth's hunger for significance and the experience of sexual rejection may all be components in generating a violent response among our less fortunate young males.'

(James Hemming)

A CHRISTIAN VIEW

'If we are to learn to live together, then we need to look at the way that men are educated and conditioned in a male-orientated, materialistic society. Often boys are not encouraged to express their true feelings and they are taught to suppress the turbulent emotions that well up deep from the unconscious. Jesus taught "Love your neighbour as you love yourself", but until society encourages boys to look at themselves hatred and division will take the place of love and peace.'

(Author's interview with a practising Christian)

FOR YOUR FOLDERS

▶ Write a paragraph about your views on the seven starting points for discussion.

▶ Explain in your own words the meaning of the Humanist and Christian views on masculinity.

Pornography – 'that which exploits and dehumanizes sex so that human beings are treated as things and women, in particular, as sex objects.'

(Christian Action Research and Education)

Pornography – 'depicting a combination of the sexual objectification and subordination of women often including violation and violence.' Pornography is big business. In the USA alone it is worth at least $10 billion a year – more than the music and film industries combined. 'Softcore' pornography portrays women in 'provocative' positions, inviting sexual arousal and penetration. 'Hardcore' pornography includes things like torture, multiple rape, women engaged in sexual intercourse with animals, and the actual killing of women on screen in 'snuff films'.

SEX STEREOTYPING

Whether it is overtly violent or not, pornography shows women in a degrading, humiliating way, often with the message that women enjoy this and want to be abused. It seems that pornography has become acceptable in our society – the top shelves of newsagents are full of pornographic magazines and tabloid 'newspapers' display half-naked women on their pages. However, images which represent women in sex stereotyped ways (such as in 'Janet and John' children's books, in Mills and Boon romances, soap powder 'housewives', 'Oxo mums', and 'Jackie' magazine heroines) are an essential part of creating and maintaining the system of sexism (see Unit 50). The portrayal of women as sex objects (newspaper page 3 pin-ups, car adverts, 'Miss World' competitions) is a powerful expression of the negative attitude of sexism.

PORNOGRAPHY AND CENSORSHIP

'We believe that pornography should be eliminated on the grounds that it contributes to sex discrimination, sexual inequality, sexual violence and sexism. We believe in free speech, free expression and freedom of information. We are totally against censorship. Censorship is about the limitation of freedom; eliminating pornography is about promoting the freedom of women. We believe in human rights and the rights of women.

Pornography silences women and censors the freedom of women. There are some so called 'freedoms' that society agrees to limit because of the harm and damage that they do to other people. The 'freedom' to manufacture and distribute pornography should be limited for the same reasons, i.e. because it causes harm and damage to women. Pornography acts as an "incitement to sexual hatred and violence" in the same way that racist and fascist literature acts as an "incitement to racial hatred" and which is unlawful under the Race Relations Act (1976). We believe that pornography should be legislated against on the same grounds.'

'Some people, usually men, argue that pornography is harmless. However, if we try and think clearly about the existence of pornography in our everyday lives we should begin to see that the effects of pornography have dangerous consequences for us individually and as a society.'

(*New Internationalist*, September 1988)

FOR DISCUSSION

Divide into pairs, if possible with someone of the opposite sex. Read and discuss the following together.

1 Pornography ruins family relationships
2 Pornography degrades both women and men
3 Pornography is offensive
4 Pornography promotes destructive fantasy
5 Pornography is addictive
6 Pornography damages young people
7 Pornography is linked with corruption
8 Pornography triggers sexual assault
9 Pornography destroys God's Creation.

TALKING POINT

'It is said that we are free not to buy such newspapers but things are not as simple as that. I have received several letters from women whose husbands buy such newspapers. Those women object strongly to those newspapers and object to them being left lying around the house for their children to see. I agree with the women who think that there is a strong connection between the rising tide of sexual crime and Page 3. Obviously this is unprovable, but the constant mass circulation of such pictures so that they are widely seen by children must influence sexual attitudes and the climate towards sexuality in our society. These pictures portray women as objects of lust to be sniggered over and grabbed at, and do not portray sex as something that is tender and private. When future generations read that in our day about 10 million newspapers carried such pictures every day to be left around and seen by children and by lots of women who did not want to see them, they will see those pictures as symbolic of our decadent society.'

(Clare Short, MP)

FOR YOUR FOLDERS

▶ Find out the meaning of the following words: exploit, dehumanize; subordination; objectification; violate; stereotype.

▶ Explain in your own words how pornography exploits, dehumanizes, subordinates, objectifies, violates and stereotypes women.

CONFESSION BY TED BUNDY, AMERICAN SERIAL SEX KILLER

'My experience with pornography that deals on a violent level with sexuality is that once you become addicted to it – and I look at this as an addiction – I would keep looking for more potent, more explicit, more graphic kinds of materials. Like an addiction, you keep craving something which is harder. Something which gives you a greater sense of excitement. Until you reach a certain point where the pornography only goes so far. I think society deserves to be protected from itself because as we've been talking there are forces at loose in this country – particularly violent pornography – where on the one hand, well-meaning, decent people will condemn the behaviour of a Ted Bundy, while they're walking past a magazine rack full of the very kinds of things that send young kids down the road to be Ted Bundys. That's the irony.'

(Ted Bundy, aged 42, was executed in February 1989 in Florida. He confessed to killing more than 20 women.)

CLASS DEBATE

▶ This house believes it should be an offence to publish in newspaper pictures, of naked or partially naked women in sexually provocative poses.

CHRISTIAN VIEWPOINT

'Not only does pornography dehumanize the person portrayed, but also dehumanizes the viewer, for to the extent to which we dehumanize others and fail to respect them as creations of God, we ourselves are dehumanized and dwarfed.'

(CARE, 1988)

'AIDS is caused by a virus called HIV (Human Immunodeficiency Virus). This can damage the body's defence system so that it cannot fight certain infections.

HIV is not passed on through everyday social contact.

HIV is transmitted in three main ways:

- *Through unprotected sexual intercourse (anal or vaginal)*
- *By injecting drug users sharing equipment including syringes and needles*
- *From an infected mother to her unborn child.'*

(Health Education Authority leaflet)

Since 1981 tens of thousands of cases of AIDS have been reported worldwide and the numbers are increasing fast. The main groups at risk are:

- practising homosexual and bisexual men
- drug users who share injection equipment
- haemophiliacs and others who have received blood products
- sexual partners of all these people
- babies born to infected people
- heterosexuals with more than one partner who do not practise safe sex.

But the infection is now spreading among heterosexual people, since it can be passed on by sexual intercourse.

The Terrence Higgins Trust, named after the first person to die from AIDS in Britain, offers the public a wide variety of services concerning AIDS. These include help and support for people with AIDS, their families and friends; health education for those at risk; and support for medical research into AIDS.

At first it was thought that only homosexuals could contract or pass on AIDS, but it is now accepted that AIDS can affect the whole community. Some people have called AIDS 'God's wrath' on homosexuals and other people who have contracted the disease through sexual relations. However, most Christians strongly disagree with this.

'AIDS is heartbreaking and challenges the Churches to break their own hearts, to repent of inactivity and of rigid moralizing. Since AIDS cuts across race, class, gender, age, sexual orientation and sexual expression, it challenges our fears. [The Churches] must work against the real danger that AIDS will be used as an excuse for discrimination and oppression and work to ensure the protection of the human rights of persons affected directly or indirectly by AIDS.'

(Source: World Council of Churches Executive Committee)

HOW TO PROTECT YOURSELF

HIV – the virus that can cause AIDS – is found in the fluids exchanged during sexual intercourse (men's semen and women's vaginal fluids).

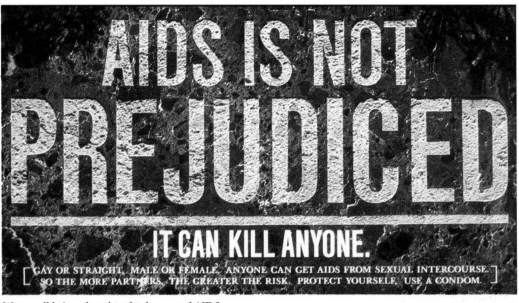

We are all being alerted to the dangers of AIDS

● **Try to make safer sex part of your life**

The more people you have unprotected sexual intercourse with the more likely you are to meet someone with HIV and become infected yourself. The same applies for your partner. You are also more likely to become infected with other sexually transmitted diseases like gonorrhoea, herpes, chlamydia and hepatitis B and to pass them on to someone else.

Some ways of having sex carry a higher risk than others

● **Unprotected anal intercourse**
This is when the penis enters the anus or back passage. It carries a particularly high risk.

● **Unprotected vaginal intercourse**
This carries a risk. The virus can be passed by both men and women to their sexual partners through men's semen and women's vaginal fluids.

● **Oral sex**
When one partner stimulates the other's genitals with the mouth or tongue (oral sex) there is theoretically some risk. The virus could pass through semen and women's vaginal fluids into the other person's body, particularly if they have cuts or sores in their mouth. However, this is extremely unlikely to occur.

● **Sharing sex toys**
Sharing sex toys, like vibrators, could carry a risk as the infection could be passed from one person to another.

It is extremely unlikely that the virus could be passed on through deep french kissing and there have been no proven cases of this happening.

USING A CONDOM
A condom can help stop the virus – and other sexually transmitted diseases – passing from one person to another. It must be used properly.

Look for condoms with the BSI Kitemark as this means that they are properly tested.

Never re-use a condom.

PHONE THE NATIONAL AIDS HELPLINE ON
0800 567 123
FOR MORE INFORMATION

(Health Education Authority)

THINGS TO DO

▶ Read about how to protect yourself. Discuss it seriously with a friend. It is very important.

▶ Look up the biblical reference *John 9: 1–3*. What does this tell us about Jesus' views of the relationship between suffering and sin?

FOR DISCUSSION

▶ 'Celibacy, chastity, virginity and faithfulness are no longer old-fashioned virtues. They are back and here to stay because of AIDS.'

▶ Why might many practising Catholics find themselves in a dilemma as regards the use of a condom?

▶ 'People must become "sexually honest" with their partners.'

▶ 'AIDS does not discriminate.' Would you agree?

FOR YOUR FOLDERS

▶ Write two short articles of about 100 words each, entitled 'AIDS: the facts' and 'The problems facing an AIDS victim and their family'.

▶ Write a paragraph explaining in your own words the World Council of Churches' statement.

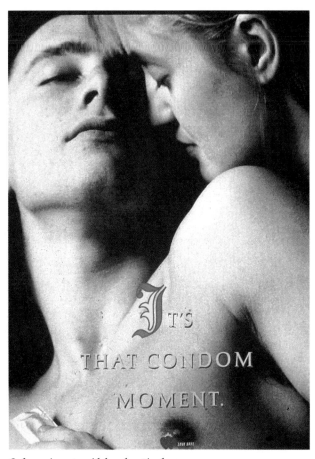

Safe sex is now widely advertised

An AIDS epidemic is something that should concern us all. It raises many moral issues.

When AIDS first hit the headlines it was assumed that it would only affect the gay community and intravenous drug users. We now read, however, of cases of people who have contracted AIDS through dental treatment, blood transfusions and heterosexual intercourse. Indeed, as we can see in the article opposite, it is estimated that by the year 2000 around 90 per cent of global AIDS cases will be among heterosexuals.

There has been great debate about the origin of the AIDS virus and, as with much information about AIDS, there has been a great deal of misinformation. For instance, some people argue that AIDS came from Africa (which can merely reinforce racist attitudes). Others argue that AIDS came about as a result of scientific and military research on germ warfare. The fact remains, however, that AIDS is a reality which is taking a terrible toll in many countries around the world. The World Health Organization (WHO) calculated that in 1991 approximately one million people would have AIDS,

with another 5–10 per cent being HIV positive.

Early on AIDS was labelled the 'gay disease', and many fundamentalist Christians believed that AIDS was God's punishment for certain types of behaviour. People who were outside the accepted norms of society, e.g. gays, drug users and anyone else seen to be 'dirty' enough to be infected were targets of persecution. For instance, in America the home of a family with two HIV positive haemophiliac sons was burnt to the ground by angry neighbours; the family had wanted to enrole their sons in the local public school.

'The real tragedy of AIDS lies in the racism, homophobia and negative responses of government, the mainstream medical establishment and society at large.'

(Kris Peterson and Corey Dubin)

AIDS raises many issues:

1 Should there be compulsory testing of people who are in the high risk groups?

2 If someone is found to be HIV positive should this information be passed to his or her employer?

3 Should babies carried by HIV positive mothers be aborted?

4 How should people be educated about AIDS so that the prejudices surrounding AIDS can be minimized?

5 In a national health system that is suffering from inadequate funding should more money be put in to help sufferers of AIDS?

6 Should the multi-national companies, who are spending billions of dollars on trying to find a cure for AIDS, be made to work together so that there is not a competitive element brought into this area of medical research? Obviously, the company that discovers a 'cure' will make enormous profit.

7 Should people with AIDS be allowed to move freely from country to country?

8 On a personal level, how can people who have AIDS be made to control their sexual activity so that they do not infect others?

9 Should condoms be made freely available in schools, colleges, places of employment, etc?

10 How can the families of AIDS sufferers be supported?

Freddie Mercury, one of AIDS' most famous victims

THE GUARDIAN   Tuesday June 18 1991

Chris Mihill at the Aids conference in Florence

Heterosexuals face epidemic onslaught

THE FUTURE spread of the global Aids epidemic in the heterosexual population will make drug addict and homosexual cases almost irrelevant in numerical terms, the chief Aids statistician of the World Health Organisation said yesterday.

Dr James Chin, head of Aids surveillance and forecasting, said that by the year 2000 around 90 per cent of global Aids cases would be among heterosexuals.

He told the seventh international Aids conference in Florence that there may be "anything from a quarter to a half billion" heterosexuals at very high risk of a sexually transmitted disease, because of multiple sexual partners.

"There may be only 10–20 million homosexual men throughout the world with multiple sexual partners, and 5–10 million injecting drug users throughout the world who share needles on a regular basis.

"The point is to say that the future of the HIV and Aids pandemic is in the heterosexual population.

"Because of the relative size, even if we were to infect all homosexuals and all injecting drug users, the future really rests with the large number of susceptible heterosexuals."

TALKING POINT

'To even begin to address the AIDS crisis a massive input of government funding is needed. This would mean a complete change in government policies and priorities. America spends more money in one day on 'defence' than was spent in total on research and treatment during the first 10 years of the AIDS crisis.'

(Kris Peterson and Corey Dubin)

> **Contraception** – 'various methods by which a couple can avoid an unwanted pregnancy.'

WHY IS CONTRACEPTION USED TODAY?

- a couple may decide not to have children
- a family may already be large enough
- it helps people to plan their future
- it enables couples to enjoy sex without worrying about pregnancy
- it helps to control the population
- in cases of pre-marital sex, it can prevent unwanted pregnancy.

METHODS OF CONTRACEPTION

- **Natural Family Planning (NFP)**
  NFP refers to the woman becoming aware of her own fertile and infertile cycles by recording the natural signals of her body (e.g. the temperature method, the Billings (or 'ovulation') method and the sympothermal method). Many Roman Catholics prefer these methods.
  Is it safe?
  The World Health Organization puts the sympothermal method in the top three methods of birth control.

  (Catholic Truth Society)

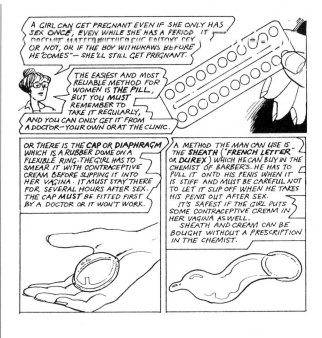

- **Rhythm method**
  Some days during the menstrual cycle a woman is not fertile – so a couple can have sex during those days. But they need to work out the 'safe' days very carefully indeed – the woman will have to take her temperature regularly – and this has to be done every month as the cycle is different every time.
  Is it safe?
  This method is not safe at all, as it is so easy to make a mistake.

- **Withdrawal method**
  The man withdraws his penis before his sperm are released, so that none of them enter the woman's vagina.
  Is it safe?
  No, because the man may not withdraw his penis in time. Also, sperm can be released at any time while the couple are having sex.

- **The Pill**
  The Pill is now taken by about 55 million women worldwide. It works by altering the hormone balance of the woman's body, so that she does not become fertile.
  Is it safe?
  As a method of contraception, it is the safest. There may be side-effects in that other parts of the body such as the breasts, or body hair may be affected. Women taking the Pill may also suffer from depression. The long-term effects are not known.

- **The vault cap and diaphragm**

  These are both rubber domes on a flexible ring. The diaphragm is wider and flatter. Both are smeared with contraceptive jelly and slipped into the woman's vagina. The cap fits over the mouth of the cervix. The diaphragm fits right across the vagina. Both must be fitted by a doctor and checked regularly or they will not work. They must be left in place for at least six hours after the couple have had sex.

  Are they safe?

  Both are reliable so long as they are fitted and used correctly.

- **The sheath or condom**

  This is the method a man can use. He pulls the sheath on to his erect penis and leaves it there until his sperm have been released. It's safer if the woman puts contraceptive cream in her vagina as well.

  Is it safe?

  Again, it is safe if correctly used. More and more people are using the sheath now because it is the best available protection against infection by the AIDS virus.

- **The IUD (inter-uterine device) or coil**

  This is made of plastic or metal and has a small piece of copper wire attached to it. It is fitted inside the woman's womb by a doctor. No one is sure how it works, but it is thought to prevent a fertilized egg from attaching itself to the wall of the womb, where it can begin to grow into a foetus.

  Is it safe?

  The IUD is a reliable way of preventing pregnancy. Side-effects may be heavy or prolonged periods, or cramp-like pains. Occasionally the woman may expel it from her body.

THREE VIEWS ON CONTRACEPTION

1 **Humanists regard sex as one of the greatest pleasures of life, not just the means of reproduction. If contraception helps a relationship, then it is a good thing.**

2 **The Catholic Church teaches that the primary purpose of sexual intercourse is the begetting of children. Intercourse is a sin unless the procreation of children is intended, or at least not hindered, because children are a gift from God. In the papal encyclical *Hymanae Vitae* (1968) all artificial forms of contraception are condemned.**

3 **The Anglican view on contraception is that a couple may practise forms of contraception that are acceptable to both partners.**

FOR YOUR FOLDERS

▶ List some contraceptives that are available for (a) men and (b) women.

▶ What contraceptives can be unsafe?

▶ Write a paragraph about some of the foolish things that Evelyn says in the cartoon.

! ▶ Write a paragraph about the following statement: 'No one has the right to create a life thoughtlessly.'

▶ In 1984 the Pope said:
'Only natural forms of birth control do not offend the moral order established by God.'

  a What do you think he means by 'natural birth control'?

  b How would he argue that 'unnatural' forms of birth control would offend 'the moral order established by God'?

FOR DISCUSSION

▶ 'The availability of contraception makes society less moral than it used to be.'

▶ 'Sex is a function primarily for having children.'

▶ 'The method of contraception is not just up to the woman.'

> **Celibacy** – 'the state of being unmarried, especially as the result of a religious promise'.

> **Virginity** – 'the state of being a virgin (one without sexual experience)'.

In 1139 celibacy among practising priests was made law in the Catholic Church. In the early Church many of the leaders were married but the Church in 1139 felt that the celibate priest is more free to devote himself fully to the work of the Church. However, over the last 20 years the idea of celibacy among priests has become a controversial issue in the Catholic Church. In 1966 the National Association for Pastoral Renewal (NAPR) was formed to work for, among other things, optional celibacy. Hans Kung, a Swiss Catholic thinker, said: 'There will be no rest about this matter in the Catholic Church until celibacy is again – as it was originally – left to the free decision of the individual.' However, successive Popes have ruled that celibacy among priests must remain. They argue that celibacy enables a priest to dedicate himself entirely to his ministry. During the Second Vatican Council (1962–5) the idea of priestly celibacy was confirmed.

'To the unmarried and the widows I say that it is well for them to remain single as I do.'

(I Corinthians 7: 8)

> **Chastity** – 'the state of being sexually pure'.

To refrain from having sexual relations (sexual abstinence) for personal reasons is known as 'chastity'. People decide to be chaste for a number of reasons:

- to practise self-control
- to concentrate all their energies in other directions
- to practise birth control
- to dedicate themselves to some religious ideal
- as an experiment within a relationship
- to follow their own desires.

In monasteries (communities of monks) and convents (communities of nuns), men and women make three vows – poverty, chastity and obedience.

IS BEING A VIRGIN IMPORTANT?

The most important thing about virginity is for a girl or boy to be sure in their own mind why they do or do not wish to have sexual intercourse.

WHY ARE THERE DIFFERENT VALUES?

Many factors will play their part in making up a person's mind about virginity (their own desires, their society, its values, their friends, families, etc.). In some countries in the past a father could kill his daughter if she lost her virginity before marriage. It is important to be sure in your own mind what you want to do and to realize that having sexual intercourse is something that should not be undertaken lightly.

IS THERE A DIFFERENCE BETWEEN MEN AND WOMEN WHERE VIRGINITY IS CONCERNED?

There is much hypocrisy here. Men may be called 'Casanova', 'Don Juan' or 'a bit of a lad' if they have a lot of different sexual partners. But if women do, they may be called names like 'tart', 'slut', 'whore'. There is no history of men being punished for loss of virginity. And until contraception was widely available, many women chose to remain virgins rather than risk unwanted pregnancy. The attitude that it is more acceptable for men to be sexually active is still common. In reality, both men and women are capable of feeling jealous if their partner has already 'slept around'. Or both may consider that a marriage is more likely to work if the partners are sexually experienced.

WHY DO PEOPLE CHOOSE TO REMAIN VIRGINS?

There may be a number of reasons.

- They may refrain from sexual intercourse because their partner does not feel that the time is right for sexual intercourse. In this way they are respecting the rights of the individual.

- They may be nervous, insecure, or unsure about sexual intercourse and its implications.

- They may wish to remain virgins so that they can make a gift to the one they really love.

- They may be deeply religious and follow the teachings of their Church. For instance, 'Every sexual act must be within the framework of marriage' (Catholic teaching in the encyclical 'Casti Conubii'); 'The Christian affirms abstinence from sexual intercourse outside the marriage bond' (Methodist Conference, 1981). In these cases they will remain virgins until they marry.

FOR DISCUSSION

What do you think about the following two statements? Compare and discuss them.

a 'It's a good idea to have sex before marriage so that you'll be able to be experienced when you meet your marriage partner.'

b 'If you sleep around you soon lose the wonder and mystery of sex, which should only be shared with your loved one.'

FOR YOUR FOLDERS

▶ Explain the following words: celibacy, chastity, virginity.

▶ There are about 1½ million individuals committed to celibacy in the Catholic Church and about 2,000 men in religious orders in the Church of England. Why do you think these people have chosen this path? Try and write down at least **two** reasons.

▶ Make a list of some of the dangers of 'sleeping around'.

▶ Dear Marj,
I am 15 and a virgin. I have been going out with this 18-year-old boy for six months. We have quite heavy petting sessions but he wants me to have sex with him. I have told him 'No' – but he's threatened to finish with me if I don't go to bed with him. I love him but don't want to lose my virginity. Help me, please.
Yours sincerely,
Confused

Write a letter back to 'Confused', giving her some advice.

The word 'homosexuality' was first coined by a Swiss doctor, K. M. Benkert, in 1869. Greek 'homo' has been added to Latin 'sex' to indicate an attraction of sexual preference for the same sex. Female homosexuality is also described as 'Lesbianism', taking its name from the island of Lesbos, where the Greek poet Sappho once lived in a female community. Evidence suggests that the incidence of homosexuality among adult men and women is about five per cent. There has been much debate among scientists about the causes of homosexuality but, because of the complexity of human sexual drives, no conclusion has yet been reached. However, it is generally agreed that homosexuality is not a matter of choice. The traditional Christian teaching has been that homosexual people must remain physically inactive, or celibate, on the grounds that the only form of proper sexual behaviour is between married men and women.

THE BIBLE AND HOMOSEXUALITY

There can be no doubt that homosexuality is not a modern phenomenon. In the book of Leviticus, written over 3,000 years ago, we can find references to homosexuality, e.g. 'You shall not lie with a man as with a woman' (*Leviticus 18: 22*). Also, in *Genesis 19* we can read the story of the destruction of Sodom and Gomorrah, supposedly destroyed because of their 'wicked ways', including homosexuality. Some experts have questioned this, saying it was destroyed not just because of homosexual practices, but for other reasons as well. However, it is clear that the writers of the Old Testament condemned homosexuality.

In the New Testament we also find references to homosexuality:

> '. . . no fornicator or idolater, none who are guilty either of adultery or of homosexual perversion . . . will possess the kingdom of God'.
>
> *(I Corinthians 6: 9–10)*

Jesus made no specific reference to homosexuality during his teaching and ministry. In his book *Christian Attitudes to Homosexuality* Peter Coleman writes: 'Jesus would presumably have regarded it as one of the types of sexual sin for which forgiveness and repentance were more appropriate than punishment.'

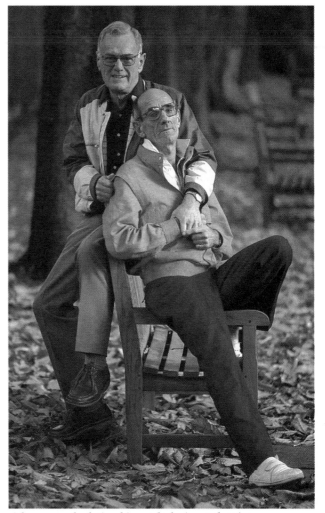

A homosexual relationship can be loving and caring

HOMOSEXUALITY AND THE LAW

Sexual relations between females have never been against the law except in the case of members of the armed services. Executions for male homosexual acts continued into the eighteenth century. Though the death penalty was removed in most European countries in the nineteenth century, it was still very severely punished by long terms in prisons. Fear of prosecution probably caused many suicides. However, by the middle of the twentieth century many states had adopted a more tolerant attitude.

During and immediately after the Second World War, there was a rapid increase in the number of homosexual offences known to the police. As a result, the Wolfenden Committee was set up to look at homosexuality. In 1967 the Sexual Offences Act removed the threat of prosecution from consenting adults (over 21) who share homosexual practices in private.

THE HUMANIST ATTITUDE TO HOMOSEXUALITY

About five in every 100 people are primarily homosexual, yet male homosexuality was against the law until quite recently, and many men were sent to prison for their homosexual activity.

Humanists, however, regarded it as nobody else's business if two adults of the same sex chose to give each other sexual pleasure. So Humanists, in cooperation with some progressive religious people, campaigned for the law against homosexuality to be altered, and eventually it was changed in 1967.

FOR DISCUSSION

▶ Read the following statements in class. Discuss what you think they mean, and whether you are in agreement with them.

'In sacred Scripture they [homosexuals] are condemned . . . this does not permit us to conclude that all those who suffer from homosexuality are personally responsible for it, but it does point to the fact that homosexual acts are disordered and can in no case be approved of.'
(Roman Catholic *Declaration on Sexual Ethics*, 1975)

'It is the nature and quality of a relationship that matters; one must not judge it by its outward appearance but by its inner worth . . . an act that expresses true affection between two individuals – does not seem to us to be sinful by reason alone of the fact that it is homosexual.'
(A Quaker essay, *Towards a Quaker View of Sex*, 1963)

'For homosexual men and women, permanent relationships characterized by love can be an appropriate and Christian way of expressing their sexuality.'
(Methodist Conference, 1979)

'Homosexuality in this culture is a stigma label. To be called a "homosexual" is to be degraded, denounced, devalued, or treated as different. It is the knowledge of the cost of being publicly recognized as a homosexual that leads many people to conceal their sexual identity.'
(K. Plummer, *The Making of the Modern Homosexual*, 1981)

'Love, security, happiness are the important things. If two people of the same sex behave towards one another in a loving and considerate way, and if their relationship brings them security, joy and contentment, then Humanists would wish them well.'
(*Humanist Dipper*)

'We believe that fear or hatred of homosexuals is a social evil, similar to anti-semitism, racism, slavery, and with the same evil consequences. It harms both the victimized individuals, and the society which tolerates it.'
(The Campaign for Reason, *Towards a Charter of Homosexual Rights*, 1978)

FOR YOUR FOLDERS

▶ After reading this section try and write an article (about 200 words) about some aspect of homosexuality.

❗▶ Which of the statements you have discussed do you agree with most? Give reasons for your answer.

More than 85 per cent of adults marry at some time in their lives. Nearly half the couples who marry have previously lived together. The average age for women to marry is 24, and 26 for men. In our society people are allowed only one partner (**monogamy**). In some societies it is acceptable to have more than one partner (**polygamy**).

WHY MARRY?

The main reasons are:
- to commit yourself to the person you love for a lifetime
- to bring up children in a secure and loving home
- to control and direct the sex instinct
- for friendship and companionship through life.

THE MARRIAGE VOWS

These can be found in the Book of Common Prayer.

'I take thee to be my wedded husband (or wife)
to have and to hold
from this day forward
for better and worse
for richer and poorer
in sickness and in health
to love and to cherish
till death us do part
according to God's holy law
and thereto I give thee my troth [promise].'

Both partners make this promise. Then the ring is placed on the third finger of the woman's hand (often men have a ring too). Then the man and the woman say separately:

'With this ring I thee wed;
with my body I thee honour and all my
*   worldly goods with thee I share*
in the name of the Father, the son and the Holy
*   Spirit.'*

THE CHURCH OF ENGLAND WEDDING CEREMONY

The vicar or minister begins by explaining the Church's view of marriage – it is a gift of God, blessed by Christ, and is a symbol of Christ's relationship with the Church. He then advises that marriage should not be approached rashly, without

Just over half the marriages in Britain take place in a church

thought or to satisfy lust, but with respect, consideration and seriousness. The core of the ceremony is in four parts:

1 'Is there any impediment to marriage?' If any reason is known why the marriage should not take place, it must be stated at this point.
2 'Wilt thou have?' The question is asked of the bridegroom first and then the bride. They reply 'I will'.
3 The vows (when rings are exchanged). The couple promise to love, comfort, honour and keep themselves for each other. The promise (vow) to 'serve and obey' is only used if the bride requests it.
4 'Those whom God hath joined together let no man put asunder.' With this declaration from the vicar or minister the couple are now married and the register can be signed.

The bride's father (or close relative) stands with the bride at the altar steps until he has completed his role – that of giving his daughter's hand in marriage to the bridegroom. The best man (a friend or relative of the bridegroom) completes his role by handing over the ring(s) which are blessed by the minister. After the ceremony the bridal party move to the vestry. Here the marriage register is signed by the bride, the groom, and two witnesses (often the best man and chief bridesmaid).

IN THE REGISTER OFFICE

The law requires that two statements must be repeated in turn by the bride and groom:

1 *'I do solemnly declare that I know not of any lawful impediment why I (say full names), may not be joined in matrimony to (say full names).'*

2 *'I call upon these persons here present to witness that I (say full names) do take thee (say full names) to be my lawful wedded wife/husband.'*

When a marriage takes place in a register office these vows are made in front of the Superintendent Registrar of the district. The register is then signed.

A HUMANIST VIEW

'In this country, marriage has always been basically a civil contract. Up to the sixteenth century a couple who wished to marry needed only to make a declaration in front of witnesses outside the church door – like the "handfasting" ceremony which was legal until quite recently in Scotland. (Nowadays the couple who marry in church are not legally married until they have signed the register in front of witnesses.)

If Humanists wish to marry they usually do so in a Register Office, and celebrate as they wish afterwards. (About half of all marriages now take place in Register Offices, some of which go to a great deal of trouble to make their premises fittingly attractive and welcoming.)'

(*Humanist Dipper*)

A METHODIST VIEWPOINT

'Christian marriage has a twofold purpose – fellowship and parenthood. Permanence in the union is an essential condition. It both expresses and develops not only constancy in affection, but also spiritual qualities of trust, faithfulness, mutual consideration, reverence and love.'

(Methodist Conference, 1980)

IN GROUPS

▶ In groups of six, with each person taking a part, write a short play about the following situation.

Kevin and Michelle are not churchgoers and they are planning their wedding. They would like to have a ceremony in a register office but Michelle's parents are keen churchgoers and would like them to marry in church. Kevin's mother, too, wants a church wedding but his father doesn't mind either way. Act out the discussion that might take place.

FOR DISCUSSION

▶ Marriage is still popular although it is frequently attacked. What are the reasons for its popularity and for the attacks on it?

▶ Discuss the meaning of the marriage vows.

FOR YOUR FOLDERS

▶ In your own words, describe why people marry.

▶ Explain in your own words what the marriage vows mean.

▶ According to Methodists, what qualities should a Christian marriage express?

❗ Can you think of any other qualities that should be included?

SOME IMPORTANT BIBLICAL TEACHINGS ON MARRIAGE

'In the beginning, at the creation, God made them male and female. For this reason a man shall leave his father and mother and be made one with his wife and the two shall become one flesh. It follows that they are no longer two individuals: they are one flesh. What God has joined together, man must not separate.'

(Jesus, in *Mark* 10: 6–9)

'The husband must give the wife what is due to her, and the wife equally must give the husband his due. The wife cannot claim her body as her own; it is her husband's. Equally the husband cannot claim his body as his own; it is his wife's.'

(St Paul, in *I Corinthians* 7: 3–4)

A ROMAN CATHOLIC VIEW

When Pope John Paul II made his pastoral visit to Britain in 1982, he spoke about marriage. He presented this vision of married life:

'A man and a woman pledge themselves to one another in an unbreakable alliance of total mutual self-giving. A total union of love. Love that is not a passing emotion or temporary infatuation, but a responsible and free decision to bind oneself completely, "in good times and in bad", to one's partner. It is the gift of oneself to the other. It is a love to be proclaimed before the eyes of the whole world.'

MARRIAGE IS NOT ALWAYS EASY

Relate is an organization concerned about marriage, and family and personal relationships. It believes the quality of these relationships is fundamental to the well-being of society. Relate provides a confidential counselling service for people who have difficulties or anxieties in their marriages or other personal relationships and in some centres provides a sex therapy service.

THE HUMANIST VIEW OF MARRIAGE

Humanists believe that marriage is a valuable institution in that it raises children and gives society stability. They believe that marriages have to be worked at and that too often newspapers, television, magazines and society in general romanticize about marriage, making it out to be the end result of a beautiful romance. It is no such thing, say Humanists. It is the beginning of a relationship. Marriage partners should be tolerant, kind and respectful towards each other. They should be sympathetic to each other, listen to the other's problems and concerns and try to take an interest in their partner. Sex is not the most important part of marriage – it is only one aspect of what should be a deep, well-developed, caring relationship.

SOME PROBLEMS WITHIN MARRIAGE

'It was OK until the baby came. Now I never see her – we never go out together.'

(Paul, aged 24)

'Since John got laid off it's been terrible. He's home all day and has lost the will to go out at all. He's under my feet – just moping about.'

(Erica, aged 35)

'We argue like hell, about money mainly. She spends money like water.'

(Lloyd, aged 23)

'I was married at nineteen. I'd never known anyone else except Richard. One day I met this lovely bloke at the keep-fit club. He's kind, charming, gentle . . . everything that Richard was until we got married. I think I would like to have an affair with him.'

(Stephanie, aged 22)

'I never see Gordon. He doesn't get home from work till eight and every weekend he leaves me and the kids and plays golf.'

(Cheryl, aged 30)

'You were born together, and together you
shall be for evermore.
You shall be together when the white wings of
death scatter your days.
Aye, you shall be together even in the silent
memory of God.
But let there be spaces in your togetherness.
And let the winds of the heavens dance
between you.
Love one another but make not a bond of love:
Let it rather be a moving sea between the
shores of your souls.
Fill each other's cup but drink not from one
cup.
Give one another of your bread but eat not
from the same loaf.
Sing and dance together and be joyous, but let
each one of you be alone.
Even as the strings of a lute are alone though
they quiver with the same music.
Give your hearts, but not into each other's
keeping.
For only the hand of Life can contain your
hearts.
And stand together yet not too near together:
For the pillars of the temple stand apart,
And the oak tree and the cypress grow not in
each others shadow.'

(Kahlil Gibran (1883–1931), *The Prophet*)

FOR YOUR FOLDERS

▶ Write a paragraph on the Christian
view of marriage.

▶ What qualities would a Humanist try
and bring to their own marriage?

▶ Make a list of the problems married
couples face.

◇

THINGS TO DO

▶ Ask two or three couples you know what
they think 'makes for a successful
marriage'.

❗▶ In pairs, decide on an order of importance
for the following qualities in making a
marriage successful:

1 Having children

2 Sexual compatibility

3 Love, affection

4 Mutual trust (no secrets)

5 Understanding and discussing things
together

6 Comradeship – doing things together

7 Good temper

8 Sense of humour

9 Financial security – no debts

10 Being considerate (give and take).

◇

FOR DISCUSSION

▶ In groups of four to five discuss the five
cases of Paul, Erica, Lloyd, Stephanie and
Cheryl. How would you try to help these
people?

▶ 'Marriage is out of date.' Do you agree?

▶ In groups of two or three discuss some of
the ideas of Kahlil Gibran on marriage.

Britain has the highest divorce rate in Western Europe, though the percentage is still lower than in the United States.

There are many pressures on marriage in our society.

- **finance** – unemployment, inflation and the high cost of living
- **lack of communication** – due to work, hobbies, children, couples do not have time to discuss things together
- **lack of companionship** – your marriage partner ought to be your best friend. But sometimes money worries, work, leisure activities and time factors separate the partners from one another
- **false hopes** – people become disillusioned when the realities of married life do not come up to their expectations
- **human nature** – everybody changes. The person you marry at 21 may be a different person at 30
- **children** – children can make or break a marriage. Sometimes they can bring couples much closer together and sometimes they can increase tensions in a home.

DIVORCE AND THE LAW

In 1857 a man could obtain a divorce if he could prove that his wife had been unfaithful. In 1878 a women could obtain a separation if the man had been cruel. By 1937 desertion and insanity were grounds for divorce as well. In 1966 a Church of England report called *Putting Asunder* stated that divorce should be allowed for the breakdown of a marriage, which included the idea of unreasonable behaviour. This brought about the 1969 Divorce Act. Some people felt that this Act made divorce too easy. In fact, many marriages had broken down before the 1969 Act, but they just had not been legally dissolved.

THE BIBLE AND DIVORCE

'Man must not separate . . . what God has joined together.'

(Jesus, in *Mark 10: 9*)

'Moses permitted you to divorce your wives because your hearts were hard. But it was not this way from the beginning. I tell you that anyone who divorces his wife, except for marital unfaithfulness, and marries another woman, commits adultery.'

(Jesus, in *Matthew 19: 8–9*)

THREE SOLUTIONS

If a couple find it impossible to live together there are three main solutions.

1 **Desertion** – One partner simply leaves the other to live elsewhere.
2 **Judicial** – The courts grant a separation, meaning the couple are not allowed in any way to interfere in each other's lives. After five years one partner can apply for divorce without the consent of the other.
3 **Divorce** – The marriage is officially declared by the courts to be at an end. After two years of living apart, and if both partners are willing, they may apply for a divorce.

A CATHOLIC VIEW OF DIVORCE

The Catholic Church teaches that a marriage between two baptized couples is a *sacrament* (a sacred ceremony) and cannot be dissolved. However, if the marriage involves one partner who is not baptized then the marriage can be dissolved under serious circumstances (i.e. if one partner converts to Catholicism but the other 'refuses to live peacefully with the new convert')(Code of Canon Law). Also, a marriage between two partners who are baptized can be dissolved if there is a just reason (Canon 1142), e.g. impotence or the inability to assume the obligations of marriage.

The Catholic Church also can *annul* a marriage. An *annulment* is 'a declaration that the marriage bond did not exist' whereas a *dissolution* is the breaking of a bond that did exist. A marriage can be annulled if there is:

- *a lack of consent* (e.g. somebody has been forced into marriage)
- *a lack of judgement* (e.g. if somebody marries without being fully aware of what marriage entails)
- *an inability to carry out the duties of marriage* (e.g. somebody might be mentally very ill)
- *a lack of intention* (e.g. if one of the partners intends at the time of the marriage not to have children).

◇

A QUAKER VIEW OF DIVORCE

There is a diversity of views on divorce by Quakers but most would agree with the Quaker report, *The Marriage Relationship*, of 1949:

'No couple, marrying with any deep conviction of permanence, would willingly give up the struggle to overcome their difficulties and seek a way of escape. But where the difficulties involved in a marriage are, of their very nature, serving to drive a couple further apart in bitterness of mind and heart, or where they reduce them to an empty and conventional semblance of living together, then there can be little reason for keeping within the bonds of legal marriage two people between whom no spiritual marriage exists. Broken marriages are always a calamity, but particularly so if there are children, since they need above all a stable home and the love and care of both parents.'

FOR YOUR FOLDERS

▶ Find out the meaning of the following words:
infidelity; separation; desertion; sacrament; annulment; dissolution.

❗▶ Write two short articles for a magazine, one entitled 'One in three marriages ends in divorce. The reasons?' and the other on 'The innocent victims of divorce'.

▶ 'Divorce should be possible only when a marriage has broken down beyond the power of restoration' (Methodist Conference 1980). Explain in your own words how it is possible to know when a marriage is beyond the 'power of restoration'.

FOR DISCUSSION

❗▶ Discuss the Roman Catholic view of divorce. Do you think it covers all the problems that cause divorce?

▶ 'Divorce is a hazard of life; not a sin,' wrote Humanist James Hemming. What do you think he meant by this?

▶ Why do you think many divorcees remarry?

THINGS TO DO

▶ Over one week of TV viewing, keep a record of the number of times (and in which programmes) divorce and unfaithfulness are portrayed. Write a letter to a magazine discussing whether television affects the level of divorce in our society.

WHAT HAPPENS WHEN YOU SMOKE?

Tobacco is made up of some 300 chemicals, 40 of which are known poisons. When you smoke, these chemicals enter the bloodstream:

- nicotine – a very powerful drug which makes the heart beat faster
- tar – which contains a number of substances which can cause cancer
- irritants – which damage the fine hairs which keep the lungs clear, producing smoker's cough
- carbon monoxide – a deadly gas which affects the blood's ability to carry oxygen round the body.

SOCIAL EFFECTS

- money – cigarettes are very expensive. Money spent on cigarettes can't be spent on other things
- pollution – non-smokers are forced to smoke because of smokers. They become 'secondary smokers'. A recent report says that non-smoking wives who live with smoking husbands have a 50% increase in the risk of lung cancer
- Health Service – smoking costs the NHS about £180 million a year. Cigarette smoking is responsible for 50,000 premature deaths a year and thousands of serious illnesses
- the third world – it takes one acre of trees to dry and cure tobacco. The long-term effects of growing tobacco are deforestation, erosion of soil and loss of land fertility. In some Third World countries land is given up to produce tobacco crops for export, and because of this the local population may go hungry.

SMOKING AND HEALTH

Smoking contributes to and causes many illnesses and diseases.

- **bronchitis** – smoking causes 75% of deaths from chronic bronchitis which kills over 30,000 people a year
- **emphysema** – this is a disease of the lung, affecting breathing
- **heart disease** – nicotine increases the heart-rate and so wears down the heart. Smoking causes 25% of deaths from heart disease
- **cancer** – 90% of deaths from lung cancer are caused by smoking
- **other problems** – smokers are less fit than non-smokers, and are more likely to get colds, flu and other infections. Smoking can damage unborn babies, and can cause problems like blood clots and stomach ulcers.

WHY DO PEOPLE SMOKE?

- from habit
- to relax
- for pleasure
- to conform
- because of advertising

Teenage smokers on 19m a week

By Celia Hall
Medical Editor

THE PROPORTION of children who smoke is increasing, with those aged under 16 consuming 19.35 million cigarettes a week, according to a new study.

Ten per cent of English and Welsh children aged 11 to 15 were regular smokers in 1990, compared with 8 per cent in England in 1988 and in Wales in 1986, the study published yesterday by the Office of Population Censuses and Surveys, said.

In Scotland, the position is worse, with 12 per cent of children aged 12 to 15 smoking, compared with 8 per cent in 1986.

Some 16 per cent of English, 15 per cent of Welsh and 20 per cent of Scottish children said they smoked regularly or occasionally. The definition of regular smoking was at least one cigarette a week, but the self-confessed regular smokers lit an average of 53 cigarettes a week in England and Wales and 50 a week in Scotland. A quarter of the regular smokers – 3 per cent of the sample of almost 9,000 pupils from 309 secondary schools – smoked more than 10 cigarettes a day.

Saliva tests for cotinine, a chemical product of nicotine, among those smoking 10 or more cigarettes a day gave similar levels to those measured in adults. The tests proved that few children lied about their cigarette consumption.

The report said smoking habits of children had changed little since the mid-1980s, despite an increasingly anti-smoking culture and a decade of health campaigns aimed at them.

David Pollock, director of Action for Smoking and Health, said yesterday that the children's cigarette consumption represented an annual market of £100m.

"The figures published today are gravely disappointing but hardly surprising, given the complacent attitude of the Government. They reflect the power of £100m of tobacco advertising – 50 times as much as the Health Education Authority has to spend on teenage smoking education." He said tobacco retailers should lose their licences if found guilty of selling cigarettes to children.

The Independent (11/9/91)

PROFILE OF A SMOKER

Name: MARCUS JONES
Age: 15

INTERVIEWER: How much do you smoke?
MARCUS: About ten fags a day.
INTERVIEWER: How much does this cost you?
MARCUS: Nearly £7 a week.
INTERVIEWER: When did you begin smoking?
MARCUS: I had my first fag when I was about nine – I felt really sick. I started smoking regularly when I was about 13.
INTERVIEWER: Do many of your mates smoke?
MARCUS: Yeah, about half of 'em, but a few are trying to give up.
INTERVIEWER: And you, are you going to give up?
MARCUS: Perhaps when I'm older.
INTERVIEWER: Why did you start smoking?
MARCUS: My mum and step-dad smoked. I started pinching their fags. I feel a bit rebellious smoking, I suppose.
INTERVIEWER: What do you mean?
MARCUS: Well, it's not the thing to do these days, is it? So it feels different to be called a smoker.

CHRISTIANITY AND SMOKING

Smoking was unknown during biblical times. However, we can apply some teachings of the Bible.

> *'Love your neighbour as yourself.'*
> *(Jesus, in Matthew 22:39)*

> *'Your body is a temple of the Holy Spirit.'*
> *(I Corinthians 6:19)*

A CHRISTIAN VIEWPOINT

'Christians hold that life is a gift from God and consequently place a high value on its preservation. The Christian ideal has been to refuse to expose life to actions or circumstances which carry with them high risks of harm ... It has been shown that smoking renders the individual prone to illness and to premature death. It can therefore be argued that it is a denial of the goodness of created existence.'

(Church of England briefing)

FOR YOUR FOLDERS

▶ Look at the biblical quotes. Write a paragraph on their relevance to smoking. (Think of 'social effects' and 'smoking and health'.)

▶ In order, write down which of the following you find the most frightening:
   a   On average, each cigarette takes 5½ minutes off your life.
   b   An average smoker loses about five years of their life.
   c   Only 6% of people diagnosed as having lung cancer survive.
   d   Cigarette smoking kills. On average, it kills 1,000 people prematurely a week.
   e   25% of heart attacks are caused by smoking.

▶ How far do you think advertising encourages young people to smoke? Design an anti-smoking poster.

THINGS TO DO

▶ Interview someone who is a smoker. Either tape-record or make a report of the interview. Ask the same sort of questions as in 'Profile of a smoker'.

▶ List as many sporting events as you can that are sponsored by tobacco companies.

FOR DISCUSSION

▶ 'The Health Service should refuse to treat smokers.'

▶ 'The government earns millions by taxing cigarettes, yet it tells us to stop smoking. How hypocritical can you get?'

WHAT IS ALCOHOL?

Alcohol is a chemical, a drug, an element, a fuel, a poison, a preservative and a solvent.

> The alcoholic content of
> **beer and cider** is 4 – 7%
> **wine** is 10 – 12%
> **spirits** is 40 – 55%
> **fortified wine** (e.g. port, sherry) is 15 – 22%

WHY DO PEOPLE DRINK ALCOHOL?

- to celebrate
- to be sociable
- to relax
- to feel adult
- for medicinal purposes
- in religious ceremonies

HOW DOES ALCOHOL AFFECT THE BODY?

- **the heart** – It increases blood pressure and heart rate
- **the nervous system** – It acts as a depressant
- **the liver** – It passes through the liver and in large amounts causes disease of the liver
- **the stomach** – Small amounts help digestion; large amounts cause vomiting
- **the skin** – It makes you feel warm but really your body is losing heat
- **the brain** – It affects the way you speak, act and think.

Research in America has shown that societies which have a low rate of alcoholism exhibit the following characteristics:

- the children are exposed to alcohol early in life
- parents drink moderately
- alcohol is often taken with food
- wine and beer are drunk at home
- drinking is not seen as good or bad
- drinking is not seen as being 'grown up'
- abstinence is socially acceptable
- people socialize without alcohol.

THE COST OF A DRINK

- Alcohol consumption in Britain rose by over 100% between 1950 and 1990.
- In 1990 24% of men and 9% of women were found to be drinking over the sensible drinking limits (21 units per week)
- A survey of 9–15 year olds found that 89% of the sample had had their first proper drink by the age of 13.
- 63% of children (11–15) believe that 'drinking is only dangerous if you are addicted to it'.

People drink alcohol to be sociable and relax

- Estimates of alcohol related mortality have ranged between 5,000 and 40,000 deaths per year. At the high estimate end, this represents 7% of the total premature deaths.
- The drinks industry spends over £2 million per year on alcohol advertising.
- Over £1600 million per year is incurred in terms of lost production and costs to the medical and social services in caring for alcohol misusers.
- People who are unemployed drink more than people who are employed.
- Heavy consumers of alcohol have a three-fold risk of cancer of the mouth and heavy drinkers have 10 times the risk of dying from chronic liver diseases than non-drinkers.
- 50% of murderers had been drinking at the time of the offence.
- Drink can be a cause of family rows, divorce, child and wife battering, poverty, absenteeism, road accidents and violence in the streets.

KEY IDEA

Alcohol if abused is extremely dangerous for individuals and society. Some Christians never drink alcohol (Salvation Army members, Methodists, Pentecostalists) and believe that the government should do more to reduce alcohol abuse. Other Christians believe that alcohol used moderately and responsibly is the best approach. In the New Testament Jesus is depicted as drinking wine.

A METHODIST VIEW

'Alcohol can give pleasure and cause harm. It is used in celebration, socialization and relaxation; it can be enjoyed for its taste. It is also a significant factor in a range of personal and social problems, and can lead to accident, illness and death ... All Methodists (should) consider seriously the claims of total abstinence, and make a personal commitment either to total abstinence or to responsible drinking.'

(Methodist Conference, 1987)

FOR DISCUSSION

▶ Comment on the American research about low rates of alcoholism.

▶ 'Without alcohol our society would go to pieces.'

▶ Some people describe getting drunk as having a 'good time'. What leads them to such a view? In what sense could getting drunk be described as having a 'bad time'?

▶ What is your opinion about total abstention or moderate drinking as the best Christian approach?

FOR YOUR FOLDERS

▶ Earlier this century there was total prohibition in America. Write an article for a magazine pretending that you believe that we should now have total prohibition in Britain because of the personal and social cost of alcohol.

THINGS TO DO

▶ Make a list of:
   a all the ads on TV in one week about alcohol,
   b the images these ads try to create,
   c the types of drink advertised,
   d the time of night the ads are on.

At some time in our lives, we almost all use drugs of one sort or another. A drug is any substance which alters the chemistry of our bodies and, consequently, affects the natural balance of our minds and emotions. Drugs which can be prescribed by a doctor include substances such as penicillin which are intended to cure infections, and sleeping pills, tranquillizers and anti-depressants intended to help us relax. Cigarettes and alcohol, which we can 'prescribe' for ourselves, have a similar function.

People turn to illegal drugs for much the same reasons. Adolescence can be a particularly difficult period. We may be under conflicting pressures from parents, school and friends, and many difficult choices may have to be made. It can also be a time of frustration and boredom. As a result, young people are always vulnerable to the offer of something which may be 'fun' or 'make them feel better'. But they often don't know about the risks involved, or how easily a serious drug problem can develop.

DRUGS WHICH CAN BE DANGEROUS

Drug	What it looks like	How it's used	What it does	Risks
Amphetamines (Speed)	A white powder, or brown powder, may be in pill or capsule form	Usually sniffed or injected	Makes people lively, giggly, over-alert; depression and difficulty with sleep may follow	Heavy use can produce feelings of paranoia
Cannabis (pot, dope, hash, grass, ganga, weed)	Hard brown resinous material or herbal mixture	Smoked in a joint or pipe, sometimes with tobacco	Heightened appreciation of sensory experience; elevation of mood, talkativeness	Risks of accidents; can cause feelings of paranoia; sleepiness
Cocaine (coke)	A white powder	Usually sniffed	Makes people lively, over-alert, elevation of mood	Can lead to dependence; withdrawal can be very uncomfortable
Crack	Crystalline rocks	Smoked	Same as cocaine	Long-term use can cause deterioration in mental functioning, irritability, social withdrawal, loss of sexual desire
Ecstasy	Tablets or capsules	Swallowed	Feelings of empathy with others at low doses, restlessness and anxiety at higher doses	Heavy use can cause psychological confusion, alienation and fear
Heroin (Skag, smack)	A brown or white speckled powder	Injected or smoked	Alertness at first, then drowsiness and drunken appearance	Overdose can cause unconsciousness; regular use leads to dependence; giving up becomes difficult
Magic mushrooms (Liberty cap)	Mushroom found growing wild	Swallowed raw, cooked or as a beverage	Heightened appreciation of sensory experiences; perceptual distortions	Mainly from eating other poisonous mushrooms by mistake
Other opiates (Dikes, 118s)	May include red or white tablets or ampoules.	Swallowed or injected	Same as heroin	Same as heroin
LSD (acid)	Tiny coloured tablets; microspots on blotting paper; small absorbent stamps	Taken by mouth	Perceptual distortions can produce hallucinations; elevation of mood; sometimes causes severe panic or anxiety attacks	Heavy use can cause psychological confusion, paranoia. Risks of accidents while under influence
Tranquillizers	Prescribed tablets and capsules	Taken by mouth	Similar to alcohol, effect increased when taken with alcohol	May lead to dependence; withdrawal symptoms can include severe anxiety

WHAT ARE THE DANGERS OF ILLEGAL DRUG TAKING?

The main dangers are:

- having an accident while under their influence
- some drugs may depress or stop breathing
- accidental overdose can lead to unconsciousness or even death
- regular use can lead to addiction or dependence

Drugs can also have nasty side-effects:

- they can bring on confusion and frightening hallucinations
- they can cause unbalanced emotions or more serious mental disorders
- first time heroin users are sometimes violently sick
- regular users may become constipated and girls can miss their periods
- later still, there may be more serious mental and physical effects
- If a drug user starts to inject, infections leading to sores, abscesses, jaundice, blood poisoning and even the AIDS virus may follow.

OTHER PROBLEMS CAUSED BY DRUG ABUSE

Personal problems

- relationships may become strained, especially with friends and family
- rather than helping you to face up to life, drugs may simply become one more problem in addition to the ones you already have.

Legal problems

- by taking illegal drugs you are risking heavy fines or even imprisonment
- if you are arrested the result may be a police record, difficulty finding a job later, and other embarrassments.

Money problems

- it costs money to take drugs – they are expensive. A heavy user may end up spending all their money on 'feeding the habit'.

HOW ABUSING DRUGS CAN HARM SOCIETY

- a heavy user will find it difficult to contribute to society
- there is a connection between drug addiction and crime.

CHRISTIAN VIEWPOINTS

'Do you not know that you are God's temple and that God's spirit dwells within you? If anyone destroys God's temple God will destroy him. For God's temple is holy and that temple you are.'

(I Corinthians 3: 16–17)

'Christians must face the serious scientific evidence about the harmful effects of drugs. A Christian's faith teaches him to use all things responsibly. He seeks to meet problems and stresses by following Christ's teachings and living by his power. To Christ he offers the undiminished vigour of his body and mind.'

(Methodist Conference)

FOR YOUR FOLDERS

▶ Find out the meaning of the following words:
addiction/dependence; speed; dope; smack; dikes; acid; overdose.

▶ Write a short article entitled 'Why some kids say "yes" '.

▶ Design a poster on the theme 'The dangers of drug abuse'.

▶ John Stuart Mill, a nineteenth-century philosopher, wrote an essay entitled *On Liberty* in which he argued that a person should be free to do whatever they want so long as it does not harm anyone else.

❗ Write an essay about whether drug abuse is entirely a matter for the individual.

▶ Write a letter to a friend who has told you that they have been offered drugs. Try and explain the dangers that they will face by accepting these drugs.

FACTFILE

- Suicide accounts for less than 1% of total deaths in Britain every year.
- Suicide rates among young people went up by 30% between 1979 and 1990.
- Men, on average, are three times as likely to commit suicide as women.
- The suicide rate amongst alcoholics is 80 times greater than for the rest of the population.
- Up to 1961 it was a criminal offence to commit suicide or attempt to do so. In 1961 the Suicide Act was passed but it still remains a criminal act, punishable by up to 14 years imprisonment, to aid or advise suicide.
- Attempted suicides are probably running at about 200,000 a year.
- Every day throughout the world at least 1,100 people commit suicide – one every 80 seconds.

CAUSES

There are many reasons why people commit suicide. Here are some of them:

- bereavement (the death of a loved one)
- insecurity (stemming from childhood)
- loneliness
- losing faith in the future
- threat of nuclear war (in 1985 a man killed himself and his family after seeing *Threads*, a film about nuclear war)
- loss of self-confidence
- deep depression caused by mental illness
- an attempted suicide can be a 'cry for help'
- old age
- disease (terminal illness or a long drawn out illness)
- money worries
- drink and drug problems
- pressures at work and at school
- depression brought on by divorce
- self-sacrifice
- to avoid capture (in war, e.g. in 73 CE, 960 Jews committed suicide at Masada rather than surrender to the Romans).

CHRISTIAN ATTITUDES

In some cultures, people believed it was perfectly honourable to take one's own life (e.g. 'hari-kiri' in Japan). However, Christians have always believed that all life is sacred and ultimately belongs to God. Therefore they believe that people have no right to kill themselves, any more than they have the right to kill others.

In the past, the Church insisted that if you committed suicide you would not have eternal life. Today, however, the Church has a more compassionate attitude, accepting that people are often under great pressure and often commit suicide when their minds are not stable.

Christians try to work for a better community and society, believing that only a caring environment will help people to live happier and more fulfilled lives.

WHAT THE BIBLE SAYS

'Every man's life is in his [God's] power.'

(Job 12: 10)

'Love your neighbour as you love yourself.'

(Mark 12: 31)

'I have the strength to face all conditions by the power that God gives me.'

(I Corinthians 10: 13)

THE SAMARITANS

In 1953 Chad Varah, a Church of England priest, was appalled to discover that three suicides were taking place every day in London. He installed a telephone in his church and publicized the fact that anyone thinking of committing suicide could telephone him and talk to him. This was the start of the 'Samaritans'. Today there are 185 centres and over 21,500 carefully selected and trained volunteers offering a 365-day 24-hour service (Christmas is their busiest time). They speak to two and a quarter of a million callers every year.

The Samaritans:

- are not all Christians
- must not 'preach' if they are Christians
- must be good listeners, sympathetic and caring.

EXIT

This is a society which is willing to help people to put an end to their lives, where the people concerned have repeatedly and strongly expressed the desire to commit suicide. Usually these are people dying of an incurable illness.

A HUMANIST VIEW

'The Humanist sees it as a fundamental human right to be able to choose to die.

Here again it is only comparatively recently that the law of this country has been reformed so as to allow suicide. Until 1961 suicide was illegal – though, of course, it was only *unsuccessful* suicide attempts that offenders could be punished for! (Except, that is, for the "punishment" of not being given a Christian funeral.)

It is still against the law to help someone else to commit suicide – and, indeed, it is obvious why this should be so. However, Humanists think that one kind of suicide help should be allowed – and that is the kind known as "euthanasia" (mercy killing), in the case of incurable illness'.

(B. Smoker, *Humanism*, 1973)

TALKING POINTS

- 'We are all responsible for those around us. Sometimes we simply need someone to talk to. The Samaritans are always there and they have time to listen.'
  (John, Samaritan volunteer)

- 'The man who, in a fit of melancholy, kills himself today would have wished to live had he waited a week.'
  (Voltaire)

- 'He who saves a man against his will as good as murders him.'
  (Horace, 1 BC)

- 'The question is whether suicide is the way out or the way in.'
  (Emerson, 1839)

FOR DISCUSSION

▶ Suicide has been called 'that most selfish of acts'. Do you agree?

▶ Discuss reasons why the attitude of some churches towards suicide has changed over the last few years?

❗▶ 'People have the right to die, and to be helped in certain circumstances to take their own life.'

FOR YOUR FOLDERS

▶ Write a piece on 'The causes of suicide'.

▶ List some of the qualities you think a Samaritan volunteer should have.

❗▶ Which talking point do you most agree with? Give reasons for your answer.

INTRODUCTION

We only have to look at the newspapers or watch the news on television to see that there are many issues in our society that are a cause for concern. As tomorrow's guardians of our world, you, the young generation, have to think seriously about the sort of society and world that you want to grow up and function in. In this part of the book you will be encouraged to explore many of the social issues and the problems they bring.

KEY WORDS

Ethics – 'Ethics are concerned with rules of conduct, with the difference between right and wrong, good and bad. Morality has the same meaning and the two words are more or less inter-changeable. Ethics and morals, however, are not concerned merely with what people do, but with what is generally accepted they should, must, ought to do, regardless of whether or not they do it.'

Social ethics – 'The ethics of society itself, which are concerned mainly with the conduct of groups of people, of society as a whole, of nations and the world community; with how they behave to other groups, other societies and nations, to animals and the natural world, and, of course, to the individual man, woman or child.'

Sometimes people say 'It's got nothing to do with me', or 'Why should I bother myself about the plight of others?' However, all things are connected and as the old saying goes, 'There but for the grace of God go I'. This means that if we haven't been affected by some terrible problem we are merely fortunate. For many of you reading this book, some of the issues that you will be discussing have been part, or will be part, of your life experience. Also, there are certain issues that **directly** affect us all.

FOR DISCUSSION

Here are some important questions that face us all. Break up into groups of four and discuss them.

1 Why are some people more violent than others?
2 Why do thousands of young people end up sleeping on the streets?
3 What sort of messages are the media trying to put across? Do these messages sometimes cause us to be dissatisfied?
4 What rights have I got?
5 What will happen to me when I get old?
6 What will happen if I get pregnant or I find that my girlfriend is pregnant?
7 Why do some of us turn to crime?
8 Will my life be ruined by unemployment?
9 Why are women treated differently from men?
10 What difference does the colour of my skin make?

BEING OBJECTIVE

It is very difficult to see things from the outside – to be objective. This is especially true of our own society and our own way of living. We forget, for instance, that we live in a capitalist world, where often the motive of profit takes priority over the needs of people. We forget that over the last decade great changes have taken place in our social structures. Things that perhaps our grandparents took for granted, like the National Health Service, are undergoing great changes.

MEDIA CONDITIONING

Through the media we are conditioned to accept certain injustices in our society and seldom are we encouraged to think about their root causes. For instance, since the 1980s there have been riots and disturbances in our towns and cities. Many thousands of dissatisfied young people have challenged the values of society with bricks and petrol bombs.

NEGATIVE VALUES

If we think about these values seriously there can be no doubt they are a cause for concern: the break-up of communities; the pressures put on people to buy more and more; the equation between possessions and happiness; the decay of any real meaning in people's lives; the strong influence of violent and sexist films and videos; the obsession with being young and 'good-looking'; our alienation from nature and the predominance of technology in all our lives.

CHRISTIAN ACTION

Many Christians are trying to improve the quality of life by working for various voluntary organizations, e.g. Christian Aid, Church of England Children's Society, Catholic Housing Aid Society, Salvation Army, etc. Some Anglican bishops have spoken out very strongly about certain Government policies that they believe lead to human despair and poverty: a document produced by the Church of England called 'Faith in the City' (1988) outlines the dreadful poverty that exists in our inner-city areas and the consequences of this poverty.

FOR YOUR FOLDERS

▶ In your own words explain what social ethics are.

▶ Write a paragraph entitled 'There but for the grace of God go I'.

❗▶ Write an article about 'Being objective about our nation'. (This should include an account of many of the issues that need attention and current attitudes to them.)

A HUMANIST VIEW

'People are more important than rules and regulations . . . A humane society should only have economic systems that improve the quality of life . . . Everyone should have equal opportunity and recognition of their talents . . .'

(*Humanist Manifesto*)

A CHRISTIAN VIEW

'A religion true to its nature must also be concerned about Man's social conditions.'

(Martin Luther King)

DEFINITIONS

Prejudice is defined as 'thinking badly of others without sufficient reason'. So prejudice is seen as a way of *thinking* about other groups of people.

Racism is defined by the formula 'prejudice + power = racism'. Sometimes, our racial prejudices are made acceptable and supported by key institutions in our society. Racism is when racial prejudice gets turned into action of some sort, and that action harms the weaker group. So racism is seen as a way of *acting* towards other groups of people.

One of the problems of looking at racism in Britain today is that people tend to think of it in terms of strong personal prejudice, with violence and with organizations like the National Front or the British Movement. However, these are the extremes. They can restrict our understanding and lead us to allow the vast majority of racist thought and action to go unchecked. Though racial violence is on the increase, few black people come face to face with this most extreme expression of racism. But all black people suffer the effects of the subtle, far-reaching institutional racism that exists in our society and culture. This is a racism that individual white people, however well intentioned, cannot avoid, for it has been built into British culture over several centuries. This makes it difficult to shake off.

'Built in' or institutionalized racism causes black people to die 20 years earlier than whites on average in Australia; and leaves them twice as likely to be unemployed in Britain. The racism that does this damage, that hems black people in on all sides, is woven into the fabric of our societies.

Racism is discrimination based purely on the colour of a person's skin. In the sections on Racism in this book the word 'black' is used to refer to any non-white group.

RACISM VERSUS RACIAL PREJUDICE

Racism is not the same as 'racial prejudice'. People have always had wild ideas about other humans who looked and talked differently. Prejudice comes out of ignorance and it thrived in a geographically isolated place like seventeenth-century Britain which had no real contact with black people. But racial prejudice on its own shouldn't have lasted any longer than other irrational ideas and should have

been destroyed by more frequent contact with Africans. Racism, on the other hand, has been going on for over 200 years and is still a ruling force in a world of mass communications, where geographical isolation is now almost impossible.

THE ORIGINS OF RACISM

In Britain, racism began in the eighteenth century because it was economically useful. The first merchants who entered the slave trade weren't doing so because they were prejudiced against Africans – they did it to make money. But once that foundation of economic profit had been laid it became very useful to think of black people as inferior, as not altogether human. So all those ignorant rumours about black people became a set of beliefs, a system that justified slavery and the building of empires. The British rulers argued that to control places in Africa or India was a noble cause – white supremacy was necessary for human progress. This belief led to the near extermination of the native Indians in North and South America and the aboriginal people in Tasmania and Australia. Charles Kingsley, a Victorian author, wrote that 'the welfare of the white race is the welfare of the world and "degenerate races" [non-whites] were better off dead'.

ECONOMICS AND RACISM

So racism is deeply ingrained in our culture. Britain became rich and powerful by treating black people as less than human, and while the rich got richer the poor got poorer. Racism has always been at the service of economic exploitation. When Britain needed all the labour it could get to start anew after the Second World War, the Government invited thousands of black people over from the Caribbean colonies. Yet as soon as there was no longer any economic need for their labour people started calling for them to be 'repatriated' (sent home).

Racism always becomes more widespread during times of economic depression. In declining inner cities, for example, when jobs become scarce and money tight, frustration is vented on the most available scapegoats – the black population.

WHITE SOCIETY

Accepting that racism is our responsibility means getting rid of the idea that the 'race problem' is caused by black people's refusal to 'integrate'. According to this idea black people should do all they can to fit in and accept white values. But integration with a white majority that holds all the economic and institutional power can only be on white terms. And how can a black person be expected to take on the attitudes of a white society which believes that she/he is inferior?

ANTI-RACISM

'The cause of anti-racism is not just the cause of the black minorities in our own country it is the cause of the millions in Africa, Asia and Latin America still suffering from the legacy of the exploitation that produced our wealth as well as our racism. It's up to us.'

(Chris Brazier)

CHRISTIAN RESPONSES

'Every human being is made in the image of God . . . To love your neighbour as yourself is one of the two great fundamental commandments.'

(Catholic Truth Society)

'Every human being created in the image of God is a person for whom Christ died. Racism is an assault on Christ's values and a rejection of his sacrifice.'

(Source: World Council of Churches)

'He created every race of men of one stock, to inhabit the whole earth's surface.'

(*Acts* 17: 26)

FOR YOUR FOLDERS

▶ Find out the meaning of the following words:
prejudice; racism; stereotype; discrimination; scapegoat.

▶ What is meant by institutionalized racism?

▶ Why is racism not the same as racial prejudice?

▶ How did racism arise?

▶ Why does racism become more widespread during times of economic depression?

▶ Explain in your own words the meaning of the World Council of Churches' statement.

A HUMANIST VIEW

'Humanists believe that prejudice is caused by ignorance and fear. Racism robs people of their humanity. Racism is a denial of human dignity.'

(*The Humanist Manifesto*)

Racism first arose out of the white desire to exploit black people economically – and it is maintained today for much the same reasons. We cannot understand racism without looking back into history.

1 There were of course black or indigenous peoples in Australasia and North America long before there were whites. But few people realise that there were black people in Britain before the English (or Anglo-Saxons) arrived – black soldiers in the Roman army helped to pacify and 'civilize' the 'barbaric' natives. And there was a continuous black presence in Britain from the sixteenth century onwards – Sir Walter Raleigh's wife started a trend by having an imported African servant and this became highly fashionable in the course of the next hundred years. Certainly there was racial *prejudice* at this time – wild notions about people who looked so obviously different and came from a world away. But *racism* – an ideology which bundled up prejudices into a package to 'prove' that black people were inferior – didn't come about until it became economically useful for white people to believe such a thing. That time came with slavery.

2 Racism emerged out of the rise in the slave trade in the eighteenth century. Black people could be bought and sold like property and treated – or maltreated – as their owners wished, because they were regarded as something less than human. The basis for this idea already existed in European culture in general and in Catholicism in particular, which held that those who were not believers in the 'one, true church' were inferior beings. Around this in the era of slavery a whole system of beliefs was erected which attempted to prove that blacks were less intelligent than whites, with smaller brains and a capacity only for manual labour. They were seen, moreover, as uncivilized and barbaric. The existence of the great black civilizations has been hidden from history – right down to the present day.

3 The abolition of slavery didn't come about because people like William Wilberforce and Abraham Lincoln were liberal and philanthropic. It was rather because it ceased to be profitable and stood in the way of economic development. Slaves were expensive to control, and developing capitalist economies needed a free market in labour and a population which could afford to *buy* the goods now being produced in factories. Slaves, who were not a mobile workforce and had no wages with which to buy commodities, obviously didn't fit this bill and thus stood in the way of 'economic progress'. This is what was behind the American Civil War – not the North's humanitarianism but instead their wish to industrialize and challenge the power of the Southern plantation-owners. Slavery was replaced with wage labour – and the US Constitution continued to regard black people as only three-fifths human.

SLAVE AUCTION

Selling their sister. Slaves were sold in London as well as in America.

Africa picks up its burden. A slave train in Zanzibar – Arab traders were often the intermediaries between white and black. If they survived the horrendous conditions on board ship these people would probably have ended up on the sugar plantations of the Caribbean.

4 In the colonial empires of the British, French, Belgian, German and Dutch, racism continued unabated to justify the ruthless exploitation of millions of people throughout the world. This plunder of natural and human resources financed industrial growth in Europe – and the notion that black people needed a firm white hand to guide them even allowed the Europeans to feel good about the theft.

Colonialism is now over – but it is no longer necessary to rule others in order to exploit them. It is partly our racism, our enduring sense of black people as somehow inferior and uncivilized, which allows the rich world to go on exploiting the poor.

5 In the years after the Second World War, racism really came home to Europe. In North America and Australasia there had always been a large black population suffering alongside the white, but it was only when mass labour was needed for the post-war reconstruction that black immigration to Europe took off. Britain had a ready source of cheap labour in the colonies, and the new immigrants were given the jobs white people refused – dirty, ill-paid work, night shifts and dead-end jobs. The country had not paid to raise, educate or house these people yet everybody made money out of them – landlords, employers, and the Government through taxes.

FOR YOUR FOLDERS

▶ After reading this section write an article entitled 'the history of racism'.

FOR DISCUSSION

'Within a few years of white Christian settlers and their missionaries setting foot in Australia 600,000 Aborigines died. The destruction of Aboriginal culture with its spiritual roots of wisdom planted deep within its sacred land, was on an appalling scale.'

(John Pilger)

Keeping their feet dry – a West African shooting party.

Only the dirtiest jobs. One of the Caribbean immigrants who swept Britain's streets in the Sixties.

6 Racism is not a historical relic that we have outgrown. In Australia and Britain, Canada and the US, racism continues to leave black people more likely to be unemployed and for longer, earning less money in lower-status jobs, living in worse housing and more liable to physical attack. And in Europe the terms of the discussion have shifted from immigration control (keeping black people out) to repatriation (getting rid of those already there).

RACIST ATTACKS

A total of 6,459 racially-motivated attacks were reported to police forces in England and Wales in 1990. It is estimated that about another 65,000 racial attacks go unreported every year.

THE MEDIA

Very often black people are stereotyped. The reporting of events involving black people usually takes the form of bad news such as crime, riots, immigration to Britain, or wars abroad. Or else they are undergoing some disaster which the West is rushing to relieve.

HOUSING

People in black households are three times more likely to become homeless than those in white ones. Black people are settled mainly in the run-down and deprived areas of our inner cities.

EMPLOYMENT

Recent surveys show that when white unemployment was around 11%, it was 21% for those of West Indian extraction, 29% for Bangladeshis and Pakistanis, and 16% for Indians.

CRIMINAL JUSTICE SYSTEM

'Young people from ethnic minorities fear the police. They do not respect them. Their fear springs from experience; they are often stopped in the streets to be questioned and searched; many are racially abused; some are beaten in police custody.'

(*The Church of England and Racism – and Beyond*, Church of England Board for Social Responsibility, 1982)

THE CHURCH

'The leadership of the Church is what I call "politely racist". It does not exercise vulgarity but it is extremely racist. Because of that they are not able to listen to the black presence in their midst.'

(Reverend Tony Ottery)

RACE RELATIONS LEGISLATION

The 1976 Race Relations Act states it is unlawful to discriminate against a person because of his/her race, colour, nationality or ethnic origins. It applies to employment, housing, education, and the provision of goods and services.

'It looks good on paper, but the reality is very different. Very few cases of discrimination are dealt with each year. In 1987, the Commission for Racial Equality, which covers the whole of Britain, conducted only 213 cases.'

(The Institute of Race Relations)

EDUCATION

'Pupils with emotional and behavioural difficulties are more likely to be Afro-Caribbean rather than white.'

(Paul Cooper, Oxford University)

BECOMING ANTIRACISTS

'As whites we frequently find it difficult to recognize when we are behaving in racist ways. When we discriminate, whether consciously or unconsciously, we are racist. When we profit knowingly or unknowingly from the past or present racism of other whites, we are racist. When we live in a segregated neighbourhood, or work for a business that exploits or discriminates, we are being racist. When we avoid contacts or friendships because of race, when we use racist language, when we tell jokes based on racial stereotypes, we are being racist.'

(Excerpt from *Education and Racism: An Action Manual (1973)*; National Education Association)

Two blacks murdered in Thamesmead . . .

"TWO BLACK people dead and everybody just turns a blind eye."

That's the feeling of a black resident on south east London's Thamesmead estate. It's the scene of two murders of black people in the last three months and a dramatic rise in the number of racist attacks.

Now the Nazi British National Party plans a march through the centre of the estate this Saturday demanding "rights for whites".

Many locals are angered by media coverage that's branded Thamesmead the "estate of racial hate".

"That's not the situation at all," says Tim, a white resident.

"There is a small number of racist idiots who make life miserable for everyone. There is a certain amount of soft racism among other residents, but that's quite different to siding with the Nazis.

"Lots of white residents are outraged by the BNP leaflet we got through our door.

"One woman chucked a bucket of water at the racists."

One gang of young white kids are thought responsible for most of the attacks. They hang around outside the pub and shout abuse at people.

They've scrawled swastikas, and "Wogs out" all over the bus shelter. They're influenced by BNP members who are getting active on the estate.

The horrific consequences of the Nazi presence have already been felt.

Fifteen year old Rolan Adams was stabbed to death by a gang of 14 white youths in February.

The boy who stabbed Rolan hung around with the gang. Before the attack he said it was his ambition to kill a black person.

Orvill Blair was stabbed to death outside his front door in broad daylight two weeks ago.

"The police are saying it was not a racist murder – they say it's all to do with petty crime. But whatever the ins and outs of it, I think it all adds up to an atmosphere that it's open season on blacks," says Tim.

"There's already graffiti up saying '2–0' and 'RIP Orvill'."

"It didn't used to be so bad here two years ago," says Dave, a local black resident.

"There used to be mingling – black people would drink down the pub. Now nobody black goes in that pub. They've written on the wall near it 'White man's manor'."

"But it's a tiny number at the centre of it," continues Dave.

"A lot of them are unemployed. Woolwich is the nearest place where anything happens and that's miles away.

"There's no life here. The whole area is just dead.'

Residents are angry that the police do nothing about the harassment.

"If a gang of blacks beat the shit out of a white kid there'd be much more trouble. Now the police are just not interested."

(*Socialist Worker* newspaper, 25th May 1991.)

FOR DISCUSSION

'No young person acquires misinformation by her or his own free choice. Racist attitudes and beliefs are a mixture of misinformation and ignorance which has to be imposed upon young people through a painful process of social conditioning – you have to learn to hate and fear.'

(*Towards a Perspective on Unlearning Racism,*
Birmingham City countil)

FOR YOUR FOLDERS

▶ Why do you think it might be difficult to make the Race Relations Act work?

❗▶ How do you think people from other cultures help to make our society a richer and more interesting place?

▶ Is racism always directed at people who aren't 'pink'?

▶ Write an article entitled 'Racism – Alive and Kicking in 90s Britain'.

Martin Luther King was born in Atlanta, Georgia, on 15 January 1929, in the heart of the American south. From an early age he was aware that black people were not treated as equal citizens in America. Four million Africans had been torn from their homes and shipped to America to work as slaves. Even though slavery had been abolished by Abraham Lincoln in 1869, most blacks still lived in poverty in the richest nation on earth. They earned half of white people's wages; many could not vote; they lived in ghettos and they were segregated (separated) in public places. Some whites (like a secret society called the Ku Klux Klan) wanted slavery reintroduced and used violence against black people.

Martin Luther King was a Christian. He became a doctor of theology and in 1954 a Baptist minister in Montgomery, Alabama. He believed that the only way to achieve equality was by non-violent and peaceful forms of protest. Not all blacks agreed with him. The Black Power movement (led by Malcolm X) believed that equality would only be achieved by violence.

In Montgomery black people could only sit at the back of buses and even the old had to give up their seat if a white person asked them. Martin Luther

King organized a 'bus boycott', (when black people refused to use the buses until they were desegregated). This movement became known as the Civil Rights movement and in 1960 Martin Luther King became its leader. In 1956 the government passed a law making it illegal to segregate people on buses.

Martin Luther King campaigned endlessly. In 1957 he spoke to a crowd of 40,000 in Washington at a 'freedom march'. He organized various forms of peaceful protest. Often the police reacted with violence. In 1960 he led a march of a quarter of a million people in Washington demanding that black people be given the vote.

Throughout his life Martin Luther King was confronted by violence. His home was bombed, he was stabbed, his family received death threats but he kept to his Christian belief that violence and hatred could only be conquered by love and forgiveness. In 1964 he was awarded the Nobel Peace Prize, and in 1965 equal voting rights were given to black people.

In 1967 America became involved in the Vietnam War. Over 400,000 Americans were fighting in the war and thousands of Vietnamese civilians had died. In a Christmas Eve speech in 1967, Martin Luther King said humankind 'is a child of God, made in his image . . . until men see this everywhere . . . we will be fighting wars.'

In 1968 a white man called James Earl Ray shot Martin Luther King dead in Memphis. The world was stunned. He was only 39. His wife Coretta later wrote: 'The killers of the dream could end his mortal existence with a single bullet but not all the bullets in all the arsenals in the world can affect his death.'

> 'I have a dream that my four little children will one day live in a nation where they will not be judged by the colour of their skin, but by the sort of persons they are. I have a dream that one day . . . all God's children, black, white, Jews and Gentiles, Protestants and Catholics, will be able to join hands and sing in the words of the black people's old song, Free at last, free at last, thank God Almighty, we are free at last!'

FOR DISCUSSION

▶ In pairs, discuss what might be said if Martin Luther King met Malcolm X.

▶ Conduct an interview between the two.

THINGS TO DO

▶ Tape the interview. It will need an introduction about what it was like to be black in America before 1970.

FOR YOUR FOLDERS

▶ What do the following words mean? How do they fit into the story of Martin Luther King?
slavery; Ku Klux Klan; Black Power movement; bus boycott; Civil Rights movement; segregation; Nobel Peace Prize; Vietnam.

▶ Copy down the three statements from the following list that you think say most about the piece you have read.
1 Martin Luther King was a troublemaker.
2 Malcolm X was right.
3 Non-violence is the best solution.
4 Martin Luther King was a brave man.
5 Black people were treated as if they had no dignity.
6 Because of the way he died, all Martin Luther King's beliefs were proved wrong.

▶ Write a diary of events plotting Martin Luther King's life.

▶ Write down a list of some of Martin Luther King's beliefs.

▶ What did Coretta King mean about her husband's death?

▶ Why do you think the Rock star Stevie Wonder has campaigned for 15 January to become a national holiday in the USA?

▶ Jesus said, 'No prophet is recognized in his own country' (Luke 4: 24). How might this be interpreted in the light of Martin Luther King's life?

▶ Why do you think Christians regard Martin Luther King's life as being so inspirational?

In the 1930s the Nazis under Adolf Hitler embarked on a programme that was planned to rid the world of all Jews and all 'Jewish blood'. It was called 'The *Final Solution* to the Jewish Problem'. The Nazis began to use the Jews as scapegoats for the problems that faced Germany. By 1945, over six million Jews had died, most of them in the gas chambers of concentration camps like Belsen, Dachau, Treblinka and Auschwitz among others. The 'Final Solution' was one of the worst examples of racism that the world has ever seen. It is impossible for us to begin to imagine the amount of human suffering involved. After the war the Jews called it 'The Holocaust'.

On 28 May 1944 Isabella (aged 17), her four sisters, mother and brother were herded, together with other Jews from the Hungarian town of Kisvárda, into cattle trucks. Their destination was Auschwitz. Her mother and youngest sister, Potyo, died almost immediately. Somehow she and her three sisters survived the Holocaust, mainly because of each other. Here are some extracts from her remarkable and moving book:

'Kisvárda was just a little town. It's where I began, where I yearned to be away from. I didn't think I could take a large enough breath there. I cannot count the times I was called a "dirty Jew" while strolling down Main Street, Hungary. Sneaky whispers: "Dirty Jew". No, "Smelly Jew" – that's what I heard even more often. Anti-Semitism, ever since I can remember, was the crude reality. It was always present in the fabric of life. It was probably so everywhere, we thought, but surely so in Hungary – most certainly in Kisvárda . . .

We were afraid. Our neighbours, we knew, would be Hitler's willing accomplices when the bell would toll. And the bell tolled.

On Monday morning, 29 May 1944, the ghetto was evacuated. Jews, thousands upon thousands of Jews – every shape and form, every age, with every ailment, those whose Aryan blood was not Aryan enough, those

In 1944 Isabella and her family were rounded up in Kisvárda

who had changed their religion oh, so long ago – dragged themselves down the main street toward the railroad station for what the Germans called "deportation". Upon their backs, bundles and backpacks – the compulsory "50 kilos of your best clothing and food" (which the Germans could later confiscate in one simple operation).

And the Hungarian townspeople, the gentiles – they were there too. They stood lining the streets, many of them smiling, some hiding their smiles. Not a tear. Not a goodbye. They were the good people, the happy people. They were the Aryans.

"We are rid of them, those smelly Jews", their faces read. "The town is ours!"

Main Street, Hungary.

Soon we are packed into the cattle cars . . . cars with barred windows, with planks of wood on the bars, so that no air can enter or escape . . . 75 to a car . . . no toilets . . . no doctors . . . no medication.

The Arrival

We have arrived. We have arrived where? Where are we?

Young men in striped prison suits are rushing about, emptying the cattle cars. "Out! Out! Everybody out! Fast! Fast!"

The Germans were always in such a hurry. Death was always urgent with them – Jewish death. The earth had to be cleansed of Jews. We already knew that. We just didn't know that sharing the planet for another minute was more than this super-race could live with. The air for them was befouled by Jewish breath, and they must have fresh air.

The men in the prison suits were part of the Sonderkommandos, *the people whose assignment was death, who filled the ovens with the bodies of human beings, Jews who were stripped naked, given soap, and led into the showers, showers of death, the gas chambers.'*

Isabella completes her book with a chapter on the birth of her second son, Richard, in 1962.

'We have another son, Mama. We have named him Richard. He is like nothing else on the face of the earth. He looks like Uncle Joe and Aunt Sara, like all our cousins, like all of our family.

He looks like nobody else.

He is the sound of your soul. He is the voice of the six million. He is Richard.

Mama, I make this vow to you: I will teach my sons to love life, to respect man, and to hate only one thing – war.'

(extracts from Isabella Leitner's *Fragments of Isabella*, 1978)

FOR YOUR FOLDERS

▶ Write a few sentences on the following:
Anti-Semitism in Hungary
The Aryans
'The Germans were always in such a hurry'

▶ Write a paragraph on:
Isabella's childhood
Auschwitz
Richard

▶ In the death camp, Treblinka, over one million Jews were gassed. A survivor, Samuel Rajzman, who lost 70 members of his family, wrote of the world's attitude: 'today it believes, tomorrow it forgets'. Try to explain in your own words what he meant.

FOR DISCUSSION

▶ 'The victims were Jews. The murderers were Christians.'

▶ 'The Holocaust story should be untiringly told and retold, making the world aware of its lessons.'

(From *The Holocaust Library*, Schocken, 1980)

In July 1941 three prisoners escaped from the Nazi concentration camp of Auschwitz. The Nazis picked ten men in reprisal to starve to death in the underground bunker. One of the men was Franciszek Gajowniczek. When he realized his fate he cried out, 'O my poor wife, my poor children, I shall never see them again.' It was then that the unexpected happened. From the ranks of watching inmates, prisoner 16670 stepped out and offered himself in the other man's place. Then he was taken with the other nine condemned men to the dreaded Bunker, an airless underground cell, to die slowly without food or water.

Prisoner 16670 was a Polish Catholic priest called Maximilian Kolbe. He was 47 years old. Before the war he had founded one of the largest monasteries in the world which was dedicated to the Virgin Mary. It was called Niepokalanow. He had also travelled as a missionary to the Far East and Russia. In 1930 he helped to start a monastery in the Japanese town of Nagasaki. In 1939 he began helping Jewish refugees.

However, in 1941 he was arrested by the Nazis and sent to prison in Warsaw and then deported to Auschwitz.

Auschwitz was a terrible place. Human beings were treated in the most inhuman ways imaginable. Thousands died every day from beatings, floggings, torture, disease, starvation and in the gas chambers. Father Kolbe dedicated his life in Auschwitz to helping his fellow prisoners. He would console them, share his food with them, organize secret church services. He tried to show others, by his own example, that even in such a hellish place God still loved and cared for them. He once said: 'Every man has an aim in life. For most men it is to return home to their wives and families, or to their mothers. For my part, I give my life for the good of all men.'

An eye-witness of those last terrible days of Father Kolbe's life tells us what happened.

'In the cell of the poor wretches there were daily loud prayers, the rosary and singing, in which prisoners from neighbouring cells also joined. When no SS men were in the Block I went to the Bunker to talk to the men and comfort them. Fervent prayers and songs to the Holy Mother resounded in all the corridors of the Bunker. I had the impression I was in a

Jews digging their own graves at Auschwitz Concentration Camp

church. Fr Kolbe was leading and the prisoners responded in unison. They were often so deep in prayer that they did not even hear that inspecting SS men had descended to the Bunker; and the voices fell silent only at the loud yelling of their visitors. When the cells were opened the poor wretches cried loudly and begged for a piece of bread and for water, which they did not receive. If any of the stronger ones approached the door he was immediately kicked in the stomach by the SS men, so that falling backwards on the cement floor he was instantly killed; or he was shot to death . . . Fr Kolbe bore up bravely, he did not beg and did not complain but raised the spirits of the others . . . Since they had grown very weak, prayers were now only whispered. At every inspection, when almost all the others were now lying on the floor, Fr Kolbe was seen kneeling or standing in the centre as he looked cheerfully in the face of the SS men. Two weeks passed in this way. Meanwhile one after another they died, until only Fr Kolbe was left. This the authorities felt was too long; the cell was needed for new victims. So one day they brought in the head of the sick-quarters, a German, a common criminal named Bock who gave Fr Kolbe an injection of carbolic acid in the vein of his left arm. Fr Kolbe, with a prayer on his lips, himself gave his arm to the executioner. Unable to watch this I left under the pretext of work to be done. Immediately after the SS men with the executioner had left I returned to the cell, where I found Fr Kolbe leaning in a sitting position against the back wall with his eyes open and his head drooping sideways. His face was calm and radiant.'

(The Catholic Truth Society)

The heroism of Father Kolbe echoed throughout Auschwitz and other death camps. Later a Polish bishop wrote: 'The life and death of this one man alone can be proof and witness of the fact that the love of God can overcome the greatest hatred, the greatest injustice, even death itself.'

In 1982 Pope John Paul II, also a Pole, declared that Maximilian was a saint. He opened his speech with the words of Jesus in *John 15: 13*: 'Greater love hath no man than this, that a man should lay down his life for his friends.'

THINGS TO DO

Franciszek Gajowncizek
Niepokalanow
Nagasaki
Auschwitz
The Bunker
John 15: 13
Martyrdom

Look at these words and phrases. How do they fit into the story of Father Maximilian Kolbe? What does each one mean?

FOR YOUR FOLDERS

▶ Write a few sentences describing the photo of Auschwitz.

▶ Write a diary of events plotting Father Kolbe's life.

▶ Imagine that you survived Auschwitz. Write a short newspaper report (about 100 words) about Father Kolbe's sacrifice.

▶ Make a list of other people you've heard of who have been martyrs.

▶ How did Father Kolbe's faith as a Christian affect his behaviour at Auschwitz?

FOR DISCUSSION

▶ 'If a man hasn't discovered something he will die for, he isn't fit to live.'

(Martin Luther King)

▶ 'Self-survival, not self-sacrifice.'

Television, radio, video, magazines, newspapers, books, advertisements and the cinema all play a huge role in our modern society. From an early age we are exposed to one form or another of the media. Its influence on our thoughts, attitudes and behaviour is not to be underestimated. Every minute of every day the media pours out pictures, images and words about the world in which we live. The time in which we live has been called the Age of Information. With the recent popularization of computers, both at home and at work, billions of hours of our attention is directed towards sources of information and entertainment. It has been estimated that the average media consumption in Britain is approximately 75 hours per person per week.

The media is one of the most *pervasive* and persuasive phenomena of the twentieth century. It is difficult for us to imagine a world without it – yet the world that our great grandparents lived in was very different from this one.

THE NEWS MEDIA

When we turn on the Six O'Clock News or read the front page of a newspaper or listen to the news on Radio 1 we blindly accept that what we are hearing is the truth. However, the people who decide what news items are to be covered are 'shaping' the news for us. They select and edit the items and this involves making decisions about relevance, importance and values.

For tabloid newspapers like *The Sun* or *The Star* headline news can mean Princess Di's holiday in Mustique rather than famine in Mozambique. And *The Sun* will put a different interpretation on events than, say, *The Independent*. What *The Independent* calls a 'demonstration' *The Sun* might call a 'riot'. When Clare Short put forward a Bill in Parliament trying to ban page three nudity, *The Sun* launched an anti-Clare Short campaign. Some 'newspapers' are known to create stories where none exist.

All British newspapers are in private hands, that is, they do not belong to the Government. However, most newspapers have particular preferences for political parties. For example, *The Sun* is owned by Rupert Murdoch, who owns other newspapers and television stations. He is one of the richest men in the world and it is likely that he would not want to encourage people to change a system that has made him so wealthy. Other newspapers are in a similar position. The news reports in his newspapers or on his television stations may be very different from those of other organizations.

'If by "truth" we mean an accurate, totally unbiased, comprehensive and objectively presented version of events, then we will never find perfection in the media.'

(David Porter)

INFORMATION TECHNOLOGY

We live in what is sometimes called a 'global village'. Satellite dishes and complex computer systems enable us to see and hear images from all over the world as they happen. Information Technology (IT), the means by which information is transmitted, first came into the public eye through George Orwell's novel *Nineteen Eighty Four*. Orwell foresaw state control, thought control and total invasion of privacy through mass media and censorship. The situation today, though less extreme, is disturbing for the following reasons:

- Around the world the mass media is in the control of state authorities and a few huge multi-national companies.

- Censorship is widespread, particularly in one-party states and the dictatorships of the southern hemisphere.

- Almost everywhere, privacy is invaded through computerization of personal files.

- The IT revolution is strongly centred in the northern hemisphere and it proceeds apace, far faster than regulations to prevent its abuse. With a few exceptions the southern hemisphere is outside the network.

- The Third World lacks many of the benefits of basic communications: 9 out of 100 people have a radio; 1 in 30 has a daily newspaper, and 1 in 500 a TV; 90% of foreign news published in the world's newspapers comes from just four Western agencies.

As long as people have sought power – whether social or economic – they have tried to control communication channels and information. The greater the extent of mass media, and the more powerful the development of Information Technology, the more people can be controlled.

With mass media, the simplest method of control is straight censorship, i.e. by banning certain types of information. Government control over radio and TV in nearly all nations has gone far beyond what is actually necessary for state security. Legal controls like libel laws and secrecy acts back up the state's control. In many countries, people are thrown into prison because of what they have written, or what they have said. And where the state can manipulate the media without opposition, what is printed or broadcast bears little resemblance to the truth.

The multi-national companies have control in the production of electronic components, computers and telecommunications technology. As national economies rely more and more on these technologies, the power of the companies will increase.

'The importance of the free communication of ideas and information cannot be over-emphasised; it is a vital key to the management of our global crises. At present many voices – of minorities and of people outside the communication network – go unheard.'

(The Gaia Atlas of Planet Management)

FOR DISCUSSION

Improved technology has on one hand made our lives more private, but on the other it has opened up increased possibilities of 'Big Brother Watching You'. Government 'bugging' is on the increase. What can be done about this secret world?

THE POWER OF COMMUNICATION

The store of human knowledge has never been greater, nor our ability to communicate it so accomplished. In today's world, split between the rich and the poor, communications technologies have huge potential for solving problems. For example, literacy rates are low in the underdeveloped world. Broadcasting could represent a lifeline to vital information and participation, boosting educational programmes in isolated rural communities. Instead, Americans alone spend $10 billion a year on pornography – another invention of the media.

TALKING POINT

'Information is power, more valuable than oil, more precious than gold. And most of it is created, stored and distributed in the rich countries. A few western nations are the judges of taste and cultural values throughout much of the world. Their news media has something close to a monopoly.'

(The Gaia Atlas of Planet Management)

THINGS TO DO

▶ Work out what your media consumption has been over the last week.

▶ Look at two newspaper reports of the same story. (One newspaper should be a tabloid.) Note any differences in the way they are presented.

▶ Watch an episode of your favourite soap opera. Try to work out what messages they are giving out about (i) lifestyles, and (ii) right and wrong.

FOR YOUR FOLDERS

▶ Write an article entitled 'A world of much information but little wisdom'.

It has been estimated that the average person in Britain will spend some eight years of his or her life looking at a television screen. Television viewing is now the main leisure activity in most families. On an average day 38 million people in Britain tune in and watch for three hours. When J. R. Ewing was shot in 'Dallas', 21 million people in Britain argued over whether the shooting was morally justifiable. Before the age of 14 the average child will have seen some 18,000 'deaths' on the screen. The British spend 80 million hours a week watching TV soap operas.

Many people, including Christians and Humanists, are becoming increasingly concerned about the massive influence television has, particularly on the young. They argue that although television has some very positive aspects – for example, it informs, educates, reduces boredom and loneliness – it also has many negative aspects that need to be studied.

TUNED IN AND SWITCHED OFF

- Television has its own set of values and behaviour patterns. It defines what a 'whole person' is; what makes us happy; what success is; what we should buy; how we should behave.

Television has a huge influence, even on the very young

- When a person spends hours in front of the box a whole range of leisure pursuits, social encounters, information sources are excluded. It keeps people switched off from life outside the living-room.

- Research at Harvard University, USA, suggests that children who are television addicts show poorer logical thinking and weaker imagination than children who don't watch much television. Television is a significant factor in failure at school.

- Teachers report that children don't know how to play any more – they don't know how to generate their own imaginative games and are so used to TV images they can't create their own.

- There is evidence that TV, as a technology which works by electronic scanning, shuts down the functioning of those parts of the brain that reason and think logically. This means that we are not able to concentrate on what somebody is saying but rather are affected just by the emotional tone of the situation.

- After parents and before school, television is the main educator of children.

- Day after day viewers are exposed to a distorted portrayal of people, concentrating almost

exclusively on the violent, the superficial, the sensational, the selfish and the apathetic. Television can distort our view of reality.

- Television's consumerism encourages a small minority of the world's population to devour a huge amount of its resources while others drown in a sea of poverty.

- People stay in and watch the blue flickering screen. Community living is a thing of the past. Television viewing is passive – people 'switch off' from their families and neighbours.

- Television works against an understanding and appreciation of life's spiritual and religious dimensions. The TV version of the 'good life' is one in which spirituality plays very little part. Programmes are set firmly in the here and now of immediately visible action and excitement. The qualities and goals striven for and the values held up as praiseworthy tend to be superficial, e.g. wealth, power, physical beauty, strength.

- Television numbs us. It hides from our sight the realities of our existence. We live in an enormous universe. We are all living together on one planet that is slowly self destructing because of our apathy and ignorance. Millions prefer to watch 'Neighbours' or 'Eastenders' than talk to their neighbours or families about the meaning of life.

TALKING POINTS

'At a time when we require the very best, we are fed a diet of the very worst. Television has become a tool of our mass-consumption society, reinforcing materialistic attitudes and wasteful habits.'

(Jonathan Porritt)

'If it is the case, as I believe, that what we call Western civilization is fast disintegrating then television is playing a major role in the process.'

(Malcolm Muggeridge)

'We need to wake up from the various slumbers of ignorance and distortion which so easily take our minds off the real world and the problems it poses . . . television has the potential to assist in the educative process of waking up (witness, for example, the impact of 'Live Aid'). As things stand at present, though, it seems more usually to act as a potent soporific.'

(Dr Chris Arthur)

'In their complacency, the British television public resembles smokers before there was any evidence that cigarettes could be responsible for cancer and heart disease.'

(Milton Shulman)

FOR YOUR FOLDERS

▶ Work out how many hours you spend watching television. Now work out how much this will add up to if you live to be 70.

▶ 'Television is exclusive.' Explain what you think this means.

▶ Write an essay entitled 'Tuned in and switched off'.

▶ Why might television give us a false sense of reality?

▶ Why do many Christians and Humanists find the attitudes and values generally promoted by television to be dangerous?

❗▶ What do you think are the positive aspects of television?

41 ADVERTISING

The average person living in a city is bombarded by over 1,600 advertising images a day. Wherever we go we are invited to spend. We are shown pictures of desirable goods and services, and we are given reasons why we're entitled to have them. We're encouraged to want more than we need. Adverts tempt us, give us glimpses into a world of luxury.

Whether we are aware of it or not adverts do affect us. Advertisers talk about us as 'targets'. They tailor their work very specifically for particular targets. They know which audiences are susceptible to their produce. When TV sells advertising space it is buying audiences. It is buying us. If offers advertisers a known audience to which to advertise. The fee is fixed according to what kind of audience it is. If a programme is mainly watched by people in their twenties to forties it will cost more to advertise in its commercial breaks than, say, in a programme aimed at older people who have less spending power.

Adverts also manipulate the audience. If you buy a certain produce you will be rewarded by having many friends or you will be happy and so on. Some adverts play on people's fears. If you buy a certain insurance policy you will be guaranteed a lifetime of peace and security. If you buy a telephone your old age won't be lonely and isolated, with relatives phoning you up from across the world. Adverts also make us discontented with what we already have – invest with the advertiser and you can enter a glamorous world. If you buy the product or service you will reach a new and higher status. Ownership will tell the world you've 'made it', you're 'in with the in-crowd'.

Advertising is a unique form of communication. Many adverts do not even need the product to be included; everybody knows what is being talked about. Others rely on simple visual clues, like the Silk Cut cigarette adverts which use photographs of pieces of cut silk, and no words at all. Advertising is more of a code than a language. Words are used in compressed and witty ways, for example, one advert for Lucozade uses three letters: NRG. It is left up to the consumer to decode the advert – the more time it takes to decode the longer we are in the advertiser's power.

Adverts also have hidden content. A Woolworth's promotional leaflet advertises toys. Boys' toys include guns, construction sets and activity toys. The girls' toys feature dolls, housekeeping and 'fluffy' toys. The hidden message is reinforced by the use of colour. Soft pastel shades for the girls and strong dramatic greens, reds and khaki for the boys. The imagery upholds stereotypes which are certainly not the primary message of the advert. But the stereotypes play a large part in reinforcing the appeal of the products.

THE DANGERS OF ADVERTISING

● Many adverts are offensive to women or are lifestyle ads that have little to do with the product.

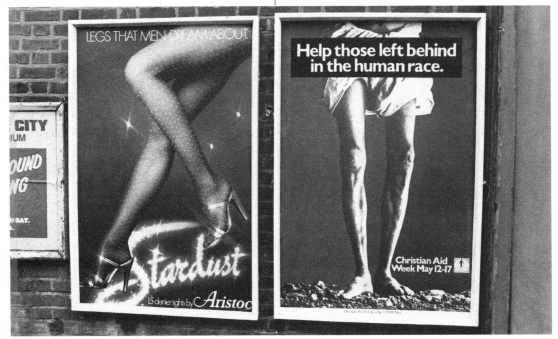

| *The power of advertising is immense*

- Adverts promise things they can't possibly deliver – like popularity or respect – creating a consumer itch that can't be scratched.

- Advertising today speaks to a society in which many people are struggling financially. It encourages people to want more and more, when they can ill-afford it, which often leads to debt.

- Advertising portrays an 'ideal' – usually built around looks, youth, glamour and material possessions – when the reality of life for many of us is very different.

- There are millions of hungry people in this world with nothing. Yet adverts encourage us to long for more things. They encourage us to hog the world's resources for ourselves. When Mr and Mrs Western are choosing their safari holiday in Africa – tempted by plush hotels, empty beaches and exotic food – children outside the hotel are dying of starvation. Adverts maintain and reinforce social evils and injustices.

- Adverts can make us feel inadequate. We don't look like the young man in his Levis or the young woman eating a Bounty. They tend to stereotype people and imply that if we don't buy the product then we are lacking in something.

- Adverts put pressure on people to be something they are not.

- Adverts tempt people to follow certain fashions that will soon be outdated.

THE BIBLE

Advertising as we know it originated in Elizabethan times. There is nothing in the Bible that speaks of advertising. One of the messages of the New Testament, however, is that material wealth and luxury do not bring true happiness.

> 'And I tell you, it is easier for a camel to go through the eye of a needle than for a rich man to enter the Kingdom of God.'
>
> (Matthew 19: 24)

> 'You say, "I am rich; I have acquired wealth and do not need a thing". But you do not realize that you are wretched, pitiful, poor, blind and naked.'
>
> (Revelation 3: 17)

FOR YOUR FOLDERS

▶ Write down details of 10 adverts that you have seen.

▶ Apart from the product, what type of lifestyle are they promoting, e.g. Levi jeans – sex appeal.

▶ Explain in your own words how adverts often have 'hidden meanings'.

▶ Why do you think advertising is such a powerful form of communication?

▶ What do you think are the dangers of advertising?

▶ Bearing in mind the two Biblical references given above, how do you think a Christian might view advertising?

TALKING POINTS

'In the thirty second dreams which are the currency of TV advertising, no mention is ever made of the animals killed to ensure the safety of some new cosmetic; the pollution which is a side-effect of producing a particular kind of container; the appalling foreign employment practices of some of the multinationals who supply us with tea and coffee; the people who will starve because of the agricultural policy which allows us to afford and enjoy certain foods. Do such omissions not mislead consumers about the products advertised, about the lives they lead, about the world they live in?'

(Dr Chris Arthur)

'Advertising – in persuading people to buy things they don't need with money they don't have, in order to impress others who don't care – is probably the phoniest field in existence today.'

(Victor Papanek)

Ageism means discrimination against people because they are no longer young. Ageist attitudes persist in the newspapers, on radio and television, in the world of work and in advertisements. As with all forms of discrimination, the 'stereotype' is common. Stereotyping means fixing something or an idea of something or someone in a mould which you are not prepared to change and then insisting that it is the only possible one. Here are some stereotypes to do with the elderly:

'Old people think they know best.'
'Old people are always talking about the good old days.'

Western societies tend to treat old people with very little respect. Old people are often seen as being a burden on families and on society in general. Ignorance about old age shapes public policy, too. Western societies dispense with the skills of the most experienced citizens and then fail to make proper provision for their needs. One possible reason for the ignorance that surrounds ageing may well be the reduced contact of young people with the old.

The United Nations estimates that by the year 2025 one person in seven will be over 60, compared with one in every twelve in 1950. The number of over-60s is the fastest growing section of world population.

TALKING POINTS

'I have often thought what a melancholy world this would be without children; and what an inhuman world, without the aged.'

(Samuel Taylor Coleridge)

'Old age is the most unexpected of all the things that happen to a person.'

(Leon Trotsky)

'We don't get older, we get riper.'

(Picasso)

'We must prepare to do battle to maintain our independence. I am haunted by the fear that unless I can dispel the assumption that I am a senior citizen the following events may reasonably occur:

1   I shall have a gang of young thugs sent to my home to paint my kitchen instead of going to prison.

2   I shall have patients from the local mental hospital drafted to dig my garden.

3   I may be forced to go to 'suitable' entertainments, drink tea and wear a paper hat.

4   I may receive vast baskets of assorted food to which I feel I am not entitled.

We pensioners are in a terrifying position. We are *recipients*. Hands off please, I'm in charge of my life.'

(Frank Adey, author's interview)

CHRISTIAN AND HUMANIST ATTITUDES

Christians and Humanists believe that the lack of concern in the way society treats old people is indicative of the uncaring attitudes of our modern world. Many churches are working to improve the care of the elderly:

'Elderly people and their families should retain as much choice as possible. Elderly people should not be removed from their existing network of relationships.'

(Church of England Board for Social Responsibility)

The Bible teaches that the old should be treated with respect:

'Honour your father and your mother.'

(Exodus 20: 12)

To many people the way that our society shunts men and women into old people's homes and geriatric hospitals illustrates a lack of compassion for the elderly. It seems that in a Western, materialistic society, if people become economically obsolete they are valueless. Yet it is so easy to forget that we all grow old, if we are lucky, and that old people have a wealth of life experience and can teach us much about living. Too often they are seen as 'old dears', too old to work, too old to learn anything new, too old to have a good time, too old to enjoy sex, too old to do anything except wait to die. Old age is not fashionable. We only have to look at advertisements to see that the 'good life' means being young.

SOME FACTS ABOUT OLD AGE

One household in seven in the UK is an old person living alone.
Nearly half a million old people have no living relatives.
One million old people have no regular visitors.
Over one thousand old people die in their homes every year from hypothermia.
Michelangelo was 71 when he started work on St Peter's, Rome.

FOR YOUR FOLDERS

▶ Explain the words 'ageism' and 'stereotyping'. List some of the stereotypes associated with the elderly.

❗▶ Prepare a three minute talk for your class on 'Ageism in Britain Today'.

▶ Explain the reasons why Christians and Humanists are concerned about the way old people are treated in our society.

▶ Imagine that the UN are devising a Charter of Rights for the Elderly. Write down some of the rights you think should be included.

HELP THE AGED AND AGE CONCERN

These organizations are dedicated to improving the quality of life for old people in Britain and abroad.

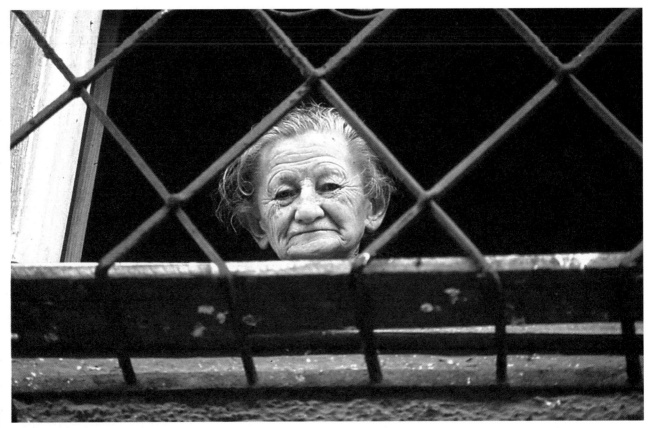

Old and alone

Ending life in an old people's home haunts many people. In this article we are taken along the corridors of a residential institution.

'"Mr H. is an ideal resident. He's most grateful for anything that's done for him." (Matron in residential home) Like a frozen frame in a film about musical chairs – no music, no movement – but everyone in a chair and every chair in its place lining the walls of the lounge. This image of an old people's home is true only too often. The lounge is not a lounge at all. It is a place to put people between meals. And old people's homes are usually not homes at all – they are total institutions where residents are "managed" and where the needs of the staff rather than the residents, determine the order of the day.

Rewarded if they cooperate and punished if they try to assert themselves, an old person's individuality is quickly crushed by remorseless regime. For those in charge any real relationship with the old people threatens the home's smooth-running schedule; talking interferes with "work", "spoils" the residents and raises their expectations.

And when the residents try to help themselves – by choosing their own clothes and making their own beds – they are often rebuked for being "too independent" and labelled "uncooperative".

The institution continues to undermine the old person's independence by removing all sources of status, identity and worth. Many elderly women wear redundant aprons or rock dolls on their knees – a sad reminder of their lost roles as householder, mother, neighbour. Even control over personal finances is removed; pension books are taken away so that contributions for board and lodging can be deducted and "pocket money" (sic) is doled out piecemeal on request.

As a final insult, there is no escape. The privacy of a single bedroom is a rare privilege. And people are denied the right to hold themselves aloof from others because the staff call residents by their first names. The whole experience is reminiscent of the effects of solitary confinement on a prisoner.

Society locks old people up and throws

away the key. The staff of the home where I worked had only meagre information about the people in their care – some residents' files only contained a list of possessions. And when people enter residential accommodation the files of doctors and social workers outside the home are often "closed" and stored – with macabre significance – together with those of the clients who have died.

People are admitted to an old folks' home because they are thought to be too fit for hospital but not fit enough to remain within the community. Many come to old people's homes straight from hospital. Others are admitted after the death of a spouse. Still others are put into care because relatives, neighbours, doctors or social workers believe they can no longer "cope" in their own homes.

It is tempting to blame the institutions themselves for the way some old people are treated. But the institutions simply reflect the attitude of a whole society. To be without possessions, property and employment or to be physically or mentally ill is a disgrace. We look at old people and see our own futures. And we banish our fear of ageing and death by setting elderly people apart from us. When they find it difficult to maintain themselves in their homes we decide they will be "better off" in an institution. But what we are usually saying is that we – the rest of the community – will be better off if the old are removed from us.

Being uprooted from familiar surroundings and admitted to hospital or into residential care can have a devastating effect on someone's ability to manage. And being deprived of one's life partner has been described as being the biggest single tragedy of old age. Bereaved partners often become depressed and neglect both themselves and their homes. Intensive rehabilitation can help dramatically and allow old people to remain in the community where they belong. It has been estimated that nearly half the people in Britain's homes for the elderly need not be there.'

(Article adapted from Pamela Martin's booklet *I Shall Wear Purple*, by kind permission of the publishers, Age Concern)

TALKING POINTS

'In society's eyes the aged person is no more than a corpse under suspended sentence.'

(Simone de Beauvoir)

'I had to come here, it had to be done. But it took the life out of me. It is something that you lose. And its only them that loses it that feels it.'

(Resident in an old people's home)

'Life ceases to have any significance for one who has been debarred from every activity and deprived of every relationship which gave it meaning. Usually the prisoner becomes indifferent to his surroundings, apathetic and incontinent.'

(Anthony Storr, psychiatrist)

FOR YOUR FOLDERS

▶ After reading Pamela Martin's article and the Talking Points, write an article entitled 'Out of Sight, Out of Mind'.

▶ What alternatives can you think of to locking old people away in residential institutions?

A disability refers to the lack of some bodily function.

A handicap refers to the relationship between the disability and the environment.

Mental handicap is caused at conception, birth, or in infancy, and is a permanent disability.

Mental illness may be experienced at any stage of life and can be treated and cured.

PHYSICAL DISABILITY – A CASE STUDY

'My name is Daniel Leech and I live in Cheltenham. I was born 14 years ago, but due to a bad birth I am disabled. Cerebral palsy has left me with no speech, no use of hands, and no ability to walk.

My parents and the head teacher of my special school thought that I should try to get into a comprehensive school when I reached 11. Bournside Comprehensive School accepted me and this has meant a great deal to me. I always enjoyed the company of other children and envied their schools as they were much more interesting than small special ones.

I cope well enough thanks to my BBC computer and my left foot. I use two foot switches to write, speak and produce graphs for maths and other subjects. All the children at Bournside have made me feel very much one of them. I do not feel different at school. No one turns to look at me or my motorized wheelchair (unless I knock into them!).

I have noticed that society is becoming more aware of the needs of the disabled, providing more toilets, ramps, lifts and other facilities.

I don't know if I can believe in God. If there is a God, then why is there so much suffering in the world?'

FACTFILE

- among the present world population of 5 billion, an estimated 500 million people are disabled in some way. Some 250 million of these are children

- every year 250,000 children lose their eyesight through lack of Vitamin A alone

- most disabled people agree that other people's attitudes, like embarrassment or ignorance, can be disabling in themselves

- one hundred million people in the world today are disabled through malnutrition.

L'Arche is a religious community that helps mentally handicapped people

THE MENTALLY HANDICAPPED

There are about 230,000 mentally handicapped people in Britain, of whom 60,000 are children. Taking the population as a whole, there are approximately 2.5 severely mentally handicapped people per 1,000 in the population. Sometimes the handicap is not visible, although it seriously impairs the intellectual capacity of the person. Often so-called 'normal' people have difficulty coping with mentally handicapped people and frequently confuse mental handicap with mental illness.

In the past, mentally handicapped people were shut away in homes or hospitals and this did little to break down people's prejudices and fears about them. However, today there is a steadily growing awareness that mentally handicapped people have plenty to give, and can develop within the community, and as a result more of them are taking their place in community life. It is estimated that about 15,000 mentally handicapped people at present in hospital – about one-third of the total – could be discharged immediately if appropriate services in the community were available.

Mentally handicapped people who do live in the community live either at home, usually with their parent(s), or in hostels within the community. Many of them go out to work. In a report on the mentally handicapped, the Church of England stated:

'Mentally handicapped people have much to give, they share our common humanity and, like us all, are children of God.'

(from *The Local Church and Mentally Handicapped People*, a report by the Church of England Board for Social Responsibility, 1984)

'Mentally handicapped people can be an inspiration to others, they can help us understand ourselves and the often inhuman values of the rest of the world.'

(Jean Vanier, founder of L'Arche, a religious community concerned with helping the mentally handicapped)

FOR YOUR FOLDERS

▶ Explain the terms:
disability; handicap; mental handicap; mental illness.

▶ What handicaps does Daniel face? How has he learnt to overcome them?

▶ What are the advantages for Daniel and for other pupils in having Daniel attend a comprehensive school?

▶ Write an article explaining some of the problems a mentally handicapped person will have to face when living in the community.

❗▶ How might mentally handicapped people be 'an inspiration to others'? How might they 'help us understand ourselves and the often inhuman values of the rest of the world'?

FOR DISCUSSION

▶ Disabled people often encounter certain attitudes like over-protection, fear, embarrassment, stereotyping and being patronized. Discuss each of these attitudes in turn.

▶ 'It has been shown that mentally handicapped people can make their marriage promises as sincerely and with as much understanding as other people.'

(Church of England report)

THINGS TO DO

▶ Imagine that you are at Bournside School in the year before Daniel joins. In groups of four draw up a report or document entitled 'Preparing for Daniel'.

The Great Miracle Baby Business

by Celia Kitzinger

The world's first "test tube" baby, Louise Brown, was born in July 1978 in England. Since then reproductive technologies have been big news in the West. Newspaper and television interviews with radiant mothers nursing newborn babies portray doctors and scientists as glamorous heroes selflessly promoting miracle cures for infertility. Reproductive technologies, it is claimed, ease the heartache for childless women, offering them a last chance to hold a baby in their arms.

Between ten and fifteen per cent of heterosexual couples are involuntarily infertile and for many this causes intense grief. There are enormous cultural pressures on women to bear children, and tremendous stigma attached to infertility.

The method used to conceive Louise Brown, *in vitro* fertilisation (IVF), is done by bringing together ovum and sperm in a dish on a laboratory bench. Usually the ovum and sperm are taken from the would-be parents, but either or both can come from other people so that a woman can bear a child with no genetic relationship to her or her husband. Once a viable embryo has been achieved it can either be deep-frozen and stored for later implantation, or it can be transferred straight into the mother's body.

The procedure presents serious health hazards for women and half the IVF clinics in the US have *never* sent a patient home with a baby. For ninety per cent of women IVF treatment means doctors appointments, hospital visits, tests, repeated examinations, surgery, tremendous anxiety, depression, disruption of work, strain on personal relationships, disappointment, hope, despair – often without a baby at the end of it. These stories are missing from the media hype.

One woman explains how she felt when her fertilised eggs failed to implant: "I had terrible feelings of guilt that my body was this damaged vessel incapable of letting life continue. It was difficult for me to think that I would be carrying around fertilised eggs that would die one more time. I didn't think I could stand any more dead babies."

Social pressures on women to produce babies are being exploited by big business. Sperm, stored in "banks", is now a saleable commodity. Surplus eggs removed from women's bodies are used for a range of scientific experiments or, in the US, sold to other women unable to produce their own ova.

Surrogate motherhood is a commercial transaction in which a man buys the services of a woman to bear him a child and perpetuate his genes. As babies become products, mothers become producers, pregnant women the unskilled workers on a reproductive assembly line.

While scientists scramble to develop wonderful technology to "solve infertility" concern about the environmental causes of infertility are overlooked. Female and male infertility is caused by pesticides, weapons testing, crop dusting, chemicals used in industry and tobacco marketing.

Reproductive technologies may offer a beacon of hope to infertile couples: they may even help a lucky few realise their dream. But while attempting this many women endure humiliating, painful, even life-threatening side effects. Most have to accept a childlessness made harder to bear by the shattering of unrealistic expectations raised to generate profits for big business. Others are forced by poverty to sell their services as human incubators to male baby buyers. The rights of the poor and vulnerable must not be sacrificed to maintain the illusion of choice for a few rich, white, westernised heterosexual couples.'

(Adapted from *New Internationalist*, March 1991)

Over the last few years medical science has advanced to such a degree that it is possible to create a normal baby with no fewer than five parents. One would be the woman who actually bears the child. Two others, its genetic parents, would supply the sperm and the egg which are 'mixed' and then implanted as a living embryo in a surrogate mother's womb. Finally come the baby's 'real parents', the infertile couple who will take the baby home and call it theirs.

One technique is called AI (artificial insemination), when live sperm are injected into a woman's uterus at the time of ovulation. Another approach, transferring embryos from a female donor, has already been used for infertile women otherwise capable of carrying a child.

With doctors and researchers achieving powers over procreation that far outstrip traditional law and conventional morality there are many questions to be answered. Should surrogate motherhood be allowed? Should we interfere with nature? What if the child is deformed? Does a sperm donor have any obligations or rights to the eventual offspring? Do all couples have a right to reproduce? How far can scientists go in using embryos for experimentation in order to push back the frontiers of medical knowledge? Have human beings the right to play God?

Because of these questions the British government in 1990 passed the Human Fertilization and Embryology Act (see Section 46).

A CATHOLIC VIEW OF ARTIFICIAL INSEMINATION

'Artificial insemination (AI) is different from natural intercourse. As used with animals this poses no moral problem. However, the Church teaches that among humans, AI violates the dignity of the person and the sanctity of marriage. It is therefore contrary to the Natural and Divine Law. In an address to Catholic doctors, Pope Pius XII condemned AI. It is condemned because a third party becoming involved in a marriage is like 'mechanical adultery': the donor fathers a child (with his sperm), yet he has no responsibility to the child; any process that isolates the sacred act of creating life from the marriage union is a violation of that marriage union (which alone is the way to create life). However, if the marriage act is preserved, then various clinical techniques designed to help create new life are not to be condemned.'

(adapted from *Modern Catholic Dictionary*)

The Catholic Church therefore teaches that new life should only be created by natural means within the bounds of the marriage union.

A baby is born

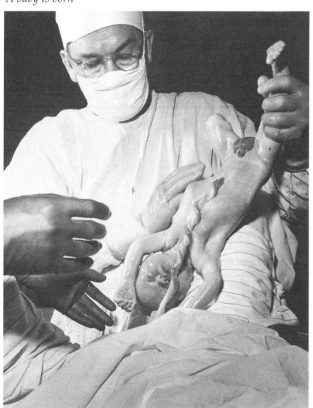

FOR YOUR FOLDERS

Answer these questions in your folders.

1 Explain the following: genetic parents; procreation; IVF; AI; surrogate mothers; commercial surrogacy; embryo research.

2 Explain how it is 'even possible to create a normal baby with no fewer than five parents'.

3 What do you think are the benefits of artificial reproduction?

4 What is the Roman Catholic view of artificial reproduction?

5 According to Celia Kitzinger, what are the dangers of 'the great miracle baby business'?

6 Can you think what the problems are that face the surrogate mother and the parents who commission her?

7 What are your own views on artificial reproduction?

8 'God is the giver of life, not man'. In the light of the extract on this page, do you agree with this comment?

FOR DISCUSSION

▶ 'The real parents are those that bring up the baby.'
▶ 'We should not interfere with nature.'
▶ 'God has given human beings the gift of scientific knowledge. We should use it.'

HUMAN FERTILIZATION AND EMBRYOLOGY ACT 1990

In 1990 the government passed a series of laws about human fertilization and embryology. Some of these include the following:

- A statutory licensing authority, with substantial non-medical membership, should be set up to regulate those infertility services and research which the report regards as acceptable, including *in vitro* (test-tube) fertilization, semen or egg donation, embryo donation following *in vitro* fertilization, and the use of frozen embryos.

- There should be complete anonymity for semen, egg or embryo donors and couples requiring their services. Both partners should give written consent to treatment. The number of children born to a donor should be limited to 10. A woman giving birth as a result of egg or embryo donation should be regarded in law as the child's mother, and the donor should have no rights or duties relating to the child.

- Frozen embryos should be stored for a maximum of 10 years, after which the right to use or disposal should pass to the licensed storage authority. Up to 10 years, an embryo's parents should have the right to decide on use or disposal; if both die or fail to agree, that right should go to the storage authority.

- The establishment and operation of surrogate motherhood 'rent-a-womb' agencies should be made a criminal offence.

- No human embryo should be kept alive outside the womb or used for research beyond 14 days after fertilization, excluding any period when it was frozen. It should be made a criminal offence to transfer to a woman any embryo used for research, or to place a human embryo in the womb of another species.

THE CATHOLIC RESPONSE

The Catholic Church believes that:

1 **The human embryo has the right to proper respect. 'Test-tube babies' are indeed babies, and embryos cannot be manipulated, frozen or simply left to die without bringing into question the whole area of human rights. Human beings are not to be treated as means to an end.**

2 **Marriage is the proper place for sexual activity, and our society depends on stable and loving families.**

3 **The demands of science do not take precedence over individual human persons, especially when they are defenceless.**

4 **There must be a careful weighing up of issues when deciding on the allocation of resources for the health service. It is, to say the least, doubtful that people's much-claimed 'right' to children should take precedence in the complex and difficult business of proper health provision for the nation.**

(The Catholic Truth Society, 1990)

SEVEN FRONT-LINE TECHNIQUES IN HUMAN FERTILIZATION AND EMBRYOLOGY

1 *Artificial insemination (husband) (AIH).* The putting of male seed into a female by means of an instrument.

2 *Artificial insemination (donor) (AID).* The semen (seed) is provided by an anonymous donor and not the husband.

3 *In vitro fertilization for husband and wife (IVF). 'Test-tube babies'.* The ovum is withdrawn from the woman and fertilized with a man's semen under laboratory conditions. The embryo is then transferred to the womb.

4 *Egg donation.* A woman donates an ovum, which is then fertilized with the semen of the husband of the women into whose uterus the resulting embryo is transferred.

5 *Embryo donation.* Similar to egg donation, except the ovum is fertilized by semen from a donor because both partners are infertile or both carry a genetic defect.

6 *Surrogacy. 'Womb-leasing'.* A women bears a child for a wife who cannot become pregnant, and hands the child over after birth.

7 *Scientific research on human embryos.* Potential research which ranges from simple study of early embryos to increase knowledge on the beginnings of human development (for infertility, etc.) to testing new drugs on embryos.

KEY QUESTIONS

! Obviously these new techniques raise
many religious, legal and moral
questions. When does life begin? Has
an embryo the same rights as you or I?
Can these techniques be exploited for
the wrong reasons? Have the donors or
other people involved any rights? Who
are the real parents? Should we
interfere with God's creation? Or is
nature a 'raw material' given by God to
experiment with? Do these techniques
help family life? What about those who
suffer infertility? These are just some of
the issues. There are many more.

AN ANGLICAN RESPONSE

The Church of England believes that:

● It is natural for couples to want to produce and
raise children. In the Bible the need and desire
for an heir led to instances in which a third
party was involved, e.g. Rachel's invitation to
Joseph to take her slave Bilhah, so that 'I may
also obtain children by her'. *(Genesis 30: 3).*

● Human beings are made in the image of God
(Genesis 1: 26). This bestows on them a unique
status in creation. To treat them, not as persons
to be respected, but as things which may be
manipulated, is to violate this God-given nature.

● Intercourse and procreation are often separate.
AIH is therefore acceptable. . .

● '. . . those engaging in AID are involved in a
positive affirmation of the family'. AID is
therefore regarded as an acceptable practice, so
long as: donors do not sell their sperm; central
records are kept to that no more than 10 children
can be fathered by one donor; at 18 the child can
have access to information about the donor.

● IVF is acceptable in cases of infertility and
inheritable disorders.

● 'It violates the dignity of motherhood that a
women should be paid for bearing a child.'
Also, 'strong bonding may take place between a
woman and the child she bears in her womb
and she may be unwilling to give the baby up'
(at birth). Many Anglicans feel that all surrogate
agreements should be illegal.

● Research on the embryo can be permitted under
certain, strict circumstances: 'We support the
recommendation that research, under licence, be
permitted on embryos up to 14 days old and
agree that embryos should not be created purely
for scientific research'.

(Church of England report *Human Fertilization and
Embryology*, 1984)

TALKING POINT

! Look at the key
questions in the
box on this page.
How would you
answer them?

FOR YOUR FOLDERS

▶ Write an article entitled 'Babies in the
Front Line of Medical Technology'.
List some of the ways that the seven
techniques could be misused.

▶ List some of the advantages of the
techniques.

▶ Try and explain in your own words the
Catholic response.

▶ List the techniques that the Anglican
Church accepts and doesn't accept,
and write a sentence about why each
is acceptable or unacceptable to the
Church.

! ▶ Write down some of your views on the
issues that have been explored in this
section.

> **Euthanasia** – 'gentle and easy death; the bringing about of this especially in cases of incurable and painful disease'.

In this section we are concerned with voluntary euthanasia, i.e. euthanasia carried out at the request of the person killed. Despite great advances in medicine, dying can be a long, painful and distressing process. In fact, advanced medical techniques can 'keep a patient alive' for much longer than in the past. Under present laws anyone (doctors included) who helps the sufferer to end their life risks the possibility of being charged with murder or manslaughter.

THE VOLUNTARY EUTHANASIA SOCIETY (EXIT)

This society aims to bring about a change in the law so that

> *'An adult person suffering from a severe illness, for which no relief is known, should be entitled by law to the mercy of a painless death, if and only if, that is their expressed wish.'*

> *'Doctors should be allowed to help incurable patients to die peacefully at their own request. The patient must have signed, at least 30 days previously, a declaration making their request known.'*

SOME FACTORS INFLUENCING A CHRISTIAN

- 'God made man in his own image' (*Genesis 1: 27*). Human life is a gift from God. It is sacred and has dignity
- death is an event in life, not the end of life
- Jesus in the New Testament heals the sick and the dying
- God gave man 'dominion over every living thing' (*Genesis 1: 28*). Humans have a responsibility to use God's gifts to the full
- the body *and* spirit of the patient need care and love.

THE HOSPICE MOVEMENT

In recent years the emphasis has moved from a debate about euthanasia to a concern for the care of those who are terminally ill. This has led to the growth of the Hospice movement, which tries to help the dying spend their last few days in a loving and sympathetic environment so that they can die with dignity. One of its leaders, Dame Cicely Saunders, has written: 'We have to concern ourselves with the quality of life as well as with its length.'

THE CASE FOR VOLUNTARY EUTHANASIA

- it can quickly and humanely end a patient's suffering
- it can help to shorten the grief and suffering of the patient's loved ones
- everyone has the right to decide how they should die
- if the law was changed, doctors could *legally* act on a patient's desire to die without further suffering
- it would help others to face death if they realized they could die with dignity
- it would help doctors if they knew of their patient's intentions
- the initial decision about euthanasia could be made when the individual was not under the stress of immediate suffering or anxiety.

THE CASE AGAINST VOLUNTARY EUTHANASIA

- there are many pain-killing drugs which can help the patient die with dignity
- a patient might not be able to make a rational decision or might change their mind but be incapable of telling the doctors
- many people recover after being 'written off' by doctors
- old people might feel they are a nuisance to others and opt for euthanasia when in their hearts they want to continue living
- life is a gift from God and only God can take it away
- euthanasia devalues life by making it disposable – it could be the first step on to a slippery slope
- the relationship of trust between doctors and patients could be destroyed. Under the Hippocratic Oath doctors must try to preserve life
- if there were better facilities for caring for the dying, there would be less need for euthanasia.

FOR DISCUSSION

VIEWPOINTS

'The argument for euthanasia will be answered if better methods of caring for the dying are developed. Medical skill in terminal care must be improved, pre-death loneliness must be relieved, patient and family must be supported by the statutory services and by the community. The whole of the patient's needs, including the spiritual, must be met.'

(Methodist Conference, 1974)

'Humanists believe that people have the right to end their own lives when they wish. They believe that death is final and inevitable, but nevertheless can be dignified, peaceful and painless with the aid of modern drugs. Some go to the trouble to discuss this with doctors, friends and relatives. Some sign the form available from the Voluntary Euthanasia Society which leaves no doubt whatever of the person's wishes about his last days.'

(*Humanist Dipper*)

▶ Why do many Christians, like the Methodists, argue that voluntary euthanasia is wrong?

▶ How do Methodists believe that better methods of caring for the dying can be developed?

▶ How might a Christian and a Humanist react to the following letter?

Case history (from a letter published by the Voluntary Euthanasia Society)

'I have no family commitments, I suffer from diabetes, failing eyesight, skin disorders, arthritis and chronic narrowing of the arteries which has already resulted in the amputation of a leg . . . I am not afraid of death, but I am afraid of the protracted suffering which would almost certainly precede my death in the natural course of events. Even more, I am afraid of the consequences of making an unsuccessful suicide attempt. During the six months I spent in hospital last year, numerous were the patients brought in for resuscitation after suicide attempts, and the memory of the sordid and horrifying sounds which ensued from behind the screens will never leave me. When the time comes, I shall need help, and it would be a great comfort to me to know that there is a doctor to whom I can turn.'

TO DEBATE

▶ 'This House believes that a person has a right to die.'

FOR YOUR FOLDERS

▶ Explain the following:
Exit; the hospice movement.

▶ Write a paragraph on
a The beliefs of Exit.
b Some of the factors that influence Christians.

❗▶ From ideas collected during your debate and from the arguments for and against voluntary euthanasia, write an article of about 200 words on your own views on this matter.

> **Abortion**
> - 'premature expulsion of the foetus from the womb'.
> - 'operation to cause this'.

THE HUMAN FERTILIZATION AND EMBRYOLOGY ACT 1990

For many centuries it was regarded as a serious crime to destroy a baby in its mother's womb. Over the last 30 years the British parliament has debated the abortion issue several times. Following the 1990 Act, the law on abortion now lists the following conditions:

a   That the pregnancy has not exceeded its twenty-fourth week and that the continuance of the pregnancy would involve risk, greater than if the pregnancy were terminated, of injury to the physical or mental health of the pregnant woman or any existing children of the family; or

b   That the termination is necessary to prevent grave permanent injury to the physical or mental health of the pregnant woman; or

c   That the continuance of the pregnancy would involve risk to the life of the pregnant woman, greater than if the pregnancy were terminated; or

d   That there is a substantial risk that if the child were born it would suffer from such physical or mental abnormalities as to be seriously handicapped.

Abortion is now legal if two doctors agree on either of the following:

i   Continuing the pregnancy means that there is a risk to the woman's health, or that of her existing children greater than if the pregnancy was terminated, allowing up to 24 weeks of pregnancy; or

ii Continuing the pregnancy would involve severe damage to the woman's mental or physical health greater than if the pregnancy was terminated, or there is a strong risk of severe handicap in the expected child, or the woman's life is at risk if the pregnancy continues without time limit.

> **KEY ISSUE**
> When does life begin? At conception? During pregnancy? At birth? Is abortion morally acceptable?

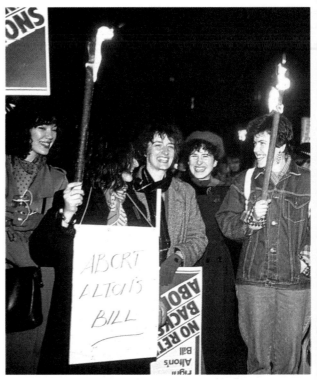

Pro-abortionists making their voices heard

> **Development of the foetus**
> 25th day   – heart beating.
> 28th day   – legs and arms begin to form.
> 6th week   – bones appear.
> 7th week   – fingers, thumbs forming.
> 10th week – organs nearly formed.
> 12th week – vocal chords, sexual organs form.
> 16th week – half its birth length.
> 5th month – eyebrows, eyelashes begin.
> Premature babies born as early as 25 weeks.

VIEWPOINTS

'The decision to terminate a pregnancy is so important that it can only be made by the person most involved – the woman. Women must always have a choice and never have the decision forced upon them. Free abortion facilities should be available on the NHS for every woman who needs them. We believe that the right of women to control their own fertility is a fundamental human right. Women will only be able to take a full and equal part in society when we can all decide for ourselves whether and when to have children.'

(National Abortion Campaign)

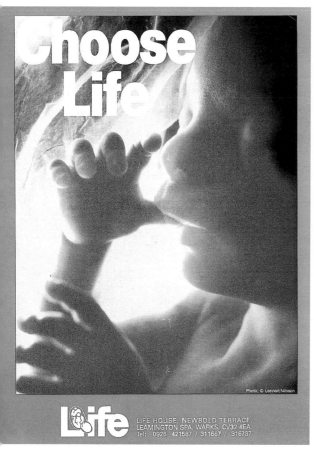

An emotive anti-abortion poster

'Since human life begins at conception, i.e. fertilization, and since all human life should be equally protected by the law from conception to natural death, whether or not the human being concerned is wanted or handicapped, it follows that the destruction of unborn life is always wrong.'

(LIFE Campaigns)

'Humanists regard abortion as better than bringing unwanted babies into the world. It is a mistake to say that Humanists are in favour of abortion; no one can be in favour of abortion, which, except in unforeseen circumstances, is the result of failed contraception. We think there will probably always be a certain number of unplanned pregnancies and that the mothers concerned should have the complete choice of either early abortion, or keeping the baby.'

(Humanist Dipper)

'We have been created by Almighty God in his own image and likeness. No pregnancy is unplanned, because no baby can be conceived unless Almighty God intends that conception and has willed that particular unique and completely individual new person into existence. What has actually happened in our society is that clever arguments have convinced those with no anchor of belief in God to cling to, that merciless slaughter of unborn babies is morally justifiable, and even essential for the happiness of the individual and the good of society.'

(Catholic Truth Society)

'The Anglican view on abortion is that although the foetus is to be specially respected and protected, nonetheless the life of the foetus is not absolutely sacrosanct if it endangers the life of its mother.'

(Church of England report, 1984)

FOR YOUR FOLDERS

▶ Explain in your own words the 1990 Human Fertilization and Embryology Act.

▶ Briefly explain why the organizations LIFE and NAC hold the views they do on abortion.

▶ What is the Humanist view and why do Catholics believe this is wrong?

THINGS TO DO

▶ In groups of three to four discuss reasons for and against abortion, then write your reasons down and compare them with those of the rest of the class.

CHOICES

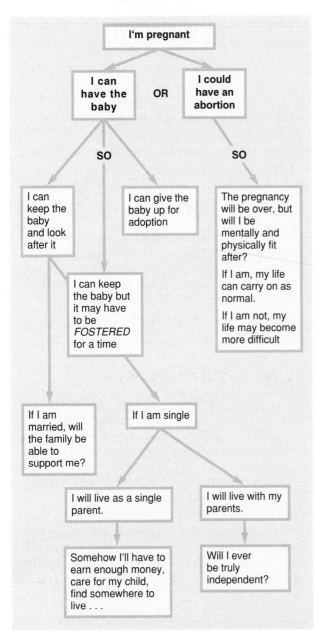

```
                    I'm pregnant

        I can                    I could
        have the        OR       have an
        baby                     abortion

            SO                       SO

  I can          I can give the    The pregnancy
  keep the       baby up for       will be over, but
  baby           adoption          will I be
  and look                         mentally and
  after it                         physically fit
                                   after?

         I can keep                If I am, my life
         the baby but              can carry on as
         it may have               normal.
         to be
         FOSTERED                  If I am not, my
         for a time                life may become
                                   more difficult

  If I am          If I am single
  married, will
  the family be
  able to
  support me?

      I will live as a single    I will live with my
      parent.                    parents.

      Somehow I'll have to       Will I ever
      earn enough money,         be truly
      care for my child,         independent?
      find somewhere to
      live . . .
```

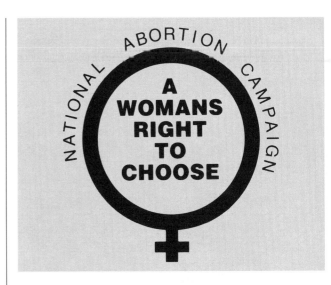

NATIONAL ABORTION CAMPAIGN

A WOMANS RIGHT TO CHOOSE

AMMUNITION FOR A CLASS DEBATE: THE CASE FOR ABORTION

- The decision to have an abortion is never easy, but no-one is better suited than the woman concerned to make that decision.

- Taking control of your own fertility is everyone's right, but there is no such thing as 100% safe and certain contraception, so women still need abortion.

- Because opinion differs as to when life begins, a minority has no right to impose its views on the rest of us.

- A foetus is only a potential human life, but there can be no argument about the humanity of the woman.

- Doctors have no special moral or ethical training which makes them fitter than pregnant women to make these sorts of decision.

- There will always be women who don't want children at all and we should respect that choice.

- No society has ever been known where abortion has not existed in some form, whatever the male secular and religious leaders have said.

- The argument is not whether abortion exists, but whether it should be legal, safe and dignified or illegal, unsafe and furtive.

- Every child has the right to be a wanted child. Abortion saves thousands of children from being unwanted and saves society from many problems.

- It is more of a trauma to give up a child for adoption than having an abortion.

THINGS TO DO

▶ This is only a very brief summary of the choices. Discuss them in pairs or groups of three and then write down some of the problems that these choices might create.

▶ Organize a class debate on the arguments for and against abortion, using the 'ammunition'.

- Even if abortion were made a crime thousands of women would still risk their lives and health in back-street abortion clinics.
- If a women is raped and becomes pregnant then offering an abortion is a humane and practical way of helping her.

AMMUNITION FOR A CLASS DEBATE: THE CASE AGAINST ABORTION

- modern science proves that the unborn child is a separate human being from conception. It is never just a part of his or her mother's body
- by allowing abortion, society is taking the easy way out. It should concentrate on improving the quality of life in society
- even in the womb the unborn child has a right not to be killed
- people with the most awful handicaps can lead happy, creative and fulfilled lives
- abortion is discrimination against the weak
- abortion is not just a matter of 'religion' – it is about murder, injustice and the denial of human rights. The UN Declaration of the Rights of the Child states that children need protection before, as well as after, birth
- unborn babies are unique, different, they have potential personalities
- every aborted foetus was a potential human being, perhaps even a Beethoven or a Curie

- abortions can go wrong. They can leave terrible mental and physical 'scars' on a woman
- if abortion is acceptable, where do we draw the line? Abortion is a form of infanticide
- if society did more in the way of contraception and education, and helped single mothers by providing counselling and places where they could seek advice, abortion would not be necessary
- killing is killing, whether done in back-streets or openly.

THREE VIEWPOINTS

Humanists say:

Abortion should be available on request.

The Catholic Church says:

Abortion is a sin in all cases.

The Protestant Church says:

Abortion in certain cases is acceptable.

IT COULD HAPPEN TO YOU

Between 1969 and 1974 on average 28 women in every 100 of child-bearing age experienced an abortion whilst by 1990 this had risen to an average of 42 in every 100. At this rate, unless there are improvements in the provision and delivery of contraceptive services, 50% of women will have an abortion at some time in their lives. In terms of percentage of conceptions ending in abortion, approximately half of all conceptions in girls under 16 are terminated, as they are for women aged 40 or over. This is the highest percentage. About 10 girls aged 15 or less in every 1000 have abortions. Also, women under 20 are twice as likely as older women to have an abortion at 20 weeks or later.

FOR YOUR FOLDERS

!▶ This section has been concerned with the 'rights' and 'wrongs' of the abortion issue. By now you will have formed your own opinions. Try to express them in the form of a letter to a Church, or to LIFE, or to the National Abortion Campaign.

'You start by sinking into his arms and end up with your arms in his sink.'

(Graffiti)

Men have dominated societies for many hundreds of years. They have wielded the power, shaped the values, controlled the wealth, formed the leading ideas and have treated women as second-class citizens. It is difficult for us today to believe some of the ways that women have been treated and still are treated in some parts of the world. We like to think that we live in a world where women are treated as equals and with respect. However, if we look closely at the way that our society is run and at many of its values we will find that still today men think of themselves as the dominant sex.

Our language is often sexist: mankind, masterful, craftsman, masterpiece, statesman, forefathers, manpower, God the father, God the son, etc. Our advertising exploits the female body to sell its goods suggesting that if you buy a certain product you have access to a woman's body. Pornography (see Section 19) is rife and one of the biggest growth industries in the Western world. Our workplaces are sexist – statistics show that women have the lesser paid jobs, are subject to sexual harassment, and are less likely to reach the so-called 'top jobs'. Our parliamentary system is sexist – over half the voting population are women and yet we only have a few women MPs. Our churches are sexist – women are not allowed to hold any positions of power. Sexism as an issue is alive and kicking and one that we all need to think about.

FOR DISCUSSION

Over the last 20 years the rights of women have become an issue on the public agenda. Read the following statement by a women's rights group, and in groups of four (preferably two boys, two girls) discuss the idea that women are oppressed.

'We believe that women are oppressed, as women within a system of sexism in which men as a group have access to power and privilege that women do not have. Within this system, women are discriminated against in employment, in exclusion from employment, in every aspect of public and private life, and by the fact that women's work as wives, mothers and carers is undervalued and under-rewarded.

We believe that women are victims of violence, sexual violence and sexual harassment, at home, at work, on the streets and in public places. Women are not only discriminated against, but regarded as "inferior" (less intelligent, less important, less able). On the one hand, women are trivialized, treated as sex objects and even treated with contempt, while on the other hand they are idealized and sentimentalized. We

believe that discrimination against women is perpetuated by these negative attitudes and these attitudes and the behaviour and practices that result from them are at the core of sex discrimination.

We believe that although men have power and privilege within the system of sexism, both women and men are conditioned to accept their roles of "subordinate" and "dominant" respectively. Both sexist conditioning and the system of sexism are damaging to women and to men.

We believe in the right of women to be free from discrimination, to be treated equally in education, training and employment and every other aspect of their lives. In addition, their work as wives, mothers and carers should be valued, rewarded and supported. Women should have freedom of movement without danger of violence or harassment and women should be regarded, represented and treated with complete respect as human beings.'

TALKING POINTS

'The most important chores on earth that are done by women are regarded as being low. In our kitchens we raise all the future Jesus' of the world or all the future serial killers. In our kitchens we wash for them and cook for them. In our kitchens they learn to love and to hate. And we send them out from our kitchens to be grown men and women. What greater work is there than that? A mother with a family is an economist, a nurse, a painter, a diplomat, a psychologist and much more. Those who wish to control and influence the future generations by giving birth and nurturing the young should not be looked down upon. With a small family, I am working over 120 hours a week. I am not getting paid. If I had my way, it would be the highest paid job in the world. We are taught that it is low because society tells us so. But it is time we said it is not so. We are the guardians of tomorrow.'

(Buchi Emecheta, author's interview)

'How many complaints would there be if women breastfed their young openly on buses, trains, in pubs, offices, on the streets, etc? Yet no-one objects to naked women in newspapers, read and displayed in all these places.'

(A man interviewed in Liverpool)

'Until men learn that delicacy, tenderness and honour are an essential part of their relationships with women, there isn't much hope for us.'

(A man interviewed in Surrey)

(Quotes from men in Liverpool and Surrey are taken from Clare Short's book, *Dear Clare: this is what women feel about* page 3, 1991)

FOR YOUR FOLDERS

▶ Can you think of examples where women on the one hand are sentimentalized (the Madonna) and on the other hand are treated with contempt (the whore)?

▶ Women are afraid to walk the streets. How can we try to create a society where this is not so?

▶ What influence do you think media pictures of women (e.g. on Page 3 and in *Playboy* magazine) have on men's conditioning?

▶ The most valuable job on earth is not paid. Do you think that mothers and carers should be paid?

▶ Write an article entitled 'You start by sinking into his arms and end up with your arms in his sink'.

! ▶ What are your views on men's treatment of women?

Throughout most of known world history we cannot examine the status of women because normally they have had none. Their achievements have gone unrecorded. Women have nearly always been dominated by men and regarded as men's personal property. This has certainly been the case during the three or more thousand years of Judaeo-Christian civilization and is symbolized by Eve being created from one of Adam's ribs *(Genesis 2: 20–23)*.

THE OLD TESTAMENT

'So God created man in his own image, in the image of God created He him; male and female created He them.'

(Genesis 1: 27)

Throughout Jewish and Christian history, however, it was Eve's role as Adam's 'helper' and inferior which was accepted universally, because her own likeness to God came only via the male spare rib. It was never forgotten also that in the story it was because Eve yielded to the temptation of the serpent, ate the forbidden fruit and gave some to Adam that they were both expelled from the Garden of Eden *(Genesis 3: 1–24)* ashamed of their nakedness. In the story Adam was condemned to work among thorns and thistles but Eve, as the cause of their 'fall' was given a worse punishment: 'I will greatly multiply your pain in childbearing; in pain you shall bring forth children yet your desire shall be for your husband and he shall rule over you.' This biblical nutshell sums up woman's lot down the ages and reflects attitudes towards women at the time that the *Genesis* story was written. Because of her biology man must be her master.

Genesis reflects the social realities of that time. The whole of the Old Testament depicts a society which was rigidly patriarchal. A women was a man's private possession. Rape or adultery were considered to be a violation of *his* ownership rights, whereas his own unfaithfulness was overlooked unless he interfered with the wife of another man. During much of their adult lives women underwent the additional burden of being considered 'unclean'. For instance, during menstruation they were untouchable for at least a week: 'If any man lies with her and her impurities on him, he shall be unclean seven days and every bed on which he lies shall be unclean' *(Leviticus 15: 24)*. Very observant Orthodox Jews still observe the Jewish laws of family purity and Jewish women do not regard the laws as oppressive or sexist. This ritual purity still exists in parts in the ban on women entering sanctuary or serving at the altar of most Roman Catholic and high Anglican Christian churches. It is also tied up with the continuing refusal to ordain women as priests.

JESUS' ATTITUDES

Jesus was born into a patriarchal society and this probably explains why none of his disciples were women. However, his attitude to women was very different and it is widely believed that women play a very *active* role in Jesus' ministry and life. He always considered them as equal and as deserving of respect as any man. It was to the Samaritan women at the well that he first made himself known as the Messiah *(John 4: 7–30)*; the story of Martha and Mary demonstrates his belief that women were fit for other things besides domesticity *(Luke 10: 38–42)*; he appeared to women first after the crucifixion *(Matthew 28: 1–10)*.

ST PAUL'S ATTITUDES

St Paul stated: '. . . there is neither male nor female for you are all one in Christ Jesus' *(Galatians 3: 28)*. He also taught that a husband should love his wife as himself *(I Corinthians 7: 3)*. However, he also warned wives to '. . . be subject to your husbands' *(Ephesians 5: 22–23)*. When it came to teaching the Word to others, St Paul was adamant that 'a women learn in silence with all submissiveness. I permit no woman to teach or to have authority over men; she is to keep silent' *(I Timothy 2: 11–12)*. To us today, these references are very sexist.

CHRISTIAN HISTORY

During the 2000 year-old history of Christianity women have had no position in society, and the Church has reinforced the general sexist attitudes of the day:

'Women should remain at home, sit still, keep house, bear and bring up children.'

(Martin Luther, 1483–1586)

FEMINIST THEOLOGY

It is only over the last few years that male Christians have seriously taken on board and thought about the sexist attitudes that have dominated the Church. Since the rise of the Women's Movement in the 1960s a new force has arisen in the Church which is sometimes called FEMINIST THEOLOGY. Women are slowly beginning to make the male dominated Church think about its attitudes and language.

Sara Maitland, a Christian feminist, writes:

> '. . . the effect of not having to regard women as fully human means that their experiences, complaints and joys do not have to be given the same validity. Male experience is declared as normal; female alternatives to this experience are regarded as being abnormal. Prostitution, for instance, has been considered in the light of what using prostitutes might mean for the moral fibre of men and their society. This, Augustine (354–430) could write, "remove prostitution from human affairs and you will unsettle everything because of lust" (men's lust presumably).'

Over the last few years the issue of women priests had taken many churches by storm. Within the Anglican church it has caused widespread division to such an extent that many Christians feel that they are beginning to see an irretrievable split within it.

> 'The language of the church is sexist too. Why does it always convey a male God? Surely God, the Creator of everything is both male and female. As women we want to be consulted about attitudes in the church and not be expected just to make cups of tea.'
>
> (Reverend Nan Peete, author's interview)

FOR YOUR FOLDERS

▶ Explain in your own words why and how the Genesis story laid the groundwork for sexism within the Christian Church.

▶ Look up the biblical references given as regards Jesus' attitudes to women. Write a paragraph on how he treated women.

▶ Why do the teachings of St Paul both support and reject the notion of women being ordained as priests?

▶ Explain in your own words what Feminist Theology is.

▶ How do you think the Church has helped to reinforce the sexist attitudes that have dominated the world over the last 2000 years?

▶ How do you feel Christians should move forward in accepting that women have as important a role to play in the future of the Church as men?

TALKING POINT

> 'Surely God, the creator of everything, is both male and female.'

In this section we will be looking at one particular type of violence – rape. In this article Clara Czerny argues that female sexual desire must be controlled or murdered and this is often done by rape.

'DEATH TO DESIRE'

We forget that up to fairly recently Western women diagnosed as "nymphomaniac" would have their clitoris cut out by male surgeons. We often fail to recognize that the West has ways of trying to sexually murder women – rape and fear of rape disempower women, telling them that their sexual desires do not count and keeping them out of the male controlled – or should we say "patrolled" – public domain.

For women sexual survival is, from an early age, rather like a game of cat and mouse set in a prison camp. Whatever decision a woman may take about her own sexuality there are still the "patrollers" whom she must be careful to evade and outwit. She must be ever watchful of the signs of possible attack and watchful of the way in which her actions might be interpreted as an "invitation" to be violated. In short to ensure her own survival she has to censor herself and her range of activities. This self-limitation becomes second nature.

Even if she does this as dutifully and carefully as she can, success is far from guaranteed. One in six women in London is raped. But the advice offered by the presumed "guardians" of society – the legislators, the judges, the police – rarely does more than reinforce the barbed wires of the prison camp. Usually it takes the form of a series of "Don'ts" whose one logical conclusion is "Don't exist". They are also absurd and misleading. What is the point of advising women not to walk alone at night if half of all rapes occur in the home? Or of advising women not to talk to strangers when most women are raped by men with whom they are already acquainted?

The only definite "do" on offer is that a woman attach herself to a man for protection. But if the man then rapes her she must not complain. Indeed, complaining is discouraged whatever the circumstances. Between 50 and 75 per cent of the women raped in Western countries do not report the incident to police because they do not believe they will be treated sympathetically.

There are, of course, laws against rape; there have been since Biblical times. But these should not be confused with the rights of women. They are, if anything, an indication of the opposite. Rape laws are essentially property laws. Even the word "rape" means "theft".

In making such laws the Patriarchs were not trying to stop violence against women – they were trying to stop men stealing each other's property. In several Western nations – including Germany, and some North American states – this emphasis remains unchanged. What the woman wants – or more accurately does not want – is irrelevant. However, rape within marriage is now recognized as a crime in the United Kingdom.

Even when the law does seem to be punishing sexual violence against women the male-centred nature of the law, both in economic and sexual terms, is apparent. Take the example of the young officer, Guardsman Tim Holdsworth, convicted by a British court in 1977 of causing grievous bodily harm to a 17-year-old by ramming his ring-studded fist into her vagina when she refused to have sex with him. The girl was left partially paralyzed and lost her job as a result of the attack. But three Appeal Judges decided that Holdsworth should be set free and receive a six month suspended prison sentence because they said they did not want to see his "promising army career in ruins". During the trial itself the girl had to endure a defence lawyer exhibiting her blood-stained underwear and suggesting she had "torn it herself". Holdsworth meanwhile was reprimanded for allowing his "enthusiasm for sex" to overcome his good behaviour. A backhanded compliment from the bench?

For men to treat women this way they have to deny these women their humanity, treat them as unfeeling objects. Patriarchy lays the foundation for this – pornography builds the edifice by presenting women as a degraded sexual commodity to be consumed by males.

Some men have taken to heart the feminist slogan: "Pornography is the theory. Rape the practice" and are genuinely trying to change their attitudes. But by and large Western societies still sanction rape – even if they do not see themselves doing so.

Ray Wyre, who counsels male sex offenders says: "Just listening to the ways schoolboys talk about girls or considering how certain popular newspapers and comedians continue to confuse sex, porn and rape persuades me that improvement remains a distant hope. In fact the more I am involved in counselling male sex offenders, the more struck I am by the fact that their attitudes reflect those of ordinary members of society."'

(Article taken from *New Internationalist*, September 1988)

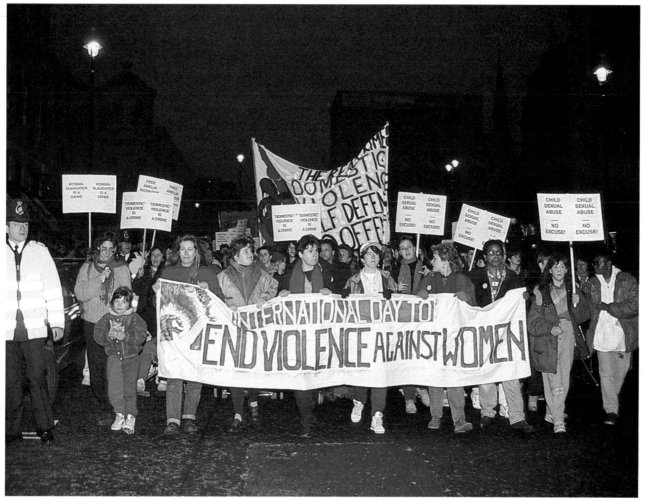

Demonstrating against sexual violence

TALKING POINT

'The underlying woman-hating motif of the *Genesis* story (Eve the temptress, the first sinner) is reiterated throughout Western culture, permeating language, law, medicine, psychology, art and literature.'

(Celia Kitzinger)

FOR YOUR FOLDERS

Write a few sentences on the following:

▶ 'For women sexual survival is a game of cat and mouse.'

▶ 'Rape means theft.'

▶ 'The law is male-centred.'

▶ Explain what you think Ray Wyre is saying about male sex offenders.

▶ What has the biblical story of Adam and Eve contributed to society's attitudes towards women?

We often see criminals in terms of stereotypes. Our vision of criminals prowling the streets and looking for trouble is thrown at us by the media. Whilst many people call for extra policing and stricter forms of punishment, Christians and Humanists feel that the root causes of crime ought to be looked at seriously. For instance, statistics suggest that for most white middle class people the risks of being directly affected by crime are negligible. Yet we are all encouraged to live in constant fear of attack, robbery and, most of all, mugging. In particular, both black and white women are encouraged, by the media and by politicians, to be frightened of going out in the dark, afraid of being alone in the house, and wary of public transport. The quality of our life as individuals and as a community is diminished by these fears. It is true that crime rates are rising, but the increase affects the poor much more than the wealthy. For instance, in some parts of London an Asian person is 50 times more likely to be attacked than a white person. So the people most likely to be victims of crime are not the comfortable white middle classes but the inhabitants of run-down inner city areas, especially if they are black. Most crime involves poor people robbing other poor people.

Many Christians and Humanists believe that the links between crime and poverty are not given enough publicity. They argue that if they were, it would become obvious that solving the crime problem would mean closing the gap between rich and poor. Western society encourages people to think of themselves as successful if they possess the trappings of wealth, e.g. big car, big house, holidays, the latest technology – stereos, CDs, videos, etc. Yet the same society prevents everyone from legally achieving this level of consumption by creating economic structures in which millions of people are unemployed or are in low paid jobs.

A HUMANIST VIEW

'As things stand, more and more money is spent on the police and on military hardware. If this money was used to alleviate poverty in ways that gave the poor some power, then the resulting change in people's thinking in inner city areas would virtually eliminate "street" crime. Such expenditure would also enable the financing of alternatives to prison, which is a major breeding ground of career criminality. Greater numbers of police often exacerbate the very problems that they are trying to cure. By arresting petty offenders they feed people into a criminal justice system that teaches them how to be professional criminals. Neither can we expect that by toughening up sentencing by the courts we will reduce crime. The sad fact is that America is one of the most crime-ridden societies *and* it has one of the world's highest rates of imprisonment.'

(Amanda Root)

WHITE COLLAR CRIME

Unlike conventional street crime, white collar crime is the work of people with high social status. It may be committed for individual gain, as in personal income tax evasion or the acceptance of a bribe. Or it may be committed by companies or governments with deceptive advertising, fraud or the marketing of ineffective and outdated products.

The crimes committed by the poor have traditionally attracted a harsh response. By comparison, the penalties for crimes committed by a company or government seem to be mild. For example, in 1985 an Australian company director defrauded the Australian government of $16.5 million in taxes. He was jailed for two years. Commenting on the crime, a senior law lecturer, Ari Friebres, said: 'A person can break into a house and steal perhaps $100 and be liable to a 14 year penalty, but a person who takes $16 million can only get a maximum of 5 years.'

CHRISTIAN RESPONSES TO CRIME

Christians look to the New Testament for their guidance and here they find Jesus consistently teaching the virtues of forgiveness:

'Pass no judgements and you will not be judged.'

(Matthew 7: 1)

'Father, forgive them, they do not know what they are doing.'

(Luke 23: 34)

Christians accept that, in a modern society, criminals need to be deterred (put off) but that society needs to look at the root causes of crime, especially those that are linked to poverty.

Many Christians would argue that society needs to work towards reforming criminals rather than merely punishing them.

FOR YOUR FOLDERS

▶ What sort of stereotypes does the media portray in terms of criminals?

▶ Why are poor people often more likely to be the victims of crime?

▶ How does society, with its images of the 'good life', in many ways encourage crime?

▶ Explain in your own words what Humanists and Christians consider to be some of the main causes of crime. Do you agree with them?

▶ What is 'white collar crime'?

▶ Try and list some of the factors that you think are the causes of crime. Write a paragraph on the theme 'Criminals are not born but made'.

TALKING POINTS

'The real criminals in this society are not all the people who populate the prisons, but those who have stolen the wealth of the world from the people.'

(Angela Davis)

'Crimes are the result of a complex of factors, a train of earlier events, a balance of both social and individual influences that differ in every case. These factors include circumstances, for example, poverty, bad housing; conflict with others and mental or emotional disturbances.'

(John St John)

What is society trying to do when it punishes an offender (somebody who has broken the law and therefore 'offended' society)? There are five main aims of punishment.

1 The theory of PROTECTION

Punishments are used to protect society from somebody's anti-social behaviour. This punishment takes many forms, the most obvious being imprisonment. Also this type of punishment can be designed to protect the offenders against themselves.

2 The theory of RETRIBUTION

If somebody does something wrong then they should receive a punishment that is fitting for the crime they have committed. 'An eye for an eye'.

3 The theory of DETERRENCE

If a person who commits a crime is punished then they will not (hopefully) commit such a crime, or any other crime, again. Also the punishment they receive will put others off (deter them from) committing crimes.

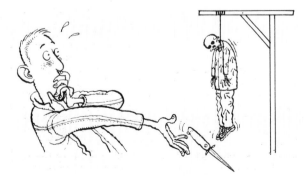

Deterrent punishment

4 The theory of REFORM

People who commit crimes often need all sorts of help. The punishments that they receive should be of a kind that will prevent them from committing further crimes, and make them responsible citizens who have something to offer society.

Reformative punishment

5 The theory of VINDICATION

In order that society is able to function securely, crime must be punished so that the law will be respected.

A CHRISTIAN VIEWPOINT

Many Christians believe that punishment and forgiveness can go together. They also lay great stress on trying to look at the motives and reasons for crime. Over the last 150 years many Christians have worked towards the idea of reforming criminals as they see the theory of reform as being the most important of all the aims of punishment.

FOR YOUR FOLDERS

▶ In your own words explain the five aims of punishment. How do you think a Christian and a Humanist would view these different aims?

▶ Try and find out what forms of punishment exist in our society. How do they relate to the five aims of punishment?

Beyond punishment

The idea of spectacular public torture is as strange to us as the notion of rehabilitation and psychological assessment would have been to the mediaeval inquisitor. Here is a brief history showing how the philosophies behind punishment have changed from retribution to the reform of a supposedly sick mind.

▲ Vicious methods of execution – such as hanging, drawing and quartering – were normal punishments in the West right up until the nineteenth century. But punishment was not limited to those guilty of secular crimes: the idea of a division between body and soul (or, later, mind) enabled the Church to torture and burn so-called heathens in South America – not to mention an estimated nine million peasant women* in Europe accused of being witches. The pretext of destroying bodies to save souls thinly masked the theft of the victims' land or livelihoods.
* Source: **New Woman, New Earth** Reuther.

◀ Public execution was a grand dramatic symbol – a theatrical confrontation between the law-breaker and the forces of justice controlled by the monarch. The condemned would make a final speech in which they could try to justify themselves. Occasionally the crowd would respond by storming the gallows to the rescue of the condemned person. Such insurrections were possible because the law was not seen as impartial but as an expression of the sovereign's control.

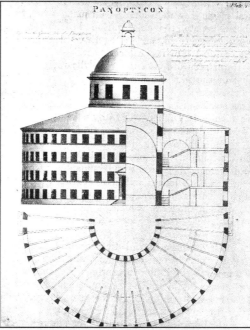

▲ This illustration shows a *panopticon,* a nineteenth-century plan of a model prison where the prisoners could be watched constantly, but could never know whether or not they were under scrutiny. From this point in history, it is the individual's own conscience that is the target of the judicial system. Torture has been superseded by the power of guilt to induce obedience in the entire population. Because everybody has internalised the norms of criminal justice, even though they may break laws, they do not question the law's right to exist.

But, elsewhere in the world, the authority to carry out punishment was not always vested in those who were distant from everyday life. In many areas of pre-colonial India, for instance, the local community assumed the right to judge its own offenders, collectively deciding which form of restitution would be appropriate. Families would meet first, and if they were unable to reach an agreement with the aggrieved person's family, then a court of older, respected members of the community would be called together. This ensured that legal power was not concentrated in the hands of a few people.

Modern psychiatry refuses to punish or put moral responsibility on the individual. Peter Sutcliffe, the 'Yorkshire Ripper' murderer of 13 women and attacker of seven others, was able to plead diminished responsibility as a schizophrenic and so was found guilty of manslaughter rather than murder. The modern legal system is caught between a diagnostic scheme which denies responsibility and the older legal one which asserts it. The resulting compromises create inconsistent judgements – some times harshly punitive and at others therapeutic – in which criminal law usually reflects the prejudices of society, punishing those who are already disadvantaged and offering psychological help to those who are more privileged.

Offenders were drawn and quartered by being partly strangled and then disembowelled while still alive, having their entrails burnt in front of them, being decapitated and then having their body butchered into four pieces. Many of these punishments were carried out in public.

In the eighteenth century you could be hanged in Britain for over 200 offences. In 1957 the British government ruled that only certain types of murder were punishable by the gallows (killing police officers; using guns or explosives; killing two or more people; killing during a robbery). In 1965, after much debate, capital punishment was suspended for a five-year trial period. In 1970 it was permanently abolished.

AMNESTY INTERNATIONAL (SEE SECTION 66)

Although 85 countries in the world no longer use the death penalty, 90 countries still retain it. Amnesty International is working towards the abolition of the death penalty worldwide. They argue that:

> 'The death penalty is irrevocable – it sends innocent people to their deaths.
> It is a particularly cruel, calculated and cold-blooded form of killing.
> It does nothing to prevent violent crime.
> It is a violation of the right to live.'

TALKING POINT

> 'Innocent men have been hanged in the past and will be hanged in the future unless the death penalty is abolished worldwide or the fallibility of human judgement is abolished and judges become superhuman.'
>
> (Arthur Koestler)

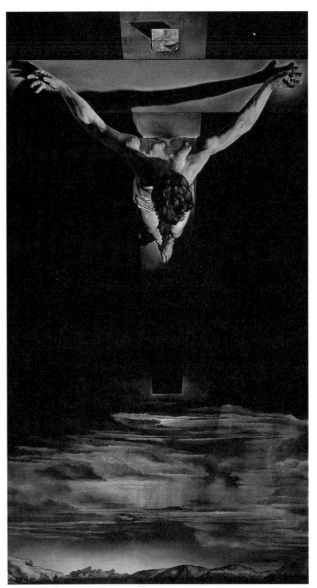

The crucifixion of Christ by Salvador Dali

In the ancient world one of the most common methods of capital punishment was crucifixion. Death was caused by exhaustion, heart failure, or suffocation brought on by having the legs shattered by an iron club. In 519 BC Darius, King of Persia, crucified 3,000 political opponents in Babylon. The Emperor Constantine abolished crucifixion in the Roman Empire during the fourth century but it was still practised in Japan until the nineteenth century.

Other forms of capital punishment through the ages have included being stoned to death; decapitation; being burnt alive; hanging; being fed alive to wild animals; being ripped apart by horses running in opposite directions; being hurled from rocks; drowning; drawing and quartering.

CLASS DEBATE

▶ 'This House believes that capital punishment should be reintroduced.' Using some of the following arguments, organize a class debate. (You need someone to propose and second the motion of both sides plus a chairperson.)

The case for capital punishment

- terrorists who indiscriminately kill people should be hanged
- it deters (puts off) potential murderers
- it has been in existence since the beginning of time, so why abolish it now?
- it protects civilians and police
- it adequately expresses society's total abhorrence of murder
- a so-called life sentence is not punishment enough
- some 'lifers' are back on the streets in a few years
- the law should be based on 'An eye for an eye, a tooth for a tooth'
- revenge is a natural human emotion
- capital punishment helps the victim's family to get over their loss.

The case against capital punishment

- capital punishment may make convicted terrorists into martyrs
- the law condemns murder and then goes on to murder in the name of the law
- it does not necessarily deter
- the death penalty is inhumane
- society turns the executioner into a murderer
- in the past the wrong person has been hanged
- in 77% of murders in 1984 the murderer knew the victim well (e.g. family rows, loss of temper)
- it makes a mockery of the idea of reform
- rather than kill so-called murderers we should begin to study their motives and the pressures society has put them under
- all life is sacred – what right has society to judge that a person's life should end?

A HUMANIST VIEWPOINT

'The abolition of capital punishment has been the concern of Humanists for years. Revenge, whether divine or human, is always destructive; never creative. It has no place in any society claiming to be civilized.'

(from Kit Mouat, *What Humanism Is About*, 1963)

AN ANGLICAN VIEWPOINT

In 1983 some of the speakers of the Church of England's General Synod made the following points:

'God is merciful and man shares in God's merciful nature.'

'The taking of life as a penalty devalues human life.'

'There is substantial doubt that capital punishment has any significant deterrent effect.'

'The abolition of capital punishment gave prison chaplains a chance to work for the reform of all prisoners rather than just some of them.'

(Report on Proceedings)

FOR YOUR FOLDERS

! ▶ Look at the arguments of Amnesty International. Do you agree with them? Give reasons for your answer.

! ▶ A local newspaper has recently had a section on whether hanging should be brought back. Write a letter to the editor either supporting or rejecting reintroduction.

! ▶ Look at the Anglican viewpoint. Write something
a explaining what is meant,
b on your views of each statement.

FOR DISCUSSION

▶ Capital punishment 'has no place in any society claiming to be "civilized" '. Do you agree?

▶ To hang terrorists would only make them martyrs.

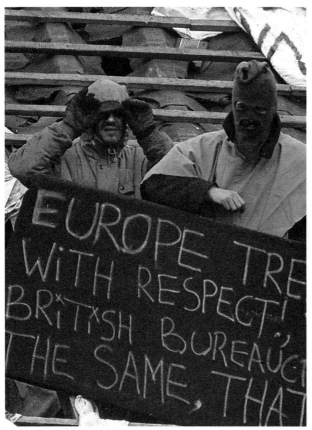

Protesting prisoners during Strangeways riot

'In the morning at ten past seven we get unlocked and then it's communal slopping out, we all empty our bowls and chambers from the night before and then we go down to breakfast, eat it in the cell, get washed, shaved, and then lounge around until nine, until they open the doors again, collect our razor blades and slop out again. And then we are locked up again until 11 o'clock, we'll have half an hour's exercise, have our dinner, go upstairs, collect the mail if there is mail, and then we are locked up again until about ten past two. Then it's slopping out again and then we're locked up again until about half past three. Then we have another half an hour's exercise, lock up again, then at 4 o'clock go down and get our tea, come back, and then we're locked up again until about six o'clock, then we slop out again, get rid of our trays – and then that's it 'til we're locked up again all night.'

(Remand prisoner in *British Prisons*, 1979)

TALKING POINTS

'The ultimate expression of law is not order – it's prison. We have hundreds upon hundreds of prisons and thousands upon thousands of laws yet there is no social order, no social peace.'

(George Jackson, *Blood in my eye*, 1972)

'To send a woman to prison is to take away from her family; her children in particular may suffer from this deprivation, which can lead to the break up of the home even where there is a stable marriage.'

(A woman prisoner)

'The most visible manifestation of the crisis in British prisons has been the crisis of conditions. Physical conditions are appalling. . . overcrowding is rife and endemic : many prisoners, particularly those on remand awaiting trial or sentence, spend up to 23 hours a day, 7 days a week in small cells.'

(Mike Fitzgerald in *British Prisons*, 1979)

'The basic evils of imprisonment are that it denies autonomy, degrades dignity, impairs or destroys self-reliance, inculcates authoritarian values, minimizes the likelihood of beneficial interaction with one's peers, fractures family ties, destroys the family's economic stability, and prejudices the prisoner's future prospects for any improvement in his economic and social status.'

(American Friends Service Committee)

'I have been in an out of nick for the last 35 years. I reckon to have spent no more than 5 of them free. I can never get a job, I have no family – it's the only place I really know. I feel secure inside – I'll die inside, I know that.'

(Billy, aged 55, author's interview)

'Prisons are the nearest things to hell on earth that have ever been created.'

(Prison Governor)

' Keep in mind those who are in prison as though you were in prison with them.'

(*Hebrews 13:3*)

'The use of imprisonment should be minimized to reduce isolation from society and weaken the society of crime.'

(British Humanist Association)

PUNISHMENT OR REHABILITATION?

All these quotes give a very negative view of prison. There are some organizations that work towards the abolition of prisons. However, many people believe that every society needs an ultimate deterrent. In some societies this might be capital punishment and in others it might be long-term imprisonment. Surprisingly, prisons in Britain are only about 200 years old, and since their conception the views on how prisoners should be treated have changed considerably. Today, more emphasis is put on rehabilitation and the idea of reforming prisoners. Many prisons provide educational facilities, counselling groups and recreational activities for prisoners. However, many people argue that prisons do not act as a deterrent (see Sections 54 and 55).

'Imprisonment does not deter. We have a record number of people in prison and a record crime rate.'

(Robert Kilroy-Silk)

Prison is still central to our system of dealing with offenders. Historically, prison has functioned in three ways:

1 custodially, to hold prisoners awaiting trial;
2 coercively, to secure repayment of a debt;
3 penally, as a punishment.

The question of how we deal with offenders in our society is becoming increasingly important. The crime rate is rising, prisons are over-crowded and people who work in the prison service are under increasing pressures. Sometimes the whole prison system erupts, as in the riots in Strangeways Prison in 1990 when prisoners claimed that up to 20 prisoners died, and numerous prison officers were injured.

Many organizations are working towards trying to reform the criminal justice system so that more offenders repay society through things like community service, compensation and probation. The cost of locking people in prison is a tremendous burden on society. For instance, 8 million working days a year are lost by men in prison; families are broken up through the imprisonment of men and women.

CONCERNED ORGANIZATIONS

RAP (Radical Alternatives to Prison) – an organization that believes that prisons do more harm than good.
NACRO (National Association for the Care and Resettlement of Offenders) – gives prisoners advice and help on their release.
Howard League for Penal Reform – puts pressure on the Government to make prisons more humane and fairer places.
PROP (Preservation of the Rights of Prisoners) – organization of prisoners and ex-prisoners trying to improve prisoners' rights.

FOR YOUR FOLDERS

▶ After reading the Talking Points write an article of at least 300 words entitled 'Our Prisons in Crisis'.

▶ Look at the five aims of punishment in Section 54. How far do you think the prison system goes in meeting these aims?

▶ Considering that prisons are expensive places to run and that the crime rate is rising, how do you think society should deal with offenders?

Prison is such an accepted form of punishment that we tend not to think about whether it does any good. In this article, Chris Tchaikovsky describes the world inside the jail and how she is trying to change it.

'My criminal career began at 17 when, with three other teenage girls I broke into a tobacconist's shop. It continued for over 12 years during which I was imprisoned for 6 months in 1963, 6 months in 1967 and for 2 years in 1973. Over the years I became increasingly professional in my chosen way of life and – in material terms at least – I became a successful criminal.

I enjoyed the excitement of crime although I did not think much about what I was doing. I believed that everyone else was endlessly corrupt and only remained law-abiding because they were afraid of getting caught.

I went along with the villain's credo, "if you can't do the time don't do the crime", because I thought that imprisonment was a fair penalty for breaking the law.

The philosophy behind punishment seems to gel around the following ideas: those who are dangerous to others must be contained and those who engage in criminal activities must be deterred. Prison was designed to allow those who are law-abiding to extract some retribution from those who aren't, and also to deter others from breaking the law through the fear of being locked up.

So far, so fair. Prisons probably do instil fear into and keep docile a labour force that on the whole, obeys the law. And certainly prisons are such filthy and brutal places that retribution is more than met. But they do more than this: having lived within a system where the punishment massively outweighs the crime I am convinced that prisons actually feed their own future. That is, they create the very people from whom they say they protect us. Sixty per cent of men and 41 per cent of women are reconvicted within two years of leaving jail.

No such thoughts occurred to me as I stepped outside the Old Bailey Court to begin my two year sentence. In the Reception Area of Holloway there were cubicles like rabbit hutches where you eat with your knees touching the door, and, underneath, a wire mesh strewn with used sanitary towels and empty cigarette packets. The dirty bath held just four inches of tepid water. The officers barked their orders in a contemptuous tone. Then the dreaded search, "Do a twirl, come on now, don't be shy", as you stand naked before them and whoever else might be passing by or dropping in. Later you are called for the doctor who asks, without looking up, "Are you fit?" . . . "Yes" . . . "Next".

When the degredation of Reception is over the prisoner soon learns that there are two sets of prison rules. One is set by the government and the other are the prisoners' unwritten rules. Both sets brutalize. If a prison is tough it becomes important to prove that you can withstand it by hiding your real feelings. This creates, in the officers, the impression we are hard, fulfils their beliefs about criminals and probably increases their desire to punish as well.

Lying becomes a way of life, almost an art. In a violent system where violence is expected at every turn, violence becomes a real and constant probability. And in a system which is ugly and brutish one can easily become an ugly brute.

One night a young woman begged the officer on duty to get her to hospital because she thought she was losing her baby. The response of the disbelieving officer was to pass a towel through the Judas Eye (spy hole) and tell the woman she should have booked to see the doctor. She miscarried in the early hours of the morning and lost so much blood she was lucky to be alive. I wanted nothing more than to see the prison pay for this neglect. I called a meeting and we drew up a list of demands and a petition that was signed by almost every woman in the wing. After taking our demands to the Governor we went on strike. The strike lasted for just one day. Woman after woman was called into the Governor's office and threatened with the loss of her parole.

Almost a decade later when crime and prison were long behind me, I met an old prison friend. She told me that a prisoner had burned to death in Holloway and that the *newly built "model" prison was far worse than the old. Women were locked in their cells for 23 hours a day and the prison was crawling with fleas and cockroaches. I began a campaigning group called Women in Prison. We have tried to publicize many cases of mistreatment and neglect but little has changed in Britain's closed and secret prisons. Perhaps because nothing can change until people realize that the kind of punishment the prison offers is counter-productive.*

Prison brutalizes people; it takes away what little responsibility a person had and gives them a deeper irresponsibility; it erodes an already small self-esteem and leaves a humiliated, broken sense of self.

What is needed is for people who have the imagination which springs from caring and not the desire to punish, to set up centres where the young and disaffected can be educated, cared for and put together again.'

(Chris Tchaikovsky, Women in Prison, 25 Horsell Road, Holloway, London N5 1XL)

FOR DISCUSSION

After reading this account on your own, break up into groups of ten and discuss the article bearing in mind the work you have done in the previous sections on Crime, Punishment and Prisons.

FOR YOUR FOLDERS

▶ Write a few sentences on the following:
  ● crime is exciting
  ● prisons feed their own future
  ● lying becomes a way of life
  ● prison brutalizes people

In February 1991 Britain experienced a spell of severe weather with temperatures dropping to below freezing for several days. In Manchester alone, seven people who were sleeping rough died. The news reports highlighted the increasing problem of homelessness in Britain. Many churches and voluntary organizations responded to the plight of the homeless. The Bishop of Chelmsford summed up the arguments: 'It is vital that in the short term the Government acts quickly to meet the needs of the homeless in critical circumstances, and that in the longer term the underlying causes of homelessness are addressed.'

Often homelessness is defined as people living on the street and prompts images of young people begging outside tube stations or people sleeping rough in shop doorways. Although street homelessness is the most visible and severe form of homelessness it should not lead to the conclusion that homelessness simply means not having a roof over one's head. A useful definition is given in the Church of England's report, *Faith in the City*:

'A home is more than having a roof over one's head. Decent housing certainly means a place that is dry and warm and in reasonable repair. It also means security, privacy, sufficient space, a place where people can grow and make choices. . . Vandalism, graffiti, fear of violence, lack of play space, all affect how people regard their surroundings. How property is managed, as well as the physical condition is important as it affects how people make decisions. To believe that you have no control over one of the most basic areas of your life is to be devalued.'

THE VULNERABLE

Young people

It is estimated that there are 156,000 young homeless people in Britain. Centrepoint (who provide hostels for young homeless people) estimates that there are over 50,000 young homeless people in central

Thousands of people live in squalor

London between the ages of 16 and 19. In 1988 general entitlement to housing benefit for 16–17 year olds was withdrawn. This has led to increasing levels of homelessness among young people, forcing them to beg and exposing them to the horrors of violence, drug trafficking and sexual exploitation.

Black and ethnic minority people

Black people form a disproportionate number of those accepted as homeless by local authorities. Many published reports demonstrate that black people suffer serious discrimination. They tend to be placed in the worst housing and have difficulty in securing decent jobs.

Women

Women are generally over-represented among the homeless. According to the Housing Advice Switchboard in London, 60% of calls received about housing problems are from women.

Lesbians and gay men

The London Gay Teenage Group found 11% of young people had been made homeless because of their sexuality.

Disabled people

The number of households accepted by local authorities as homeless because of physical disability has increased by 35% since 1985.

Psychiatric patients

Over the last ten years more than 23,000 psychiatric hospital beds have been lost, displacing increasing numbers of people.

Shelter

Shelter was formed in 1966 by several charities concerned with homelessness and housing problems. It provides practical help for people with housing problems, advice on homelessness, benefits, landlord and tenant disputes, disrepair and mortgage debt. It campaigns to change policies and attitudes to bad housing and homelessness. Recent campaigns have highlighted the growing number of young people sleeping on the streets. An estimated three million people are without homes of their own in Britain today. Official figures show that homelessness has more than doubled over the last ten years. Despite this council house building is at its lowest level since the War because the Government has cut back money from local authorities.

FOR YOUR FOLDERS

▶ Briefly explain the work of Shelter and Centrepoint.

▶ Write a paragraph on 'the vulnerable and homelessness'.

▶ Explain in your own words how the Church of England defines homelessness.

▶ What problems might a 16-year-old homeless person face?

▶ Try and list some of the reasons why there are so many homeless people in Britain today.

THINGS TO DO

Imagine you are a 17-year-old person living in a large inner city without a job or a home. Write a letter to a politician explaining what your life is like.

FOR DISCUSSION

'Homelessness is not about individual inadequacy as the government commonly implies. It is caused by the simple fact that there is not enough decent, secure and affordable housing to go round.'

(Shelter)

TALKING POINT

'A home is more than having a roof over one's head.'
(Church of England)

WHAT IS WORK?

Work has been described as 'purposeful activity' It is an activity natural to people but not all human activity is of this sort. Some of it is play or rest and some of it is thought and using the mind. For many people work is what they get paid for, but often people do not stop working when they are not paid for it.

WHAT PURPOSES DOES WORK SERVE?

In a report produced by the Church of England, five purposes of work are highlighted:

1 **Work is necessary.** Work is necessary for human survival and without work the structures of our societies and cultures would not exist.

2 **Work is creative.** By controlling the elements of nature humans are able to create things.

3 **Work is painful.** Work can be physically and mentally exhausting. It can be dangerous, repetitive, boring, meaningless, monotonous and soul destroying.

4 **Work is healthy.** Work brings us into relationship with other people. It helps us to belong to a community by giving us a place, status, belonging and value.

5 **Work is good.** Work is a way of obtaining the necessities of life and enriching our lives with beauty and enjoyment. It is regarded as a means of sharing with God in being creative in the world. During the centuries work to some Christians, especially Protestants, became a sort of religious duty. Hard work was seen as being a virtue. This became known as the 'Protestant Work Ethic'.

VOCATION

> '**Vocation** – a job which one does because one thinks one has a special fitness or ability to give service to other people. A special call from, or choosing by, God for the religious life.'
>
> (Longman's *Dictionary of Contemporary English*)

Many Christians and Humanists believe that work should be a vocation and that work in itself should be a fulfilling and valuable thing. Humanists do not believe that they are called by God but rather that their conscience and reason help them to find worthwhile and fulfilling work.

> 'Through the right use of his time a Christian offers his life, gifts and effort to God. A sense of vocation means that we see what we do as an expression of our faith and a response to God's love for us.'
>
> (*What Does Methodism Think?*, 1990)

UNEMPLOYMENT

One of the major problems of industrial society is the problem of full employment. Millions of people have no access to work and this can bring great distress to their lives.

> 'Unemployment is the worst evil, in the sense that the unemployed feel that they have fallen out of the common life . . . they are not wanted, that is the thing that has the power to corrupt the soul of any man.'
>
> (William Temple 1881–1944, Archbishop of Canterbury, 1942–44)

> 'There are social and personal costs. Local communities and amenities decline; social order is threatened; crime increases; the integrating effect of having a job and belonging in society is lost; individuals suffer psychological shock; they feel humiliated, angry and depressed; health problems increase; families suffer extra strain; there are increases in heart disease, suicide and other deaths, mental illness, loss of self-esteem, violence, the use of alcohol and tobacco. . .'
>
> (Church of England report, 1982)

LEISURE

Over the last 30 years, because of factors like the 40 hour week, increased mechanization, etc, people are finding that they have more leisure time. On the one hand this can lead to great possibilities for people, but on the other it can lead to boredom and frustration. Traditionally in our society Sunday has been a day of rest but over the last few years this has changed considerably. Many Christians believe that whether people are religious or not they need one day a week when they can have rest and recreation.

> 'Every society needs a publicly expressed day of rest and "re-creation" such as the Christian Sunday has provided. Society needs symbols

which point beyond market forces as the determining aspects of our lives in the community.'

(Church of England report, 1985)

'The traditional concept that work is good while leisure is a necessary breathing space must be replaced by the understanding that both work and leisure are good if used for the glory of God.'

(Methodist Conference, 1974)

TALKING POINT

'Whatever you do, work at it with all your heart as though you were working for the Lord and not for man.'
(Colossians 3: 23)

FOR YOUR FOLDERS

▶ Write a paragraph explaining the purposes of work as outlined by the Church of England.

▶ List some types of work that you would regard as being 'creative', 'painful', 'healthy', 'good'.

▶ Describe in your own words what a vocation is.

▶ According to the Church, what are the problems faced by people who are unemployed?

▶ Why do you think that leisure time is regarded as being so important by Christians?

▶ List some jobs that you think Christians and Humanists would regard as being dangerous for the well-being of society.

MATERIALISM

Our society is often called 'materialistic'. This can mean two things: firstly, that the meaning of life can be answered and explained without any reference to a spiritual dimension; secondly, money, possessions and wealth are the main driving forces behind people's lives. To have money is necessary for survival but we need to ask whether the obsessive acquisition of money and wealth is the most important thing in life.

Many Humanists and Christians believe that the divide between the 'haves' and the 'have nots' in our society is a cause for great concern. For instance, a single parent with two children has to live off £90 per week from the State, whereas the earning of, say, the Chairman of a large supermarket chain is nearly £30,000 per week.

> 'A humane society should only have economic systems that improve the quality of life.'
>
> *(Humanist Manifesto)*

> 'The love of money is the root of all evil.'
>
> *(I Timothy 6: 10)*

The reality of urban poverty

If we think about this quote we can see there is much truth in it. It is relevant when we consider some of the major social and global issues facing us today, e.g. exploitation of the Earth's natural resources (see Section 89); war and the arms trade (see Section 80); pornography (see Section 19); advertising (see Section 41); and even medical ethics (see Sections 45 and 46). Many problems in the world are quite simply caused by people's greed.

The teachings as given by Jesus in the New Testament are felt by many, Christians and non-Christians alike, to be relevant to the world today. In a world of increasing poverty, injustice and materialistic attitudes Jesus' teachings consistently point to the dangers of wealth.

> 'You cannot serve God and money.'
>
> *(Matthew 6: 24)*

> ' "Good master, what must I do to win eternal life?" . . . and He said, "Go, sell everything you have and give to the poor and you will have riches in heaven." '
>
> *(Mark 10: 17–21)*

The rich at play at the Derby

'It is easier for a camel to go through the eye of a needle than for a rich man to enter the kingdom of God.'

(Luke 18: 25)

'Beware. Be on your guard against greed of every kind, for even when a man has more than enough his wealth does not give him life.'

(Luke 12: 15)

Many of these teachings may seem extreme to us, for instance, the statement in Mark chapter 10. However, as with much of the Gospel teaching we must look beyond the literal meanings and try to find the deeper, hidden truths. Jesus' message is that humans must turn away from selfish greed and think about those people who are less fortunate than themselves. Wealth does not bring wisdom or happiness but rather can become an obsessive driving force which makes people forget their true priorities.

GAMBLING

One type of gambling that is on the increase among young people is 'fruit machines'. Gambling gives people a false sense of excitement and always promises but very seldom delivers. Many Christians believe that gambling can be a very dangerous habit. In the past people have lost their homes through excessive gambling and, for some, their addiction to gambling takes over their lives.

'Gambling may become a sin, even a serious sin, when it goes to excess that would destroy personal honesty, or expose a person to loss so great as to jeopardize society, and above all, their family dependents.'

(Modern Catholic Dictionary)

'Gambling appeals to chance and therefore cannot be reconciled with faith in God. Because we belong to one another, we must live by love and mutual obligation. Gambling disregards moral responsibility and neighbourly concern.'

(Methodist Conference)

USURY

Usury means 'the practice of lending money to be paid back at a large rate of interest'. It has always been regarded as wrong by Christians and in the Old Testament it says:

'If you advance money to any poor man amongst my people, you shall not act like a money lender: you must not exact interest in advance from him.'

(Exodus 22: 25)

THINKING POINTS

Materialism
in the end, there's no meaning ...

WHAT do you think?

The Gospel is war to the death against the motive of acquisition

(Jose Miranda)

FOR YOUR FOLDERS

▶ Write a sentence about the two photographs. How do you think the people in the photographs' attitudes to money might differ?

▶ 'Five per cent of the population own 40% of the nation's wealth and 50% of the population own 4%t of the nation's wealth.' Do you think that we live in a society which has a fair attitude towards the distribution of wealth?

▶ Write a paragraph on Jesus' attitude to money and the rich. Do you think His words are relevant to us living today?

▶ What are your attitudes to gambling and usury?

There are around four hundred million motor vehicles in the world today. Few objects could be more commonplace. The car like no other human tool is, very often, idealized in modern imagination. Cars are used to represent 'freedom', 'the good life' and excitement. We assume now that cars are 'natural' while human beings walking on foot are somehow unnatural.

It's a strange world where biological diversity is declining at a dangerous rate, while the artificial diversity of the machine is exploding. We are repopulating our dying world with creatures of our own invention.

Cars symbolize raw power. Speed is a key selling point in most advertising: How fast does the car accelerate? What is the top running speed? The humble family car is advertised alongside wild animals (usually horses or jungle cats): sleek, smooth, erotic and slightly dangerous. Speed and sex are strong selling points.

We all take cars for granted and often forget that it was not many decades ago that our roads were free from the pall of grey smoke, the smell of petrol fumes and the hum of traffic. However, cars are causing untold damage not only to our environment but also to our psychology.

FUEL FOR THOUGHT

- In America alone, 50,000 people a year are killed and a quarter of a million are injured in traffic accidents. In cities like Delhi and Jakarta 'rush hour' is all day. In London, rush hour traffic averages about 8 miles an hour. The world's four hundred million cars pump more than five hundred million tonnes of carbon into the atmosphere every year.
- There are less than 1,000 Siberian tigers alive today, 660 of which are in zoos. There are four hundred million motor vehicles
- Every day, one hundred thousand cars roll off the world's assembly lines.
- Car engine pollutants are a major cause of smog, the thick yellow haze that encases many cities.
- Nearly a million human beings die each year in car crashes.

PSYCHOLOGICAL DAMAGE

Two of the largest American car companies have their headquarters in Detroit. Everything in the city is built around the car – like, for instance, the huge shopping mall which you can only reach by car. Detroit also has the highest per capita murder rate of any city in the West. A local resident says: 'Everything has been removed from the streets except cars and hoodlums. The more people you take off the streets, the more people become sitting ducks for crime. In cities like Detroit, cars are used more for protection than for transportation.'

Relate, who counsel people about marriage, describe the wear and tear that commuting can inflict on a marriage:

'The husband comes home exhausted, is not very communicative to his wife and is fit only to snooze in an armchair.'

Traffic is literally driving people crazy. United States psychiatrists note that some of their patients are so stressed by driving they spend half their $200 an hour session talking about commuting.

Sometimes drivers undergo a Jekyll and Hyde transformation when they slip behind the wheel. Strapped into a lethal cocoon of steel and glass, normally polite people curse, shake their fists and scream abuse at their fellow motorists.

'Such anger comes from the emotions innate to being in a car. People have the illusion they can't be tracked down, that they are going to get away with it. For that reason people will do things they wouldn't normally do if they felt they could be identified.'

(Jack Levin)

In southern California police have established a special task force to stop the growing number of freeway murders.

TALKING POINTS

'Time in the car can be a dream state where one's sense of power and discipline are exaggerated. On a global scale the car is a destructive force that threatens to sever our last ties with the natural world. What a strange beast we urban nomads have chosen as our own. We must look beyond the car into the artificial heart of modern society if we are to save ourselves from an object that is but a projection of our own unsatisfied desires.'
(Jeremiah Creedon, American writer)

'There is no quiet place in the white man's cities. No place to hear the unfurling of leaves in spring or the rustle of insects' wings. The clatter only seems to insult the ears. The white man does not seem to notice the air he breathes. Like a man dying for many days, he is numb to the stench . . . Continue to contaminate your bed, and you will one night suffocate in your own waste.'

(Chief Seattle, 1855)

WHAT CAN BE DONE?

Although some car manufacturers have produced cars that can average 124 miles a gallon, car makers are not yet anxious to tackle the problems they cause. They concentrate on the luxury market where they can make huge profits. As Henry Ford II once said 'Small cars make small profits'.

Cars are the single largest drain on the world's natural resources and also a major source of waste and pollution. Here are some ideas that society will have to start thinking about in the very near future.

1 **Cut the car space.** In some towns and cities now roads have been pedestrianized.

2 **Support public transport**, e.g. railways, trams and buses.

3 **Stop the sprawl.** Bring jobs and people together to reduce the need for long-distance commuting.

4 **Boost the bike.** Bikes are efficient, cheap and much quicker than cars in our towns and cities. Also, in some Third World countries, the rickshaw is coming back into fashion.

5 **Make drivers pay.** In Hong Kong, for example, drivers are penalized for using the centre of the city. In Singapore drivers are penalized if there is only one person in a car.

THINGS TO DO

▶ Over the next week keep your eyes open for car adverts. Write a list of some of the symbols they use and try to explain what the hidden messages are.

▶ In groups of five or six discuss some of the ideas in this section and then write an article of about 300 words on Car Chaos.

CHILD ABUSE AND NEGLECT

During and since the 1980s the issue of child abuse has received considerable publicity. People are shocked by the widespread abuse and neglect of children in our society.

WHAT DO WE MEAN BY CHILD ABUSE AND NEGLECT?

Neglect – the persistent or severe neglect of a child which results in serious impairment of the child's health or development.

Physical abuse – physical injury to a child, including deliberate poisoning, where there is definite knowledge, or a reasonable suspicion that injury was inflicted or knowingly not prevented.

Sexual abuse – the involvement of dependent, developmentally immature children and adolescents in sexual activities they do not truly comprehend, to which they are unable to give informed consent, or that violate the social taboos of family roles.

Emotional abuse – persistent or severe emotional ill-treatment or rejection which results in severe adverse effects on the behaviour and emotional development of a child. All abuse involves some emotional ill-treatment; this category should be used where it is the main or sole form of abuse.

Grave concern – children giving grave concern are those whose situations do not currently fit the above categories, but where social and medical assessments indicate that they are at significant risk of abuse.

(Adapted from *Working Together: A guide to arrangements for interagency co-operation for the protection of children from abuse*, DSS, July 1988)

CAUSES OF ABUSE

The National Society for the Prevention of Cruelty to Children (NSPCC) identified the following **causes** of child abuse: overcrowded and inadequate accommodation; social isolation; rootlessness; marital disharmony; and children being unwanted at their time of birth. A further factor was identified, namely the 'cycle of disadvantage', whereby parents who have been abused as children are more likely than others to become abusers themselves.

THE CHURCH OF ENGLAND

In 1988 the Church of England published a report, *Child Abuse and Neglect*. Some of its comments include:

'The effects of child abuse are long lasting. Many people take years before they can begin to talk about what has happened. For many the ability to form trusting close relationships with other adults and with children is badly damaged by their childhood experiences.'

'It is often assumed that sexual abuse is done by someone who is a stranger to the child but research suggests that in most cases the child knows the adult already.'

'Does our society really affirm the importance of children? Are they believed and taken seriously? Deep down do we see children as a gift of God or a nuisance?'

'Sexuality and power. The majority of reported cases involve adult males abusing girls, usually within a family relationship. Complex issues about male sexuality, gender roles and boundaries within the family have to be addressed so that girls and boys grow up knowing they have a right to their own bodies.'

'Child abuse and neglect damages young lives in ways which must be of enormous concern to the Church. It occurs in all levels of society; the effects are frequently devastating and long lasting. In a world marred by cruelty, violence and lack of respect for others, Christians can contribute to greater public awareness, to supporting families and helping build a healthier community for all.'

Health Department investigating "bizarre and often violent ceremonies"

NSPCC says ritual child abuse rife

By Libby Jukes and Richard Duce

Children as young as five are being forced to take part in bizarre sex and satanic rituals, the National Society for the Prevention of Cruelty to Children said yesterday.

The charity is calling for Government and police to act after seven investigating teams have reported ritualistic abuse.

My Jim Harding, the NSPCC child care director, said that in many cases of ritual abuse "threats are made to the children to control them and to try and keep them silent about what has happened".

He described a horrifying catalogue of reported ceremonies in which urine and blood were drunk while children aged only five and adults wore masks and costumes.

"Sometimes animals are abused and killed. Sometimes there is sexual activity between adults in view of the children. Drugs or alcohol are often used, and the children are made to drink the alcohol or administer the drugs."

Ritualistic abuse "has connotations with some kind of supernatural symbolic behaviour," he said.

Seven NSPCC teams reported finding evidence of children caught up in ritual abuse, while another seven expressed fears that they had found youngsters who could have been involved in similar activities. Scotland Yard says it has no firm evidence of satanic or ritualistic abuse, but concedes that young victims might be terrified into silence.

The spokeswoman said police were working closely with the charity in the areas where the first seven teams operated.

"We cannot identify those areas, because to do so would endanger the lives of the children and the social workers involved."

Superintendent Leslie Bennett, head of the new Child Pornography Squad at Scotland Yard, is particularly concerned that his staff will be unable to cope with the volume of pornography expected to flood into Britain when customs barriers within the European Community are removed in 1992.

About 80 per cent of pornography in Britain is imported from countries such as The Netherlands, Denmark, Sweden, Thailand and Japan.

With a 10-minute video costing up to £200, child pornography is a lucrative business and over the past three years it has become the main target of the Obscene Publications Squad.

Although Britain is the only country in Europe in which it is an offence to possess an obscene photograph of a person under 16, police are frustrated by their lack of powers to arrest and detain suspects.

(Adapted from *The Times, March 31 1990*
© Times Newspapers Ltd. 1990)

CHILDLINE

If you are worried about any of these issues, phone Childline: **0800–1111**

FOR YOUR FOLDERS

▶ Explain in your own words the types of child abuse and neglect that exist.

▶ What do you think are some of the main causes of child abuse?

▶ Write an article based on some of the findings in the Church of England's report, *Child Abuse and Neglect.*

❗▶ After reading *The Times* article how do you think society can begin to protect children against such things as satanic rituals and child pornography?

❗▶ How do you think victims of child abuse should be encouraged to talk about their experiences?

Harrowing cases detailed in report by society

The NSPCC annual report details a number of harrowing individual cases of abuse.

• "Karen Jones", aged seven, was sexually abused by her father, with her 10-year-old brother copying his example. She complained to her teacher, and the NSPCC arranged for her to demonstrate the abuse in the presence of a policewoman, using anatomically correct dolls.

Although her father denied the allegations and a prosecution failed for lack of evidence, both children were placed with foster parents.

• The mother of "Darren Lawton" reported to the NSPCC that her son, aged nine, was often beaten by his father, from whom she was separated. A child protection officer found that Darren and his younger sister "Allison", aged five, were covered in bruises and cuts.

Darren said his father had forced him to eat chilli powder, and rubbed salt into his wounds. That affected the behaviour of both children, who became temperamental and withdrawn.

It also emerged that their mother had taken part in the abuse. Brother and sister are now in local authority care.

• "Debbie", aged 22, mother of a three-year-old girl, started playing truant from school at the age of 15. A friend told her of a place where she could watch pornographic video-films.

Debbie was offered £20 for sex by the man living there, and when she refused she was drugged and raped. Over the next six months she was sexually abused by 14 other men who visited the house, and witnessed many assaults on other children of both sexes.

Years later Debbie talked about her experiences and admitted she physically abused her own daughter. She said the sex ring in which she had been involved still operated from the same address, but feared she and her daughter would be harmed if she gave evidence to the police.

• "Tony", aged 10, the youngest of four children, received little attention from his separated parents. While playing football in the local park, he was approached by a stranger, asked if he liked computers, and invited back to the man's house to play computer games.

There he was shown a pornographic video-film, and persuaded to take part in sexual acts. Although Tony's statement to the police was corroborated by stories from other children, he later retracted his information and refused to talk about his experiences.

We have virtually conquered the planet, explored the moon, overcome the natural limits of travel and communication; we stand at the dawn of a new age, ready to move farther into space and perhaps inhabit other planets. Using technology wisely, we can control our environment, conquer poverty, markedly reduce disease, extend our life span, significantly modify our behaviour, alter the course of human evolution, unlock vast new powers, and provide humankind with an unparalleled opportunity for achieving an abundant and meaningful life. The future is, however, filled with dangers.

In learning to apply science to life, we have opened the doors to ecological damage, over-population, political repression and nuclear and biochemical disaster. Humanity, to survive, requires bold and daring measures. The ultimate goal should be the fulfilment of the potential for growth in each human personality – not for the favoured few, but for all of humankind.

For these reasons Humanists have submitted this new 'Humanist Manifesto', for the future of humankind: for them it is a vision of hope, a direction for satisfying survival.

1st   While there is much that we do not know, humans are responsible for what we are or will become. No deity will save us. We must save ourselves.

2nd   There is no evidence that life survives the death of the body.

3rd   Human life has meaning because we create and develop our futures. We strive for the good life here and now.

4th   Reason and intelligence are the best instruments that humankind possesses. We also believe in the cultivation of feeling and love.

5th   All human life is precious and dignified. Also, whenever possible, freedom of choice should be increased.

6th   The right to birth control, abortion and divorce should be recognized. We wish to cultivate the development of a responsible attitude towards sexuality, in which humans

Ecological disasters such as famine have horrific human consequences

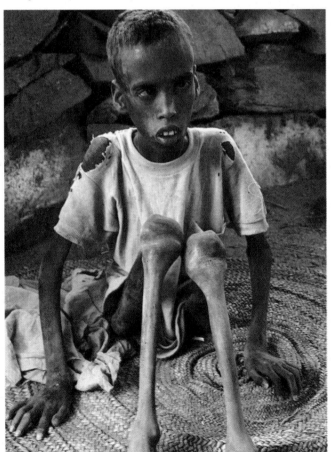

are not exploited as sexual objects, and in which intimacy, sensitivity, respect and honesty in interpersonal relations are encouraged.

7th   The individual must experience a full range of civil liberties in all societies (e.g. freedom of speech and the press, democracy, religious liberty). It also includes a recognition of an individual's right to die with dignity, euthanasia and the right to suicide.

8th   We are committed to an open and democratic society. People are more important than rules and regulations.

9th   The church and the state, and the state and any other ideologies, should be separate.

10th   A humane society should only have economic systems that improve the quality of life.

11th   All discrimination should cease. Everyone should have equal opportunity for and recognition of their talents. We are concerned for the aged, the infirm, the disadvantaged, the outcasts (addicts, prisoners, abused children, mentally retarded, the abandoned) – for all who are neglected or ignored by society. We believe in the right to universal education. We are critical of sexism, or sexual chauvinsim – male or female.

12th   We deplore the division of humankind on nationalistic grounds.

13th   The world community must condemn the resort to violence and force as a way of solving international disputes. With the possession of biological, nuclear and chemical weapons, war is obsolete. Military spending must be reduced and these savings put to peaceful and people-orientated uses.

14th   We must free our world from needless pollution and waste . . . exploitation of natural resources uncurbed by social conscience must end.

15th   The developed world has a moral obligation to assist the developing world.

16th   Technology must be used humanely and carefully.

17th   Travel restrictions across frontiers must cease. We must learn to live openly together or we shall perish together.

(Adapted from an article first published in *The Humanist*, September/October 1973)

FOR YOUR FOLDERS

▶ Make a list of the things Humanists would like to see in the future.

▶ Think of some things that are happening in the world today that Humanists believe are wrong.

! ▶ What do you consider the five most important points in the Humanist Manifesto?

▶ If we are to truly change the world, we must learn how to change ourselves. This can only come about by the search for self-knowledge.

THINGS TO DO

▶ Design a poster with the theme 'A Humanist view of the future of humankind'.

▶ Collect three articles from recent newspapers that illustrate some of the things that need changing in the world.

TALKING POINTS

- 'Using technology wisely we can control our environment.'

- 'We must learn to live openly together or we shall perish together.'

1 ORIGINS

The name 'United Nations' was devised by President Franklin D. Roosevelt of the United States and was first used in 1942.

The UN Charter was drawn up by representatives of 51 countries in 1945, on 24 October. That date is now celebrated all over the world and is called United Nations Day.

2 PURPOSES AND PRINCIPLES

The *purposes* of the UN are:

- to maintain international peace and security
- to develop friendly relations among nations
- to cooperate internationally in solving economic, social, cultural and humanitarian problems and in promoting human rights and fundamental freedoms
- to be a centre for helping nations achieve their ends.

The UN acts on the following *principles*:

- all member countries are equal
- all member countries must fulfil their obligations
- countries must try and settle their differences by peaceful means
- they must avoid using force or threatening to use force
- the UN will not interfere with the domestic affairs and problems of any country
- countries should try to assist the UN.

So the UN's main concern is with world peace. Also, it aims to secure a world of justice, peace and progress for all people. It seeks to make nations think 'globally', not nationally, when facing the problems of the twentieth century (e.g. arms race, poverty, pollution, human rights, wars, nuclear weapons and conservation).

3 THE CHARTER

The Charter of the UN helps us to understand its hopes and aims.

PREAMBLE TO THE CHARTER OF THE
UNITED NATIONS

We the peoples of the United Nations determined

- to save succeeding generations from the scourge of war, which twice in our lifetime has brought untold sorrow to mankind and
- to reaffirm faith in fundamental human rights, in the dignity and worth of the human person, in

the equal rights of men and women and of nations large and small, and

- to establish conditions under which justice and respect for the obligations arising from treaties and other sources of international law can be maintained, and
- to promote social progress and better standards of life in larger freedom.

4 ORGANIZATION

The General Assembly

The General Assembly is composed of all **member states**. It makes recommendations to governments on a variety of issues.

The Assembly's work includes:

- dealing with things such as peace-keeping, disarmament, apartheid and colonialism
- helping bodies within the UN (e.g. the UN Children's Fund).

The Security Council

This organization has the main responsibility for maintaining peace and security. There are 15 members. Five of these (USA, USSR, China, France, Great Britain) are permanent members. The other 10 are elected by the General Assembly for two-year terms. Each member of the Council has one vote. Any major decision requires all the five permanent members to vote the same way together. If they do not this is called the **veto**.

The Secretariat

This is the 'civil service' of the UN. It helps to administer the programmes and policies laid down by the UN. At its head is the Secretary-General.

5 SOME OTHER UN ORGANIZATIONS

- **UNCTAD – United Nations Conference on Trade and Development**

- **UNDP – United Nations Development Programme**
  This deals with the economic and social problems of low-income countries.

- **UNICEF – United Nations Children's Fund**
  The Fund's purpose is to help developing countries improve the condition of their children and youth.

- **FAO – UN Food and Agriculture Organization International Court of Justice**

- **UNESCO – United Nations Educational, Scientific and Cultural Organization**
- **WHO – World Health Organization**
  This works to promote the highest possible level of health throughout the world.

6 ACHIEVEMENTS

The UN's achievements since 1945 include:

1 helping 1 billion people gain national independence,
2 helping poorer countries,
3 providing a meeting ground and a talking place during the worst periods of the 'cold war',
4 providing a code of international morality,
5 containing would-be conflicts,
6 producing more understanding around the world, proving that talking and listening are the beginning of wisdom and peace in human relations,
7 providing a platform for the hopes of humanity including liberty, equality and fraternity (brotherhood),
8 helping racial equality throughout the world,
9 warning people that they are capable of destroying the world if they are not careful,
10 generally helping the world to be a more ordered and safe place.

7 FAILINGS

The UN was set up with many ideals in mind in 1945. There can be no doubt that it has helped to make the world a safer place. However, it is open to much criticism. The world is faced with huge problems but it seems that often countries within the United Nations are more concerned with their own nationalistic worries and security than with global problems. It is tragic that despite the fact the nations of the world can meet under one roof, the main underlying problems of world poverty, inequality of trade, global pollution, the destruction of indigenous peoples and war haunt us like at no other time in human history.

There is also a fear that many smaller countries can be manipulated into voting certain ways by the larger, more powerful countries which can dictate the small countries' futures by economic means. Owing to the decline of the Soviet empire the United States of America now has, to a large extent, unprecedented control over world affairs.

A good example of the way the United Nations is not always able to put into practice its ideals is the Palestinian issue. Millions of Palestinians live under Israeli military occupation in the West Bank and Gaza Strip. They live as second-class citizens and often have their human rights violated. The United Nations has passed many Resolutions on Palestine and an independent state has been recognized by the majority of its members. However, the Resolution has never been implemented because the USA has not accepted the idea. This illustrates one problem of the UN – one member can block a humane resolution that has been supported by other members.

THINGS TO DO

▶ Think of some modern-day examples where work still needs to be done to add to the achievements of the UN.
▶ **Role play.** Each one of you represents a country of the Security Council. A small country in Asia has been invaded by one of the permanent members. Organize a discussion on what should be done. What problem might the **veto** cause?

FOR YOUR FOLDERS

! ▶ What do you think the purposes of the UN are? What is their order of importance in your opinion? Give reasons for your choices.

▶ After reading this section write an essay describing the work and importance of the UN.

TALKING POINTS

- **What are the most important problems facing humankind?**
- **What can be done to solve them?**

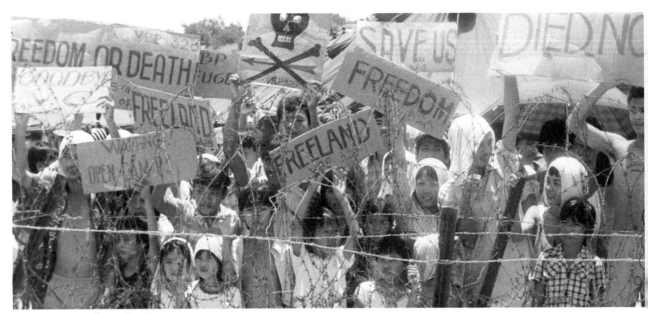

Vietnamese boat people have fled to Hong Kong to escape human rights abuses

In December 1948 the United Nations produced its Universal Declaration of Human Rights.

- All human beings are born free and equal.
- Everyone has the right to life, liberty and freedom from fear and violence.
- Everyone has the right to protection of the law without discrimination.
- No-one shall be subjected to arbitrary arrest, detention or exile.
- Everyone has the right to a fair and public trial.
- Everyone charged with a penal offence has the right to be assumed innocent until proved guilty.
- No one shall be subjected to arbitrary interference with his privacy, family, home or correspondence, nor to attacks on his reputation.
- Everyone has the right to freedom of movement within his own country and abroad.
- Everyone has the right to a nationality.
- Adults have the right to marry and found a family regardless of race or religion.
- Both men and women are entitled to equal rights within marriage and in divorce.
- Everyone has the right to own property. No-one should be arbitrarily deprived of his property.
- Everyone has the right to freedom of thought, conscience and religion and the right to express their opinion both privately and publicly.
- Everyone has the right to attend meetings and join associations.
- No-one should be forced to join an association.
- Everyone has the right to take part in the government of his or her country.

- Everyone has the right to work and to just and favourable conditions of employment.
- Everyone has the right to equal pay for equal work.
- Everyone has the right to fair pay to enable him and his family to live with self respect.
- Everyone has the right to join a trades union.
- Everyone has the right to rest and leisure, including reasonable working hours and holidays with pay.
- Everyone has the right to a standard of living adequate for their health and well-being, including housing, medical care and social security in the event of unemployment, sickness, widowhood and old age.
- Everyone has the right to an education.
- Everyone has the right to enjoy the cultural life of the community and to share in its scientific advancements and benefits.
- Everyone has duties to the community to ensure the full recognition and respect for the rights and freedoms of others.

CHRISTIAN VIEWPOINT

'Each individual is truly a person, with a nature that is endowed with intelligence and free will, and rights and duties . . . these rights and duties are universal and inviolable.'

(Encyclical letter of Pope John XXIII)

FOR YOUR FOLDERS

▶ Describe in your own words what each picture in this section shows.

▶ Look at the Universal Declaration of Human Rights. Write down which part of the Declaration is being violated in each case.

▶ Design a poster illustrating a violation of human rights. On your poster write down the relevant words of the Declaration.

! ▶ Why do you think the UN Declaration of Human Rights is so important?

▶ What rights do you think are being violated by the Chinese Government in Tibet? How do you think members of the United Nations should respond to the violations of human rights in places like Palestine and Tibet?

FOR DISCUSSION

▶ 'Human rights are fundamental to our nature. Without them we cannot live as human beings.'

(UN Office of Information)

▶ 'No rights are possible without the basic guarantees for life, including the right . . . to adequate food, to guaranteed health care, to decent housing . . .'

(Source: World Council of Churches)

PRISONERS DIE UNDER TORTURE

Allegations that prisoners have been tortured and beaten to death continue to emerge from Tibet.

According to Tibetan refugees interviewed in Dharamsala, Lhakpa Tsering, aged 20, was beaten to death in prison in December. Witnesses claim he died shortly after a meeting in which prisoners were warned not to make anti-Chinese statements during a visit by journalists. Lhakpa announced that he would tell any visitors that he supported independence for Tibet.

Lhakpa's body was handed over to his family on 16 December. He had been in prison since 4 November 1989, when he was arrested with five others from Lhasa middle school for putting up pro-independence posters and making copies of the banned Tibetan flag. He is not known to have been tried or sentenced, although charges were announced against him in a Radio Lhasa broadcast.

Following demands by his family, a post mortem was carried out. The findings were not published, but eyewitnesses say that the body was badly bruised. Inmates in Drapchi prison had heard him being beaten, and crying out that he was going to be killed.

Amnesty International called for a full-scale inquiry into the death, and expressed concern that results of the post mortem had not been published.

After inquiries at the UN Committee on Torture in Geneva in January last year, the Chinese authorities in Beijing admitted that a number of people had died as a result of torture and ill-treatment in Chinese-run prisons.

This admission followed reports that two prisoners, Yeshe and Choeze Tenpa Choenphel, died within days of their release from prison in August 1989, apparently as a result of being beaten.

(Tibet Support Group UK Newsletter, March 1991)

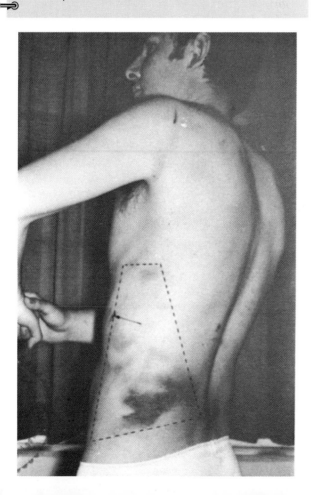

As we saw in Section 65 there are many examples in the world today where human rights are being violated. In a world where one billion people, nearly a fifth of the world's population, live in extreme poverty, human rights are a major issue.

AMNESTY INTERNATIONAL

We live in a world in which millions of people every day have their rights denied or violated. This section is concerned with the denial and violation of civil and political rights. One organization that works towards highlighting and alleviating violations of human rights is Amnesty International. In many parts of the world people are imprisoned and tortured for speaking out against injustices in their societies. These people are called 'prisoners of conscience'. A prisoner of conscience is a man, woman or child who is locked up for having the 'wrong' beliefs or being born into the 'wrong' race. Or for following the 'wrong' religion. Or reading the 'wrong' books. Or even for speaking the 'wrong' language. Amnesty has become an international watchdog to investigate and try to stop violations.

Founded in 1961 by a British lawyer called Peter Benenson, Amnesty is the world's largest voluntary body working for human rights today. It has over one million members in 150 countries. Amnesty International is independent of any government, political faction, ideology, economic interest or religious creed.

This little boy was the victim of a chemical weapons attack in Iran

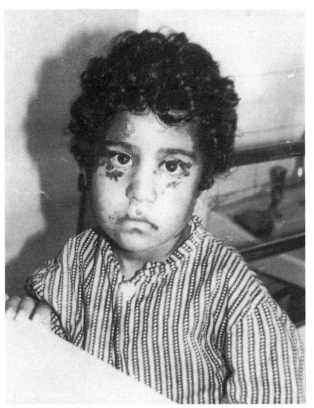

'*Human rights is the umbrella which protects all the other issues, because very often the people who are going to effect change are the people in prison. And the fact that Amnesty International focuses on individuals – real people with real names in real photographs – appeals to me more than just throwing money at a problem in a willy-nilly way. Amnesty's currency is the written word. Its weapon is the letter.*

We who live in Western Europe and North America have a fair belief that if we are arrested, we won't be tortured, we won't be imprisoned without a trial, we won't be murdered. But this is not the case in the developing world. The people there live in a medieval atmosphere – the police do torture you, you can be shot in the street. When you sit and talk to a Prisoner of Conscience – someone who has been tortured, arrested in the night, beaten up, imprisoned – the drama in your own life is suddenly diminished.'

(Sting)

It is a sad fact that in many parts of the world people have their freedoms taken away just for thinking in a different way from their government or just by speaking to a friend against government policies. Amnesty is also concerned about human rights violations in Britain and has publicized things like the treatment of political prisoners in Northern Ireland, the treatment of remand prisoners in our jails, the immigration laws which prevent women from joining their husbands, and the erosion of civil liberties in our society.

Amnesty aims to:

1   seek the release of all prisoners of conscience;

2   obtain a fair and prompt trial for all political prisoners detained without charge or trial;

3   abolish torture and the death penalty in all cases.

Members of Amnesty write letters to the government of a particular country and usually 'adopt' two prisoners and try to publicize their plight.

ACT (ACTION BY CHRISTIANS AGAINST TORTURE)

ACT is a Christian organization based in Britain which campaigns for the abolition of torture. Its members believe that torture is a crime against God and humanity and they say

'God is the source of life, the upholder of justice, the origin of goodness. So we should affirm the things of life and fight against all those of death which includes torture.'

(ACT)

CASE STUDY

'Members of my family – my mother, 73 years old, three sisters and three brothers with five children aged between five and thirteen – were arrested and brought in front of me. They were subjected to beatings and electric shocks. They also made me listen to a cassette of the cries and moans of my family undergoing torture. The detention centre is extremely filthy. Usually they keep children in a separate cell next to the mother or father's cell and deprive them of milk to force the parent to confess. I saw a five month old baby screaming in this state.'

(Iraqi student)

TALKING POINT

'First they came for the Jews and I did not speak out – because I was not a Jew. Then they came for the communists and I did not speak out – because I was not a communist. Then they came for the trades unionists and I did not speak out – because I was not a trades unionist. Then they came for me and there was no one left to speak out for me.'

(Victim of the Nazis)

THINGS TO DO

The case study above is very disturbing. Every day in our world there are thousands of people being tortured. These people have done nothing to warrant this inhumane treatment. Some of the cases that Amnesty deals with are too disturbing to include in this book. If you are concerned about the world in which you live and would like to do something then write to Amnesty International (please include a SAE) because as Sting says, 'Human rights is the umbrella that protects all other issues.'

FOR YOUR FOLDERS

▶ Explain in detail the work of Amnesty International and ACT.

❗▶ Why do you think people have their rights taken away?

▶ Try to list some of the violations of human rights that take place in the world today.

▶ Look at the following. Make a list of some of the human rights that have been violated in each case:

a) The Birmingham Six; the Guildford Four; the Tottenham Three.

b) Allies fire missiles into Iraq's Amirya shelter during the Gulf War — 300 women and children die.

c) A 'shoot to kill' policy has been adopted by the British Army in Northern Ireland.

d) The aparteid system of white South Africa.

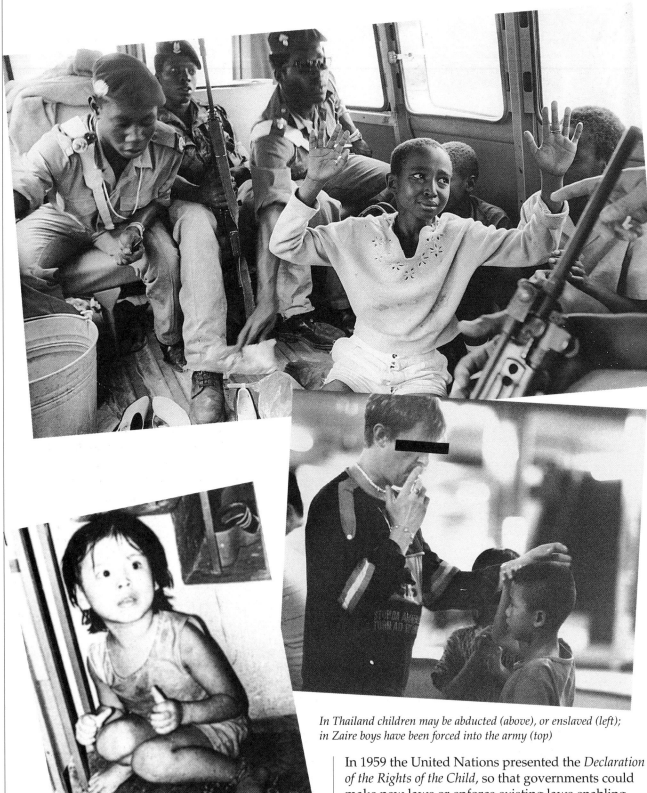

In Thailand children may be abducted (above), or enslaved (left); in Zaire boys have been forced into the army (top)

In 1959 the United Nations presented the *Declaration of the Rights of the Child,* so that governments could make new laws or enforce existing laws enabling each child to have the following: the right to an identity; the right not to be discriminated against; the right to equal treatment; the right to family life; education; and the right not to be abused or exploited.

The rights, in full, are:

'1 *The enjoyment of the rights mentioned,
    without any exception whatsoever,
    regardless of race, colour, sex, religion or
    nationality.*

2 *Special protection, opportunities and
   facilities to enable them to develop in a
   healthy and normal manner, in freedom
   and dignity.*

3 *A name and nationality.*

4 *Social security, including adequate
   nutrition, housing, recreation and medical
   services.*

5 *Special treatment, education and care if
   handicapped.*

6 *Love and understanding and an
   atmosphere of affection and security, in
   the care and under the responsibility of
   their parents whenever possible.*

7 *Free education and recreation and equal
   opportunity to develop their individual
   abilities.*

8 *Prompt protection and relief in times of
   disaster.*

9 *Protection against all forms of neglect,
   cruelty and exploitation.*

10 *Protection from any form of racial,
   religious or other discrimination, and an
   upbringing in a spirit of peace and
   universal brotherhood.'*

The United Nations Declaration is an ideal. Sadly, in our world today the reality is very different:

- A quarter of the deaths in the world this year will be of children not yet five years old, two thirds of them still infants. And 97% of those deaths will occur in the developing world.

- An estimated eight million children around the world live on the streets with no homes or families.

- Millions of children around the world work as slaves – working long hours in dreadful conditions for a few cents. In India alone there are an estimated 44 million child slaves.

- The use of child soldiers around the world is widespread.

- According to the United Nations, 'Hundreds of thousands of children are disappearing without trace'. The children end up in baby cribs of childless couples, on the streets as thieves or in brothels as child prostitutes. They have been ripped from their family roots, often dumped in a foreign country and given new names.

- Both rich countries and poor countries spend more on arms than on education (e.g. USA spends $530 per person on arms and $490 on education).

- Of the 1500 million children in the developing world, 715 million are without places in school. If they all held hands they would encircle the Earth four times.

THE BIBLE

'And they were bringing children to him, that he might touch them; and the disciples rebuked them. But when Jesus saw it he became indignant, and said to them, "Let the children come to me, do not hinder them; for to such belongs the Kingdom of God".'

(Mark 10: 13–15)

FOR YOUR FOLDERS

▶ Look at the *Declaration of the Rights of the Child*. Write down which parts of the Declaration are being violated in today's world.

▶ Study the pictures opposite. Then write an article entitled 'Children's Rights and the adult world'.

Women and girls are half the world's population yet they do two thirds of the world's work; they earn one tenth of the world's income; they own less than one hundredth of the world's property.

When people say, 'A woman's work is never done' what do they mean? Have you ever tried to count the number of hours of shopping, cooking, child care and housework your mother or another woman you know does each week? Yet women make up almost half the wage-earning workforce too.

Women produce at least half of the world's food. In Africa, as well as working in the fields they go back home and do all the work there too. For many women such workloads are often combined with frequent pregnancy, childbirth and breastfeeding. In factories all over the world the mundane and repetitive assembly work is traditionally done by women, often in very unsafe conditions.

In many countries women get no education. Two thirds of the people in the world who can't read or write are female. However, in some countries a special effort has been made to overcome the problems of illiteracy.

In many societies women are still regarded as the property of their husbands or fathers. In some rural areas women cannot say what their problems are or share their experiences – they are accustomed to keeping silent.

In some parts of the world, however, women are beginning to speak out. They are beginning to organize so that their voice can be heard and the days of exploitation and discrimination brought to an end.

In order for women to attain truly equal rights, the very structures of society must be changed radically. This needs to be in the broadest sense; for instance by changing attitudes through education, as well as on a day to day basis, such as equal sharing of paid and unpaid work.

TALKING POINT

'Because woman's work is never done and is underpaid or unpaid or boring or repetitious and we're the first to get the sack and what we look like is more important than what we do and if we get raped it's our fault and if we get bashed we must have provoked it and if we raise our voices we're nagging bitches and if we enjoy sex we're nymphos and if we don't we're frigid and if we love women it's because we can't get a "real" man and if we ask our doctor too many questions we're neurotic and/or pushy and if we expect community care for children we're selfish and if we stand up for our rights we're aggressive and "unfeminine" and if we don't we're typical weak females and if we want to get married we're out to trap a man and if we don't we're unnatural and we still can't get an adequate safe contraceptive but men can walk on the moon and if we can't cope or don't want a pregnancy we're made to feel guilty about abortion and . . . for lots and lots of other reasons we are part of the women's liberation movement.'

(NUS Women's Campaign)

African women bring their children with them to work

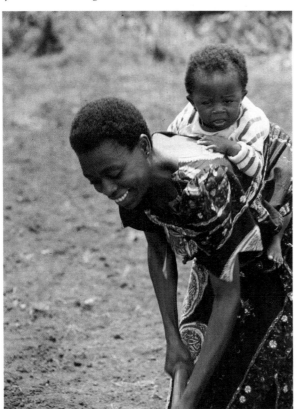

EDUCATION

Romualda de la Torre lives in Mindoro in the Philippines. She is the mother of the human rights campaigner Father Edicio de la Torre. Here she talks about what things were like when she went to school:

'I was the first to school in the morning and the last home at night. I cried when my father put the lamp out at 8 p.m. and made us go to bed. Then when I finished elementary school my father wouldn't let me go to high school. He wanted me to stay at home and help my mother. He didn't want a maid to help my mother because he said no one should cook and wash for another. Then I stayed at home to help my mother fetch water and wood and run a little sari-sari store we had. I'm going to go to school, I told myself, even if I have to run away, but where could I run? I thought I'd die. A woman's place is in the house, my father said, but my sister and I didn't believe that.'

Romualda had to wait until she was older, a widow with young children, before she managed to go to high school – she had to work at night to be able to afford it but she was very determined.

FOR YOUR FOLDERS

▶ After reading this section write an article explaining why women around the world need to struggle against the values and attitudes of their societies.

▶ Why is education so important in this struggle?

▶ What are the reasons for women around the world getting such a bad deal, do you think?.

FOR DISCUSSION

▶ 'What we look like is more important than what we do.'

THE FACTS

1 SIMILARITIES

Humans have much in common with other animals . . .

Genetic structure Humans share 99% of their genetic structure with chimpanzees.

Pain Humans share the capacity to suffer and feel pain with all vertebrates including fish.

Altruism Humans share the capacity for altruistic behaviour with mammals such as elephants, whales and dolphins. Elephants will administer first aid to wounded companions, applying clay to stop the flow of blood.

Communication Humans communicate with one another – as do other animals.

Dexterity Humans, like apes, are tool makers and users.

2 COMPANIONS

Humans love some animals. They have them as . . .

Pets Pet keeping is most popular today in the West. North Americans spend $7.5 billion a year on looking after their pets.

Healers Early Christians believed that pet animals had healing powers. The idea has recently been revived with pets being used as an aid in therapy to help bring out extremely withdrawn children and elderly people.

3 WORK AND CAPTIVITY

Humans use animals for **work**, e.g. working dogs on a farm, guide dogs for the blind, donkeys carrying loads and horses pulling the plough.

Circus animals are also working animals but deprived of dignity, confined to small cages and forced to perform unnatural tricks in alien environments.

Zoo animals . . . more than one million animals are kept in an estimated 5000 zoos around the world.

4 FOOD

Humans eat millions of animals every year :

Quantity People consume around 140 million tonnes of meat a year worldwide – about 30 kg per person.

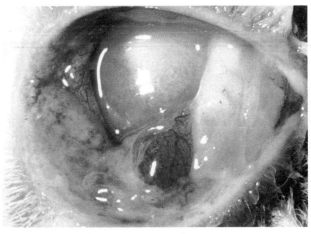
A chemical test has inflamed this rabbit's eye

Methods Much of today's meat is produced by cruel, unhygienic factory farming methods. Many animals die in transit.

Hunger Meat production is a waste of resources. Every steak a meat-eater consumes could have provided enough food for five people who do not eat meat. Ten hectares of land will support 61 people on a diet of soya beans, 24 on a diet of wheat, but only two on a diet of beef.

5 RESEARCH

Humans use animals as **laboratory tools** . . .
An estimated 200 million animals are subjected to painful experiments in laboratories around the world each year. They may be given electric shocks, injected with diseases or experimented on with drugs, subjected to toxic chemicals or radiation. In the UK over 70% of experiments on animals are conducted with no anaesthetic.

Medical research Experiments on animals for medical research are judged to be 71% unreliable. If penicillin – which has saved millions of human lives – had been tested on animals we would not have it now because it kills guinea pigs. Thalidomide, which causes severe disabilities in unborn children, passed animal safety tests.

Product testing Unless they state otherwise, nearly all cosmetic and household products are tested on animals. Over 200,000 animals are used for this purpose worldwide. In the UK testing of raw ingredients and finished products claimed the lives of over 17,000 animals in 1990. Standard international tests include the Draize eye test.

Substances are dropped into the eyes of rabbits for seven days and the effects observed. Rabbits cannot blink – so the substances may eat away at the eye. Pain killers are not usually used.

6 HUNTING, TRAPPING

- Humans hunt animals for **profit and fun** . . . 100 million animals are killed world wide every year for their fur.

- Only 1% of North American animals trapped for their fur are hunted by native people whose livelihood depends on hunting.

- There were 100,000 tigers at the turn of the century; now fewer than 8,000 remain in the world.

- Over 1,000 animal species are under threat of extinction, thanks largely to human actions.

- The world's elephant population has declined by 60% in the past decade.

- In the UK blood sports claim the lives of 63,000 foxes a year; about 12 million pheasants and 1 million wild fowl are also shot for sport.

CHRISTIAN RESPONSES

Human beings' treatment of animals leaves a lot to be desired. Some of our attitudes regarding the rights of animals come from the interpretation of *Genesis 1: 28*:

> 'God blessed them and said to them "Be fruitful and increase; fill the earth and subdue it; rule over the fish in the sea, the birds of heaven and every living thing that moves upon the earth." '

> 'Human beings have both an affinity with and an obligation to animals.'

(Church of England report, 1986)

> 'Scientists must abandon laboratories and factories of death.'

(Pope John Paul II)

FOR YOUR FOLDERS

▶ After reading the information in this section, write an article of at least 300 words discussing the way that humans treat animals.

▶ Do you think there is a conflict between being a Christian and (a) mistreating animals, (b) eating animals, (c) using products that have been tested on animals? Think about the quotation from *Genesis 1: 28*, and whether Christians might feel differently about animals.

FOR DISCUSSION

The facts above raise many important moral issues about the way humans treat animals, e.g. should circuses be banned, should people eat meat, should animals be used as laboratory tools? In groups of four or five discuss these and other issues that arise from reading this section.

THINGS TO DO

Write to one of the Animal Rights groups in the addresses section on p.190. Try to find out which cosmetic companies test products on animals. Then visit your local Body Shop to learn about alternatives.

Doomed to die for the beauty business

INTRODUCTION

Over the last few years people's attitudes to animal rights have changed. In the 1980's and since, much publicity has been given to the controversial Animal Liberation Front who are at the sharp end of campaigning. They have broken into laboratories, fur shops, and butcher's shops, adulterated products and even made death threats and bomb attacks on vivisectionists. To many people they seemed like terrorists, yet to others they appeared to be altruists. There can be no doubt that the publicity given to them, both negative and positive, raised the moral issue of animal rights in the general public's mind. In this article, Jenny, a former fashion model who spent two years in prison for her part in raids on laboratories, speaks about her beliefs.

I made contact with the Animal Liberation League when I started going on national anti-cruelty demonstrations. I was 21.

My first action was the raid on the Unilever headquarters in Bedfordshire in 1984. It was a fact-finding mission, carried out in the middle of the day. Three hundred of us entered the building – we were after a 'saturation' effect. We did as little damage as possible. The idea was to bring out documents, take photographs and show the public what we knew was going on.

We didn't find any animals that day but we got good information on the kinds of animal experiments they were doing. The people on the raid were ordinary but very committed people from varied backgrounds.

My next raid was on the Royal College of Surgeons, who have their experimental labs in Downe, Kent. There we found animals that weren't bred for experiments. They were the wrong breeds and showed social skills which led us to the conclusion that they were stolen pets. The dogs had been operated on and sewn up again in the most appalling way. We found documents and progress reports which showed some of the animals had been in considerable pain and had had to be put down. We gave the photos to the press. The publicity was amazing – it got onto the national TV news that evening.

We also found photos of primate experiments. The surgeons had been vain enough to take their own photos. These were not 'tame' photos – they were of animals screaming, being held in a vice-like grip. There were charts of monkeys which showed they had been left over the weekend with no water. One had died. The Royal College of Surgeons was prosecuted as a result.

Then I took part in a raid on the Wickham Laboratories in Hampshire. This was a lab which would test anything for anyone on animals. The raid did not go as well as it might have done. I was arrested, tried, found guilty of conspiracy to burgle, and given a one-year prison sentence. While I was serving this I was put on trial for the Unilever raid and was given another year. So I served two years in prison, without parole. This is unusual and virtually unheard of among women prisoners.

I have not gone on any raids since coming out. It isn't that prison has knocked the stuffing out of me. It's because I go about things in a different way now. I still believe that there is a place for that kind of action as long as it is productive and as long as it does not involve violence against people – which I think is such a mad, stupid thing to do, it makes you wonder if it's the work of the opposition. Anyway, I've got different responsibilities now, with a couple of small children to bring up, and I feel I've done my bit in terms of illegal action. But I'm still a campaigner and fund-raiser – and a vegan!

I think the whole tempo of the animal rights movement has changed. The campaigning organizations are much more slick. Everything is geared towards informing the public. As people become more aware of what is done in the name of feeding oneself, clothing oneself, they will revolt. And that is why it is all cloaked in secrecy because the meat and cosmetic and chemical companies know that if the public know what they are up to then they will protest.

For me it was knowing what was going on that put a block on my modelling career. I would not go to certain castings. I turned down a fur show; turned down a magazine cover where they wanted me to wear a leopard skin hat.

But I have no regrets. All of the raids produced good information in their own way, caused an embarrassment to major companies, major institutions. Given the same circumstances I would do it all again. Perhaps I would run a bit faster . . .

I just hope that by the time my daughters grow up they won't have to get involved in animal liberation. It's just a shame that some us have to be sacrificed for anything to change . . .

(New Internationalist January 1991)

FOR DISCUSSION

▶ 'The Church must say to worldly rulers whose laws are at variance with the laws of God "We had much rather obey God than man".'

(*Acts 4: 19*, Archbishop Desmond Tutu)

▶ 'In order to publicize the evils of a society it is necessary to sometimes break the law.'

(Mark, ALF raider)

FOR YOUR FOLDERS

▶ 'One person's freedom fighter is another person's terrorist.' What do you think this means?

▶ Find out what alternatives to animal experimentation there are for testing the safety of drugs, cosmetics, detergents etc.

▶ Imagine that a possible cure for AIDS has been found. Should it be tested on animals?

TALKING POINT

'If the public knew what the cosmetic and chemical companies get up to, they would protest.'

INTRODUCTION

The twentieth century has seen the largest and bloodiest wars in history. Weapons today are, from the military point of view, 'very efficient' – they can kill more people. In the media war is mostly portrayed as being a glamorous affair full of glory, bravery and bravado. The realities of war, however, are very different.

At the beginning of this century, nine out of ten victims of war were soldiers. Today, due to technology, the arms trade (see Section 80), and the nature of war itself, the situation is reversed. Nine out of ten victims now are civilians, and the vast majority of these are women, children and the elderly.

The First World War (1914–18) caused the death of nearly 9 million and the serious wounding of over 21 million men. The Second World War (1939–45) was responsible for the death of 15,600,000 soldiers and 39,200,000 civilians.

These figures are hard to imagine. Even more difficult to take in are some of the other facts about twentieth century warfare:

● In the first battle of the Somme (1 July–19 November 1916) over 1,030,000 men died in the trenches. In the Nazi death camp known as Auschwitz during the Second World War, it is estimated that 6,000 Jews died in just one day. On 6 August 1945, 140,000 died when the Japanese city of Hiroshima was hit by a uranium bomb. Again during the Second World War, in February 1945, Allied planes bombed the beautiful city of Dresden in Germany killing 135,000 people, mostly civilians, in just 14 hours.

● Since 1945 there have been hundreds of wars all over the globe, and it is estimated that nearly 30 million people have been killed using 'conventional' (non-nuclear) arms. The average

Toxic smoke and burning oil fields, the legacy of the Gulf War

death toll from armed conflict is put at between 33,000 and 41,000 *a month* since 1945.

- The Gulf War in 1991 cost $53 billion – before the damage to the area was taken into account.

Total global military expenditure runs at approximately £1.5 million a minute.

The economic cost of warfare is staggering. The developed countries spend about 20 times more on their military programmes than on economic aid to the poor countries of the world where millions face starvation. To keep military expenditure at its present level, every working person will have to sacrifice about four years' of their income to the arms race. This is one of the major causes of world poverty. In the last two years more people have died from hunger than were killed in both the World Wars.

The cost of war in human terms is tragic. Millions of people are maimed and tortured. As well as shattered bodies there are shattered minds. Between 200,000 and 400,000 women were raped in Bangladesh during a nine-month conflict there in 1971. It is estimated that there are over 15 million refugees in the world, many of them victims of war. And one of the greatest ironies of the Gulf War was that while they were there, Allied Soldiers used 20 million gallons of oil a day on their military machinery.

This century has seen the use of chemical weapons in modern warfare. In 1988 Iraq gassed the Kurdish town of Halabja with nerve and mustard gas, killing 4,000 and injuring 30,000 people.

FOR YOUR FOLDERS

▶ Write an article entitled 'War in the Modern World'.

! ▶ *'And you will hear of wars and rumours of wars.'* (*Matthew 24: 6–7*). In your opinion, will we ever see a world free of war?

▶ Look at the quotes by Javier Perez de Cuellar, Mahatma Ghandi and Pope John Paul II. What do they mean by the words 'choice', and 'moral about-face'?

TALKING POINTS

'World peace is not only possible but inevitable. It is the next stage in the evolution of this planet. For the first time in history we can view the entire planet. It is time for the planetization of humankind, the unification of all the peoples of the world in one universal family. Humanity stands today at the crossroads. The path of the future remains open, subject to a **choice** which has yet to be made. One road leads to peace, the other to self-destruction.'

(Javier Perez de Cuellar, former Secretary-General of the United Nations)

'Put up your sword. All who take the sword die by the sword.'

(Jesus, in *Matthew 26: 52*)

'Our future on this planet . . . depends on one single factor; humanity must make a **moral about-face.**'

(Pope John Paul II)

'An eye for an eye and the world will soon be blind.'

(Mahatma Ghandi)

THE 'JUST WAR'

Many Christians believe that there is such a thing as a 'just war'. This is a war which it is morally right to fight.

For a war to be just, three conditions were laid down in the thirteenth century by St Thomas Aquinas. They were:

1 The war must only be started and controlled by the authority of the state or the ruler.

2 There must be a just cause; those attacked are attacked because they deserve it.

3 The war must be fought to promote good or avoid evil. Peace and justice must be restored afterwards.

Later, two other conditions were added:

4 The war must be the last resort; all other possible ways of solving the problem must have been tried out.

5 There must be 'proportionality' in the way the war is fought, e.g. innocent civilians should not be killed. You must use only enough force to achieve your goals, not more (It would not be 'proportionate', for example, to bomb a whole village because the enemy was hiding in one house.)

THE 'HOLY WAR'

'Declare a Holy War, call the troops to arms.'

(Joel 3: 9)

Holy wars are wars fought by people who believe either that God is on their side or that they have righteousness on their side. The Crusades were holy wars. They were campaigns against the Turks, in the eleventh and twelfth centuries, to liberate the holy places of Palestine from the Muslims. The Christian Church identified the Muslims with Satan and the Crusades with God. However, from a Muslim point of view their wars were holy too. Often holy wars are very viciously fought wars and the people who fight them are stirred up by their church or religion.

Holy wars have been fought through the centuries but morally they pose many questions:

• who really knows what is right?

• is it right to kill for a religion or a set of beliefs?

• how can anyone know that 'God is on their side'?

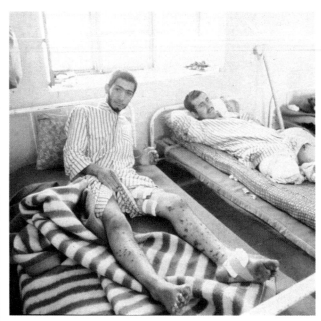

Victims of the Iran-Iraq war, recovering in hospital

'The Lord said to Joshua, "Look, I have delivered Jericho and her King into your hands. You shall march round the city with all your fighting, making the circuit of it once for six days running . . ." thus the Lord was with Joshua.'

(Joshua 6: 2–4)

BIBLICAL VIEWS OF PEACE

'Because everyone will do what is right there will be peace and security forever. God's people will be free from worries and their homes peaceful and safe.'

(Isaiah 32: 16–18)

'You have learned that they were told "eye for eye, tooth for tooth". But what I tell you is this: do not set yourself against the man who wrongs you. If someone slaps you on the right cheek turn and offer him your left.'

(Jesus, in *Matthew* 5: 38-39)

TALKING POINTS

'Since wars begin in the minds of men, it is in the minds of men that peace must be constructed.

(UNESCO)

'Peace can't be kept by force it can only be achieved by understanding.'

(Albert Einstein)

PACIFISM

'I believe that all war and violence is wrong. They are acts against God's will. We are all God's children; we all have a right to live. Violence only breeds violence. Nothing good can come out of something evil. We have been fighting for too long. Untold millions have died at the hands of others. Now is the time to stop. There is a better way. Pacifism has never been tried. We must resist violence. We can explore outer space. Let us now explore inner space and reject that most base thing – to hit out blindly. We can do it. It takes far more courage to resist violence than to engage in it. The world is crying out for us – for you   to take our destiny in our hands and bring peace into this beautiful world of ours.'

(A pacifist, author's interview)

THE PEACE TESTIMONY OF THE SOCIETY OF FRIENDS (QUAKERS)

'We utterly deny all outward wars and strife, and fightings with outward weapons, for any end, or under any pretence whatever; this is our testimony to the whole world. The Spirit of Christ by which we are guided is not changeable, so as once to command us from a thing as evil, and again to move unto it; and we certainly know, and testify to the world, that the Spirit of Christ, which leads us into all truth, will never move us to fight and war against any man with outward weapons, neither for the kingdom of Christ, nor for the kingdoms of the world.'

(from *A Declaration from the Harmless and Innocent People of God, called Quakers*, presented to Charles II, 1660)

FOR YOUR FOLDERS

▶ In your own words explain what you think the difference is between a 'just war' and a 'holy war'.

▶ Under what sorts of circumstances do you think a Christian would be prepared to go to war?

▶ Try to find the meaning of the phrase 'conscientious objector'. What do you think makes some people refuse to serve in the armed forces?

▶ Explain in your own words the meaning of Einstein's words.

▶ Write a paragraph on the beliefs of a pacifist (take into account the Peace Testimony of the Society of Friends).

INTRODUCTION

Northern Ireland has been torn apart by internal division, and the religious conflict between Roman Catholics and Protestants is often said to be the root cause of this conflict. There are many historic reasons for the conflict today including the way the Irish were treated by the English landowners during the Potato Famine in the 1840s when over a million people starved to death. The community of Northern Ireland remains ensnared in a divide between Catholics and Protestants. By sending troops to control 'terrorism' the British gave the Irish Republican Army (IRA) grounds to declare itself a liberation movement, combatting an occupying army. Whatever the reasons, the level of death and destruction in Northern Ireland is of serious concern to all in the UK.

CORRYMEELA

Protestant and Catholic Christians are working all over Northern Ireland towards achieving peace. Corrymeela was founded in 1965 by Christians, both Catholic and Protestant, who wanted to do something about the deep divisions in their country. The main aim of the community is reconciliation. At Ballycastle, a Centre provides a place where people from different traditions can meet and talk freely. Groups visiting the Centre include families of prisoners; those bereaved in the violence; those from areas of tension and social deprivation; school, youth and church groups; the unemployed; the disabled. Conferences and discussions are arranged on a whole range of issues that affect these people.

An important part of the work of Corrymeela concerns trying to help young people understand themselves, their relationships and their communities. The community at Corrymeela run what is known as a 'seed group'. This involves about 20 young people meeting every weekend for six months.

> 'Jesus uses the way seeds grow as a parable to help his followers understand God's message of hope for all who in each generation long for the spread of God's kingdom and through their own lives seek to become tools through whom it is nurtured.'
>
> (The Reverend Douglas Taylor)

The aims of the 'seed groups' are as follows:

- **to reflect** on all of the experiences and influences which have shaped who we are – on the issues and choices which confront us in terms of who we shall become;

- **to understand** ourselves and our relationship to others;

Teenagers at the Corrymeela Community learn about themselves and their relationships with others

- **to relate** the Christian faith to our own experience;
- **to build** bridges of trust, understanding and personal friendship;
- **to encourage** the development of ideas for reconciliation.

Corrymeela is a *symbol* of the fact that Catholics and Protestants can work together in real Christian fellowship. It is a *channel* through which all sorts of people can work together, using their unique talents to build a new society. It is a *challenge* not a surrender to apathy or despair, but to work courageously for peace and understanding wherever we are.

FOR YOUR FOLDERS

▶ Write an article of about 150 words on 'reconciliation in a land of division'.

▶ What problems may arise for young people after they return to their homes from the Corrymeela community?

! ▶ In the article, 'Our anger is justified . . .' what do you think Father Reynolds means when he says 'It's so hard to say the right thing'?

▶ What do you think the churches in Britain can do to work towards peace in Northern Ireland?

THINGS TO DO

Visit your local library and try to find out more about the history of the troubles in Northern Ireland.

Our anger is justified . . .

It is, he confesses, not easy being a priest in Belfast today. Clonard Monastery is right in the heart of the Lower Falls area, 50 yards or so from the green barricades that mark the border with the Protestant Shankhill district. He gazes out of a window over the neat Protestant estate just over the wall: "I used to be afraid to go there until quite recently."

He points to a picture of a young monk, Brother Michael Morgan, on the wall opposite the window. "He was shot here as he looked through this window on July 22, 1920. Shot by a British soldier. They thought the monastery was an arsenal for Republicans. They couldn't make the distinction. When the steam gets up every Catholic is a Provo. You can see the parallels."

He is still profoundly shocked by the savagery on view last week: his colleague, Father Alec Reid, was the priest who attempted the kiss of life on one of the soldiers murdered at Saturday's funeral. At times he finds speech difficult and lowers his head into his hands.

A year ago he and Father Reid attempted to negotiate a ceasefire between the two factions of the Irish National Liberation Army indulging in a mutual bloodbath.

He has little sympathy for the argument that Catholic priests should not involve themselves in the funerals of known terrorists. "We will pray for a dead republican, but that's true Catholicity. We will pray for everybody. We'll leave the judgement to God. I will go on trying to be a priest to everybody, to be a witness to the fact that there are no outsiders in God's heart. Gerry Adams comes for Mass here from time to time." He pauses. "We don't say to him 'You can't come' . . ." His voice trails off.

He recites his own poem calling on freedom fighters to end their war and accept "the violence of God's love." He hesitates before the last verse because "it seems to be almost aligning yourself with the butchery." It runs:

Go home to your children,
  British soldier
Go home to your wife with
  your pay
Go home . . .
With our Father's love upon you
And we'll surely find His way

He lowers his head again. "It's so hard to say the right thing . . . I know I must forgive . . . In my heart I know I am so far from that, but that's the only kind of love that will transform the situation."

Father Reynolds believes the mainland churches now have a crucial role to play: "If I say things it sounds as if I'm talking out of cultural prejudice. More and more I'm coming to be convinced that it is for the church in Britain to help the British people to understand and to forgive."

INTRODUCTION

Since the first nuclear bomb was used on Hiroshima in 1945 (see Section 75) the world has seen a huge expansion in nuclear technology. The awesome power of nuclear weapons has threatened death and destruction on a massive scale for nearly half a century.

Despite recent disarmament measures by Russia and the USA, the threat has not gone away. For instance, there are nearly 30,000 nuclear warheads in what was the Soviet Union. It is known that the following countries have nuclear weapons or are trying to develop them: Egypt, France, Israel, Iran, Iraq, Argentina, India, Pakistan, N. Korea, S. Korea, Taiwan, China, Russia, Brazil, UK, Syria, USA and S. Africa. The way in which so many countries have since developed nuclear weapons is called **proliferation**.

SOME DEVASTATING FACTS

Modern nuclear weapons have immense destructive power. For instance:

- A Trident missile with eight warheads has 853 times the explosive power of the Hiroshima bomb.

- The nuclear load carried by a single Trident submarine is equivalent to eight times the total fire power used during the whole of the Second World War.

- Today's nuclear arsenals contain the combined potential fire power of over one million Hiroshimas.

- The warheads carried by a single Trident submarine have the explosive capacity to destroy all the peoples and major cities of the northern hemisphere.

THIRD WORLD WAR

A nuclear war could begin in many ways, including the deliberate decision to launch a nuclear strike, some form of nuclear terrorism, a systems malfunction, or escalation from conventional war. The last is the most likely; a new war breaks out in the world almost every month. Escalation becomes more likely as more states gain a nuclear strike capability. In the Gulf War during 1991 we became used to seeing troops wearing protection from both chemical and nuclear attack. In a way it is not difficult to see how the world could begin to accept the use of nuclear weapons in a conflict.

TARGET EARTH

Many of the world's leading scientists are involved in military research. Billions of pounds are spent on making nuclear weapons more effective and more destructive. Missiles are so accurate today that they can be fired across continents and make direct hits on objects no bigger than a car. Over the last 20 years the Superpowers have engaged in a policy known as 'deterrence'. This is based on the idea of 'mutually assured destruction' (MAD) – they won't destroy us because if they do we will destroy them.

CHRISTIAN ATTITUDES

For Christians the idea of using weapons of mass destruction is evil because it means that millions of human beings will die, the environment will be shattered, and plant and animal life will come to an end. For Christians the use of nuclear weapons can never be justified.

> 'The monstrous power of nuclear weapons will have fatal consequences for life on earth. Justice, right reason and humanity therefore urgently demand that the arms race should cease . . . nuclear weapons should be banned.'
>
> (*Pacem in Terris*, Roman Catholic statement, 1965)

A HUMANIST VIEW

> 'The world community must condemn the resort to violence and force as a way of solving international disputes. With the possession of biological, nuclear and chemical weapons, war is obsolete. Military spending must be reduced and the savings put to peaceful and people-orientated use.'
>
> (*Humanist Manifesto for the Future of Humankind*)

THINKING POINTS

'And I looked, and behold a whirlwind came out of the north, a great cloud and a fire unfolding itself and a brightness was about it . . .'

(*Ezekiel 1: 4*)

'Nuclear war is seven minutes away, and it might be over in an afternoon. How far away is nuclear disarmament? We are waiting. And the weapons are waiting.'

(Martin Amis)

NUCLEAR WINTER

If there was a nuclear war the smoke from the conflict would block out so much sunlight that temperatures could drop to below freezing over much of the northern hemisphere. It is estimated that about 60% of the world's population would die of starvation after a nuclear war even if only half of today's nuclear arsenals were used.

THE PSYCHOLOGICAL BOMB

In a recent survey done in a comprehensive school it was found that 60% of 15 year-olds had dreamt about nuclear war. The threat affects us all on a deep level. Many people fear the future and have a sense of helplessness. This helplessness is deepened by the fact that even when the majority is strongly opposed to nuclear weapons, political leaders go ahead with their deployment. So great are the vested interests in nuclear weapons that military affairs are simply not dealt with in a democratic manner. Fortunately there is hope. Human instincts for survival are strong and we can learn. Millions of people are now actively seeking an end to fear and a new world that is at peace.

FOR YOUR FOLDERS

▶ Design a poster with the message 'We are on the brink'.

▶ Write a short article entitled 'Nuclear weapons in the world today'.

▶ Explain in your own words the Christian and Humanist attitudes to nuclear weapons.

❗▶ 'Despite the fact that America and Russia are reducing their nuclear stocks, the world is not a much safer place.' Do you agree with this statement?

▶ What do you think an organization like the United Nations can do to bring about world peace?

TALKING POINTS

'The Stone Age may return on the gleaming wings of science and what might now shower immeasurable blessings upon mankind may then bring about its total destruction. Beware, I say, time may be short.'

(Winston Churchill)

'The world now stands on the brink of the final abyss. Let us all resolve to take all possible steps to ensure that we do not, through our own folly, go over the edge.'

(Earl Mountbatten)

On the morning of 6 August 1945, a B29 bomber called the 'Enola Gay' dropped an atomic bomb on the Japanese city of Hiroshima. This is an account of what happened. It was written by Lord Philip Noel-Baker, Nobel Peace Prize Winner in 1959, and was read to the House of Lords in 1980.

Aftermath of a nuclear explosion

'Hiroshima, 6th August 1945, 8.15 a.m., a perfect summer morning: gentle breezes, sunshine, a blue sky. A blue sky is for happiness in Japan. The streets are full of people: people going to work, people going to shop, children going to school. The air raid siren sounds but no one runs, no one goes to shelter. There is only a single aircraft in this enemy raid. The aircraft steers a course across the city. Above the centre, something falls – 20 seconds, 30 seconds, 40 . . . and then there is a sudden searing flash of blinding light, hotter and brighter than a thousand suns. Those who are looking at it have their eyes burned in their sockets. They will never look on men or things again.

In the streets below, other people are walking – a lady as beautiful as she is elegant, a businessman in charge of great affairs, a clever student, the leader of his class, a little girl, laughing as she runs. They are in the street walking. Then suddenly they are not there. The beautiful lady, the businessman, the brilliant student, the scampering little girl have vanished, utterly consumed in the furnace of the flash. There are no ashes, even on the pavement – nothing but their black shadows on the stones.

Then comes the blast. For two kilometres in all directions, every building, every structure is levelled to the ground. The people inside are buried in the ruins of their homes. Lorries, vans, men and women, babies, prams, are picked up and hurled like bullets, hundreds of feet through the air. The blast piles its victims in huge heaps on the corners of the street – heaps seven, eight layers of corpses deep. I know a man and woman who looked for seven days for their little grandson. When they found him, one layer below the top, he was still breathing, but all the doctors in Hiroshima could not save his life.

Then the fireball touches the earth. Conflagrations spring up in every quarter. Swept by tornado winds they rush together in a single firestorm. Tens of thousands more, trapped by walls of flame that leap higher than the highest tower in the city, swiftly, or in longer agony, are burned to death. And everything goes black. The mushroom cloud rises to the very vault of heaven. It carries with it many thousand tons.

The first atom bomb weighed two kilogrammes – less than five pounds. It was a little larger than a cricket ball. It killed 140,000 people on that August day. In 1978, more than 2,000 died in Hiroshima from its long-delayed effects.

Today there are very many young adults who were only embryos in their mothers' wombs when the bomb exploded. They have leukaemia and shortly they will die. Babies are being born with tiny, deformed heads – and that first atom bomb was what the science editor of **The Times** called a "nuclear midget".'

There are many different theories as to why the Allies dropped the bomb on Hiroshima and then three days later dropped one on Nagasaki. One thing is sure – the world has never been the same since.

◇

'Before the bomb, man had to live with the idea of his death as an individual; from now onwards, mankind has to live with his idea of death as a species.'

(Arthur Koestler)

THOUGHTS FOR THE FUTURE

'Those that survive a nuclear war would envy the dead.'

(Nikita Krushchev)

'On the assumption that a Third World War must escalate to nuclear destruction, I can tell you that the Fourth World War will be fought with bows and arrows.'

(Albert Einstein)

'We are now faced with the fact that tomorrow is today. There is such a thing as being too late. Over the bleached bones of numerous civilizations are written the pathetic words "too late". If we do not act, we shall surely be dragged down the dark corridors of time reserved for those who possess power without compassion, might without morality and strength without sight.'

(Martin Luther King)

FOR YOUR FOLDERS

▶ Write a telegram (maximum 30 words) dated 6 August reminding a friend about 'Hiroshima Day'.

▶ Using the thoughts for the future opposite, write a letter to a magazine about the dangers of nuclear war.

▶ Write a paragraph answering the question 'Can a nuclear war ever be called a Just War?' (See Section 72.)

! ▶ It has been argued that the atomic bombings of Hiroshima and Nagasaki brought the war to a quick end and therefore saved the lives of countless people. In the light of this, do you think that the devastation of Hiroshima and Nagasaki was morally justifiable?

FOR DISCUSSION

▶ 'The use of nuclear weapons can *never* be justified.'

▶ 'The world now stands on the brink of the final abyss.'

(Lord Louis Mountbatten)

> 'To resist without bitterness
> To be cursed and not reply
> To be beaten and not hit back.'
>
> (Martin Luther King, explaining the
> Non-Violent Creed)

Violence is:

- wasteful – it uproots and destroys precious human lives; it consumes huge quantities of wealth and intelligence
- indiscriminate – it is hard to limit its deadly effects to those who are 'guilty'
- sexist – historically it has been done by men
- unjust – often the innocent suffer
- destructive – it encourages brutality and treats people like objects
- a vicious circle – it sets off a spiral of violence.

Non-violence is:

- humane – it avoids killing other human beings
- creative – it cuts across barriers of sex, race and class
- a civilian method – everyone can become involved
- voluntary – people are not forced into a military type machine
- radical – it can change society for the better
- dignifying – it depends on people standing up for themselves and refusing to let go of their argument however much they are provoked.

'In non-violence the masses have a weapon which enables a child, a woman, or even a decrepit old man to resist the mightiest government successfully.'

(Gandhi)

A Greenpeace worker takes non-violent direct action to protect a seal pup from culling

Non-violent direct action is designed to:

1 raise people's knowledge about an issue,
2 put pressure on people in authority to change things,
3 object to some injustice in society,
4 ultimately change the situation.

Protesting against Cruise missiles at Greenham Common

GROUP WORK

 'Council to close youth club!'
In groups of four or five plan a campaign to prevent this (e.g. letter writing, demonstrations, petitions, publicity, meetings and posters).

FOR DISCUSSION

▶ 'Let every person be subject to the governing authorities. For there is no authority except from God . . . therefore he who resists the authorities resists what God has appointed.'

(St Paul, in *Romans 13: 1–2*)

'Do not think that I have come to bring peace on earth; I have not come to bring peace, but a sword.'

(Jesus, in *Matthew 10: 34*)

What do you think St Paul and Jesus mean?

▶ 'In a democracy it is wrong to try and change things by non-violent direct action.'

'In an undemocratic state it would be a waste of time trying to change things non-violently.'

Discuss these points of view.

FOR YOUR FOLDERS

1 Write a few sentences about each picture, explaining exactly what the protestors want to change.
2 Can you think of other forms of non-violent protest?
3 List some of the things that you would like to see changed in the world today, giving your reasons.
4 Write an article on 'Violence and non-violence'.

Between 1978 and 1980 leading political figures from all over the world worked together to see if the enormous problems of world poverty could be solved.

In his introduction to the report the group's chairman, Willy Brandt, wrote:

'Our report is based on what appears to be the simplest common interest. Mankind wants to survive and, one might even add, has the moral obligation to survive. This not only raises the traditional questions of peace and war, but also how to overcome world hunger, mass misery and alarming differences between the living conditions of rich and poor . . . we want to emphasize our belief that the two decades ahead of us may be fateful for mankind.'

(North–South: A Programme for Survival, 1980)

Here is a brief summary of ten of the main suggestions made in the report.

- There must be an emergency programme to help the world's poorest countries in the poverty belts of Africa and Asia.

- There must be an end to mass hunger and malnutrition. This means more funds for developing agriculture, irrigation, agricultural research, crop storage, fertilizers and other aids.

- There should be more international support for family planning programmes.

- Funds and skills being put into arms production must be channelled into peaceful needs.

- World trade should be encouraging the developing countries to have more part in the processing, marketing and distribution of their own commodities, to increase their earnings.

- Flows of overseas aid should be enlarged.

- There should be an international 'income tax' to spread wealth from the rich to the poor.

- The international monetary system must be reformed, giving greater participation and advantage to poorer countries.

- A new World Development Fund could act to distribute resources raised on a universal and automatic basis.

- More attention must be paid to educating public opinion, and the young especially, about the importance of international cooperation.

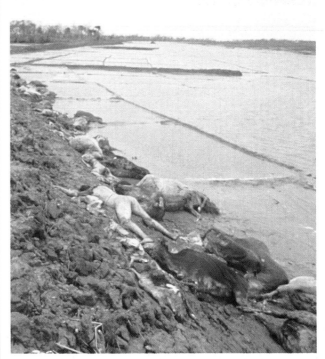

After a cyclone in Bangladesh

KEY IDEA

North–South is a very simple way of showing how the world divides into rich and poor countries. The rich **North** includes North America, Europe, USSR, Japan, Australia, and New Zealand. The poor **South** includes most of Asia, Africa, and Latin America.

Countries of the **South** are sometimes called the **Third World**, **underdeveloped** or **developing** countries

'Even in the United States this division (between rich and poor) can be seen. In countries like India, Portugal and Brazil, the contrast between the wealth of the few privileged individuals and the dire poverty of the masses is a crying scandal. And looking at the world as a collection of nation states, we see the same problem repeated; there are a few wealthy nations which dominate the world economically and therefore politically, and a mass of smaller and poor nations.'

(Julius Nyerere, president of Tanzania)

NORTH–SOUTH

North:

- $\frac{1}{4}$ of the world's people
- $\frac{4}{5}$ of the world's income
- a person can expect to live on average more than 70 years
- most people are educated at least through secondary school
- over 90% of the world's manufacturing industry
- about 96% of world's spending on research and development, nearly all the world's registered patents
- dominates most of the international economic system and institutions of trade, money and finance.

South:

- $\frac{3}{4}$ of the world's people
- $\frac{1}{5}$ of the world's income
- a person can expect to live, on average, to about 50 years
- $\frac{1}{5}$ or more of the people suffer from hunger and malnutrition
- $\frac{1}{2}$ of the people still have little chance of formal education

TALKING POINTS

'Love your neighbour as yourself.'
(*Leviticus 19: 18*)

'All things are connected like the blood which unites one family.'
(Chief Seattle, 1855)

'The world is a unity and we must begin to act as members of it who depend on each other.'
(*Brandt Report*)

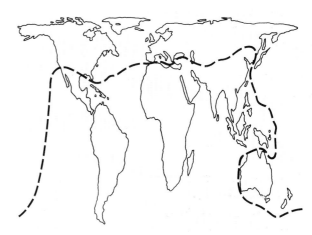

The North-South divide

PROBLEMS

The Brandt Report is in many ways an ideal. since its statements were made little appears to have changed in terms of world poverty. The Brandt Report pins its hopes for the world's poor on negotiations between governments. But the majority of Third World governments represent only the interests of a wealthy elite with too much to lose to allow any major redistribution of wealth. Quite simply, rich people anywhere are anxious to keep their wealth and to avoid too much upset, commotion or revolution. The gap between the North and the South is as wide as ever.

At the beginning of the 1990s we witnessed the historic reunification of Germany and disintegration of the USSR. On many levels this has been good news as regards world peace and security, but many people fear that the effects on the Third World will be catastrophic. The rich nations are already beginning to redirect 'aid' from the developing nations of the South to the countries of the East. The USA cut its economic support to the Third World from $545 million to $350 million in 1990 alone. In a world of limited resources no-one gets more unless somebody has less.

FOR YOUR FOLDERS

! ▶ Write an article of about 100 words outlining what you consider to be the most important part of the Brandt Report.

DEFINITION

Absolute poverty A condition of life so characterized by malnutrition, illiteracy, disease, high infant mortality and low life expectancy as to be beneath any reasonable definition of human decency.'

(Robert Macnamara)

Absolute poverty is a trap that holds about one billion people, nearly a fifth of the world's population. Ninety per cent live in the countryside, more than half are small farmers and a quarter are landless labourers. **Whilst we in the North worry about diets, 35,000 people every day starve to death.** Even if people are somehow able to survive a malnourished childhood they will never be given the opportunity to realize their full human potential. All the routes out of the trap are firmly shut because of lack of education, technical aid, employment, sanitation or safe water, access to health services,

Ethiopians are among the world's poorest people

transport or communication. Most Southern governments are unlikely to change their policies because often resources are too scarce. The poor are left with the greatest toll of death and misery – and they fall prey to exploitation by landlords, merchants, employers and the police. They are the powerless ones.

The majority of people in developing countries manage to survive on an income of under £70 a year. Many people live on less. There are over 825 million illiterate adults in the world, mostly in the South, the majority are women. In 60 countries over 40% of houses have no piped water. Some 1.4 billion people do not have access to clean water.

Over 450 million people are mentally or physically disabled; 800 million have no access to health care. **At least 15 million children die every year.**

While you are reading this some 450 million people are starving or malnourished and do not know whether they will be living by this time next week.

THINKING POINTS

'I must try and show you this. There is a child, I think maybe it's four months old. The Doctor says, "No, it's two years old". It squats on baked mud, a tattered dusty piece of cotton hangs from one shoulder onto its distended stomach. Its face is huge. A two-year-old face on a four month body.

The eyes are moons of dust and flies caked by tears so big they don't dry until they reach the navel.

The child stares. Between its legs flows a constant stream of diarrhoea. The immediate earth around its legs is damp with it. I am watching a child die. In total silence and surrounded by its family it eventually begins to shit out its own stomach.

I am tired with grief and despair and a consuming rage for humanity.

He dies soon. He just dies. Big deal. A jumble of bones and dry skin, wet eyes, flies and shit.

In that place where humans have abandoned, humanity thrives. A handful of grain each. The shame, the shame, the shame.'

(Bob Geldof)

'They sell newspapers they cannot read, sew clothes they cannot wear, polish cars they will never own and construct buildings where they will never live. They cannot make history, they are condemned to suffer it.

Welcome to the fall of the Berlin Wall. But the other wall, the wall that separates the poor world from the rich world, is higher than ever. A universal apartheid: racism, intolerance and discrimination erupt increasingly in Europe, punishing all intruders who scale the wall to reach the citadel of prosperity.

It's plain to see. The Berlin Wall has died a timely death. But it lived no more than 30 years. The other wall, which was built in 1492, celebrates its fifth centenary. Unequal exchange, financial corruption, capital bleeding away, the few owning the technology and information – these are the bricks that build up day by day as wealth drains ever faster from the South to the North of the world.

The Pope in Rome forcefully condemned the killing of a priest in Poland. But nobody listens when the priests of Latin America have their eyes gouged out for standing up for human rights. That's normal. They impose contempt on us in the South. Now they sell us contempt as destiny.'

(Eduardo Galeano)

TALKING POINT

'A church that is in solidarity with the poor can never be a wealthy church. It must sell all, in a sense, to follow its master. It must use its wealth and resources for the sake of the least of Christ's brethren.'

(Archbishop Desmond Tutu)

FOR YOUR FOLDERS

▶ List some of the problems facing the millions of people who are living in absolute poverty.

! ▶ 'There but for the grace of God go I.' We have been fortunate in being born in the rich North. Do you think that we have any responsibilities towards our brothers and sisters in the poor South? If so, what are you prepared to do?

▶ Many Christians today are concerned about world poverty yet they belong to one of the richest institutions on earth. After reading Desmond Tutu's Talking Point, how do you think the Church should respond to the fact that 35,000 of God's children are dying of hunger every day?

▶ After reading Eduardo Galeano's Thinking Point, answer the following questions:

i)   What is the 'other wall'?
ii) What are its 'bricks'?
iii) Why, in his opinion, are people in the North selling the South 'contempt as destiny'?

FOOD

Food helps us grow and develop. Without the right amount of food or the right kinds of food, people suffer from malnutrition which can result in death. At least one in eight of the world's population does not have enough to eat.

> 'When you have gathered your grapes once, do not go back over the vines a second time . . . they are for the foreigners, orphans, and widows.'
>
> *(Deuteronomy 24: 21)*

WATER

Clean, safe drinking water is essential for life. It is vital for the control of diseases such as diarrhoea, typhoid and cholera.

The World Health Organization estimates that 80% of all sickness and disease can be attributed to inadequate water and sanitation. Such diseases cause an estimated 50 million deaths each year. And children are hardest hit: one child in seven in the developing world dies before its fifth birthday. Most of the deaths could have been prevented.

Everyone has a basic need for food

HOUSING

Housing provides us with protection and security. Today, as more and more people in Third World countries are drawn to cities in search of work and a better life, overcrowding becomes a major problem.

> 'Everyone has the right to a standard of living adequate for their health and well being, including housing.'
>
> *(UN Declaration of Human Rights)*

HEALTH

Health care is important to 'ensure a state of complete physical, mental and social well-being and not merely the absence of disease or illness' (World Health Organization). This requires adequate food, access to safe drinking water, sewage disposal, health education and health care. Yet 70% of the population in Third World countries do not have access to any organized health care and 90% of child deaths are linked with malnutrition, contagious diseases and unhygienic living conditions.

> 'Heal the sick, raise the dead, cleanse those who have leprosy, drive out demons. Freely you have received, freely give.'
>
> *(Matthew 10: 8)*

EDUCATION

We take education for granted but in the poorest countries of the world only four adults in ten can read and write and less than one in four children go to secondary school.

> 'Every child shall be given an education which will promote his general culture and enable him on a basis of equal opportunity to develop his abilities, his individual judgement and his sense of moral and social responsibility and to become a useful member of society.'
>
> *(UN Declaration of the Rights of the Child)*

WORK

Work can give us identity, security and the means to meet many of our other basic needs. Today world unemployment stands at around 500 million – 300 million of these are in the Third World.

> 'All of us should eat and drink and enjoy what we have worked for. It is God's gift.'
>
> *(Ecclesiastes 3: 13)*

In Haiti many people live in shanty town communities

FOR YOUR FOLDERS

▶ Write an account of some of the basic needs of the Third World.

▶ After reading the biblical passages and the UN Declarations, write a letter, using some quotes, to a friend explaining what responsibilities Christians and non-Christians have towards countries in the Third World.

FOR DISCUSSION

▶ 'More people have died as a consequence of hunger in the past six years than have been killed in all the wars, revolutions and murders in the past 150 years.'

(The Hunger Project, 1987)

INTRODUCTION

The world spends more on arms than it spends on anything else. In a world of poverty where one billion people can barely survive, the arms trade (the buying and selling of weapons) is an issue that we need to address. In the 1980s alone $8,000 billion were spent on arms – which could have provided all the people in the world with an income for three years.

In 1991 there was the Gulf War. The cost of mounting 'Operation Desert Shield' – not including devastation caused by the Gulf War itself – was $53 billion. This is almost as much as the total annual foreign assistance that Third World countries get.

THE FACTS

1 WORLD PRIORITIES

- Six times as much public money in the world goes for research on weapons as for research on health protection.

- The Third World spends 66% more on the military than on education.

- There is one soldier per 240 people in the Third World, one doctor per 1950. Yet the chance of dying from social neglect, malnutrition and preventable disease is 33 times greater than dying from war.

2 BIG SPENDERS

Since the end of the Cold War the big spenders are cutting defence budgets but they still spend a lot. Both the USA and what was the USSR are still spending over 30% more than they did in 1980.

3 THE ARMS

Among the countries which export the most arms are the USA, France and Britain. The countries which buy the most arms are India, Iraq, Japan and Saudi Arabia. Developing countries buy over half of the world's arms. Saddam Hussein, before the Gulf War, was supplied arms by the USA, USSR, Britain, France and China.

4 REAL COSTS

If redirected, the money consumed by the military could eliminate Third World poverty. For instance, a Tornado bomber costs $40 million. The price of five of these could feed 20 million Africans for one month. One Patriot missile costs $1 million . . . the price of 23 of these could keep two million Mozambicans in seeds, clothes, pots and storage facilities for one year. A B52 bomber uses 3,600 gallons of fuel per hour of flight.

5 BIG DEALS

The people who sell arms want to see a world where war is commonplace. War or threat of war means money for them. Since the Gulf War the USA is negotiating sending $20 billion of military equipment to Saudi Arabia, Britain is negotiating with five Middle East states for orders worth $2.5 billion.

6 CHANGING TRENDS

The arms trade is scaling down in many parts of the world but gearing up in others. In 1990 there was a reduction in nuclear forces for the first time ever. Fewer nuclear tests were conducted than in the past 30 years. However, more than 20 countries in the world can make or acquire biological and chemical weapons seen in the Third World as the 'poor man's atom bomb'. Experts predict a chemical arms race. India's defence spending has recently gone up to $450 million in one year.

A CHRISTIAN AND HUMANIST VIEW

Like many people, Humanists feel that the arms trade is one of the major evils of our time. Many Christians and Humanists are involved in some of the campaigning organizations which work to try and make the world a safer and fairer place (for names and addresses see page 190). The fact is that only a tiny minority of people own the means of production within the arms industry and these are the people who make enormous profits through the suffering of others.

It was explained in the section on war that at the beginning of the century whereas nine out of ten victims of war were soldiers, in the 1990s nine out of ten victims are civilians, usually women, children and the elderly.

FIVE STEPS TOWARDS A NEW FUTURE . . .

1 CAMPAIGN

Nearly all arms-producing countries sell weapons to nations with poor human rights records or with military dictatorships. CAAT (Campaign Against the Arms Trade) works towards putting pressure on the British Government to stop selling arms to such countries.

2 EDUCATE

Children need to be taught that war is obscene. They should be encouraged to resolve disputes peacefully. They should also be discouraged at an early age from playing with war toys which make war and violence seem an inevitable part of life.

3 EXPOSE

The arms trade thrives on secrecy. Organizations like CAAT and some MPs are demanding that the Government publish details of all arms dealings.

4 WORK

Many people work in the arms industry. Some trade unions have put pressure on companies to redirect their resources away from arms manufacturing towards socially worthwhile projects.

5 THINK

We have all got used to the idea that war is somehow inevitable. However, in a world of chemical and nuclear weapons it is imperative that people learn how to discuss and debate things rather than resort to violence.

FOR YOUR FOLDERS

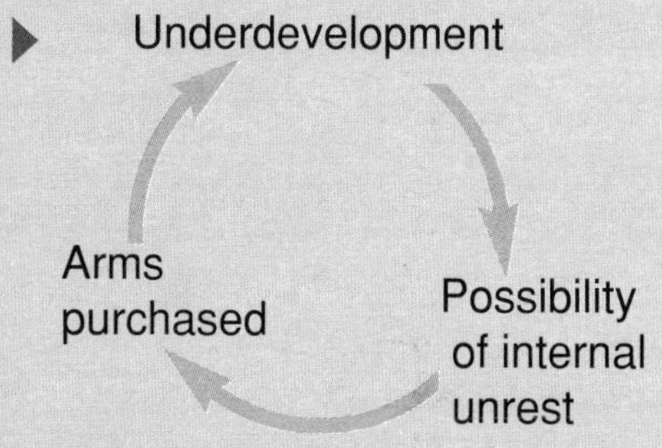

▶ Underdevelopment

Arms purchased

Possibility of internal unrest

▶ Try to work out why so many Third World countries feel the need to buy arms. Who buys the arms for them? Why are they often used against their own people? How does poverty link in with arms purchasing? Look at the above diagram to help you.

▶ Write an article of about 200 words on the arms trade today.

▶ Try to find some biblical quotes that are relevant to the arms trade. List them.

▶ Write a letter to someone in a position of power about the arms trade. (You can use some of the statistics quoted in this section.)

We live in a world of mass communication. This means that we in the so-called 'developed world' are very much aware of the horrifying existence of world hunger. Over a billion people do not get enough food – one-fifth of the world's population. However, we often make assumptions about the causes of, and real facts about, world hunger, which are not founded in reality. This section is designed not only to prompt you to think more deeply about the problems of world hunger, but also to dispel some of the myths that have been created around the subject.

THERE ARE TOO MANY PEOPLE.

Overpopulation – *the* bogey word. But which countries are overpopulated? Those which consume the most, like the USA with 6% of the world's population consuming over 30% of the world's resources? Or one of the poor countries?

THERE'S NOT ENOUGH FOOD.

There is. The world is producing enough food to feed every man, woman and child. Enough grain is produced to provide every person with more than 3,000 calories a day.

And that's without counting beans, fruit and vegetables. But that's not all! Often enough food is available even in those countries where many people go hungry. The poorest people, with little power or influence, are to be found on the worst land, while the best and most productive land is used for cultivating crops for export – sold to earn money to pay off debts and to buy much needed imports.

NOTHING GROWS WITH ALL THOSE DROUGHTS.

In the Third World, droughts and floods are not the unexpected disasters we always imagine. In the Sahel region of Africa drought is practically part of the environment cycle, and in Asia everyone knows that floods will occur regularly.

The problem is that as the poor get poorer, their ability to cope with such disasters is reduced, and they become more vulnerable to these environmental 'shocks'.

ALL THAT TEA AND SUGAR WE BUY, DOESN'T THAT HELP?

Yes, we buy food and other crops from Third World countries. They sell such commodities to help pay off their debts and to earn money to develop their economies. But the prices paid for their exports are generally decreasing, while at the same time the imports they need to buy from the developed world are getting more expensive. In the 1980s Tanzania received less and less for its exports of coffee and cotton, but at the same time it had to pay more and more for imports, such as tractors and machinery. This vicious circle is repeated across the Third World.

WE'VE GOT FOOD MOUNTAINS, SO WE'LL JUST SEND MORE FOOD.

Food aid is a lifesaver in many situations, but in other cases it does more harm than good. Only 10% of all food aid sent is used for vital emergency relief. The remainder is distributed in a variety of ways, but rarely gets out to the poor.

And the biggest myth of all –

IT'S GOT NOTHING TO DO WITH US.

It's got everything to do with us. The problem starts here, not 'out there'. The connections between us and world hunger are numerous. Take the debt crisis for one – relegated to those pages of newspapers we barely read. It is, we are told, a problem for our high street banks. The poor of the Third World don't read about it either, they live it.

Third World countries struggling under huge foreign debt are forced to take drastic measures to make regular payments. Less money is spent where

it's needed most – on the poor. Health services are cut to the bone, and infant mortality and disease are rising. And they must earn more foreign exchange by boosting their exports. More and more land is used to grow export crops. This can be at the expense of the food needs of the poor.

(Adapted from Oxfam's *Seven Myths about World Hunger* leaflet)

FOR YOUR FOLDERS

▶ Write out the myths about world poverty. Now try to write down what Oxfam says about each of these myths.

▶ Design a poster 'Myths about world poverty'.

▶ Imagine you work for Oxfam. Try to work out a programme for educating people about world poverty. Describe how you would go about it, e.g. advertising, TV, local radio, teenage magazines, schools and cinemas.

▶ Do you think that 'it's got nothing to do with us'?

TALKING POINT

'Poverty kills a small child every 2.4 seconds.'

Some people believe that the greatest threat to the survival of the human race is overpopulation. It is predicted that by the year 2000 there will be about 6 billion people on Earth. The so-called 'population explosion' creates some huge problems for humankind. Millions of people in the poor world suffer from malnutrition. Many cities are desperately overcrowded with millions of people living in terrible conditions. Millions of people throughout the world, including Britain, are homeless. Our skies, seas, wildlife and rivers have become poisoned by masses of human generated waste. The world's energy resources are dwindling. Our societies seem to be getting more violent and people more despairing and frightened of the future.

The population explosion also raises many moral problems. Should governments impose compulsory birth control? Why do we in the rich world consume so many of the Earth's resources, yet by comparison have less of a population problem? How are poverty and population related? Should we only be allowed to have a certain number of children? Should people be sterilized? Or should we follow the teaching in *Genesis (1: 28)* which states 'Be fruitful and increase'?

It is very important to think about the relationship between overpopulation and world poverty and this section shows different aspects of this relationship. Very simply, the relationship between poverty and overpopulation can be shown like this:

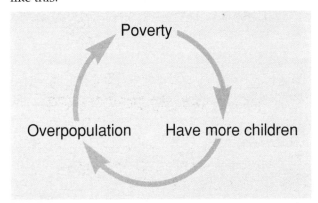

The population vicious circle

Also linked to the problem of overpopulation is the issue of birth control. The Roman Catholic Church, however, teaches that most types of birth control are unnatural (see section 22) and that sexual intercourse is primarily for the purpose of reproduction. Many Catholic priests working in the developing world believe that the levels of poverty cannot be reduced by birth control programmes but only by a massive redistribution of wealth.

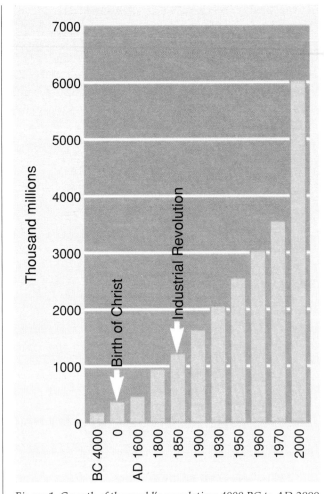

Figure 1 Growth of the world's population: 4000 BC to AD 2000

OTHER TEACHINGS

'Human beings must enter into absolute control of their birth-rate. Without this they will lose their birthright.'

(Church of England report)

'It is the moral obligation of the developed nations to provide birth control techniques to the developing portions of the globe.'

(Humanist Manifesto)

Many experts believe that there is easily enough food in the world to feed everyone adequately. They also believe that people could use new techniques to feed an even more densely populated world (e.g. better farming methods, use of foods in the sea). However, at the moment the richest 10% of the world consume 90% of the world's resources.

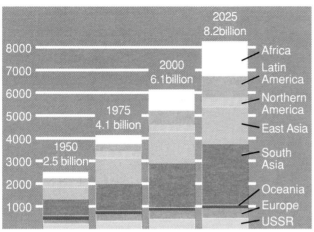

Figure 2 The growth and distribution of the world's population: 1950 to 2025

FACTS

- There are 3 births every 2 seconds,
  90 births every minute,
  200,000 births each day.
  World population doubles every 35 years.

- In 1935, there were 56 cities with more than a million inhabitants.
  In 1960, there were 100.
  In 2000, there will probably be about 500.

'Why do people in poor countries go on having more children than they can afford? The answer is: they don't, usually. Where you are living without any of the aids to living which we have, where each day is a long grind of many hard jobs, just to survive, children are needed as helpers. When there is only a 50-50 chance of your children living past five years, you've got to plan to have many children. And when there is no social security, old age pension or health insurance, who else is going to look after you if not your children? If we looked at life from the point of view of those who say 'my children are my only wealth' would we still be so keen on birth control?

We in the West are afraid that more people in the poor world will mean lower standards for us, or will cause trouble for us through revolution. We do not necessarily know best. The poor of the world will start using contraceptive devices very quickly indeed, just as soon as real development and a fairer deal in life lets them do so.'

(*How the Other Half Dies* by Susan George)

TALKING POINTS

'All Christians and Humanists would agree that the present distribution of the world's resources leads to poverty. However, they might disagree on the use or non-use of birth control. What do you think?'

'The only way to deal with the population explosion is by compulsory birth control.'

'We can't expect the poor to limit their family sizes when they need children to help support their family. The real problem is not overpopulation but poverty and the unequal distribution of wealth. This must be tackled first.'

FOR YOUR FOLDERS

▶ Equation:
poverty ↔ overpopulation.
How does Susan George explain this equation?

▶ Write a paragraph about figure 1.

▶ Figure 2 shows a breakdown of world population. List the areas where the 'population explosion' is occurring.

! ▶ List some of the problems you think this will cause, especially in the developing South.

> **Refugee** — a person who flees, especially to a foreign country, because of political or religious persecution or an invading army.

The number of official refugees in the world now stands at a record 16 million, more than half of whom are children. This is double the number of a decade ago. Over the past 10 years an average of over 3,000 people a day have been forced to leave their homes, but provision for them is dwindling.

Most refugees live in the world's poorest countries. Many suffer hunger and disease. Despite news coverage of some groups, like the Vietnamese and the Kurds, refugees remain forgotten by many of the powerful. The Office of the UN High Commissioner for Refugees is the main agency which tries to protect and assist refugees and to find permanent solutions for them.

REFUGEES – THE FACTS

- While the numbers of refugees are increasing, government contributions to the international agencies set up to provide for refugees are not keeping pace.

- People who have been made homeless within their own countries are not included in official figures on refugees, although estimates suggest they number over 30 million. For instance, there are four and a half million homeless in the Sudan and over four million in South Africa.

- Many people are so desperate to escape poverty or persecution that they enter Western countries illegally. Such immigration is increasing. Those fleeing to escape poverty, for other economic reasons, are not regarded as true refugees by agencies or governments.

REFUGEE CHARTER

Many aid organizations are working desperately hard against the increasing flood of refugees. Oxfam, Christian Aid, the British Red Cross, CAFOD, the Refugee Council, Christians Aware and Amnesty International have devised a Refugee Charter. Some of the main points are:

1   Rich nations should contribute increased amounts to programmes helping refugees.

2   Western governments should adopt less restrictive attitudes to refugees who want to live in the West ('asylum seekers').

There are millions of refugees worldwide, even in remote parts of China

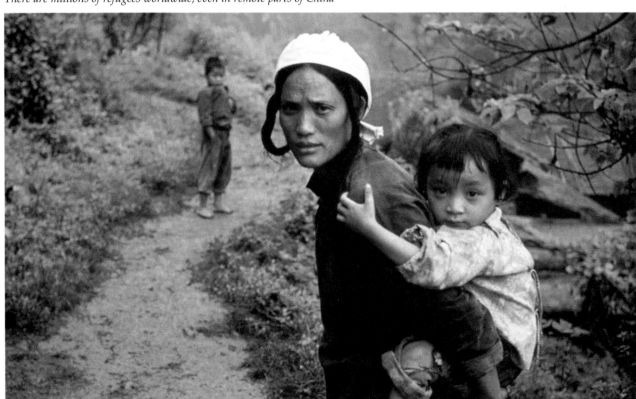

3 Every asylum seeker must have a fair chance to appeal if they are not allowed to stay in the country.

4 Refugees must be fully involved in the planning of schemes designed to provide help and support.

5 People who have fled their homes but who have not crossed an international border are entitled to protection.

6 Programmes for refugees should make sure that the needs of vulnerable groups like the disabled, the elderly and children, are met.

7 Support should be available for refugees who choose to return to their homeland.

8 Refugees and asylum seekers should have the right to be joined by their immediate family.

9 Refugees bring a wealth of different skills. Overseas qualifications and work experience gained abroad should be recognized.

10 Governments must act to end the war, human rights abuse and environmental degradation which force people to flee their homes. Foreign policy should be geared towards promoting human rights.

CASE STUDY

'I am sixteen years old. My name is Maria da Silva. When the famine struck my village in Brazil it was a nightmare. My youngest brother, who was five, and my sister who was eight, died in front of our eyes. My mother and father stopped talking. Their eyes were hollow. One day we put everything on a cart and walked away from the village to a new life in the interior. We walked for ten weeks. My mother's feet were so sore that at the end of the day she was screaming with pain. Many of the other people from the village died on the way.

When we got to the interior, to the great forest of Amazonia, all we found was a huge village sprawling and disease-ridden, a shanty town. I had expected to see colourful birds and beautiful lizards but all we found were rats and swarms of insects. My mother died of malaria two weeks after we arrived. I wanted to die but I knew that somehow I had to stay alive to look after my family. At night I would pray to God for help.

Finally, we found a small piece of land and managed to grow some crops. My father found work on a cattle ranch but after a year he lost his job. When the rains came they stripped away our fragile soil and we had to start all over again. Some days, if you climb to the hill, you can see huge clouds of smoke rising into the sky. My father tells me that they are burning the Amazon down to make way for more people like us. I wonder if it is all worth it because for me the future seems as black as the clouds of smoke that cover our forest.'

(Author's interview)

TALKING POINT

'As long as there is poverty in the world I can never be rich, even if I have a million dollars. I can never be what I ought to be until you are what you ought to be.'

(Martin Luther King)

FOR YOUR FOLDERS

▶ Explain in your own words what a refugee is.

▶ What do you think are some of the causes that make people refugees?

▶ Write an article entitled 'The Rights of Refugees'.

▶ Imagine that you are a refugee. Write a case study of your life, like Maria's.

▶ Many people have criticized the British Government's immigration laws. Do you think that we should allow more people who are refugees to come and live in our country?

▶ Can you explain the distinction that governments make between 'genuine' and 'economic' refugees?

WHO ARE FUNDAMENTALISTS?

'They worship the authority and wisdom of the past and they hope to regain a lost past. They have an absolute set of rules and are not always strictly religious but encompass secular forms of belief. Any obsessive preoccupation with a single explanation of the cosmos or a single "answer" to the problems of society can slip easily into fundamentalist belief. They reassert an old truth as the answer to modern doubt.'

(Richard Swift)

When we think of fundamentalism we often picture the media image of 'fanatical Muslims' beating their chests or American TV Evangelists calling on viewers to donate money for 'eternal salvation'. However, there are fundamentalists who put on three-piece suits, work in the Stock Exchange and believe that all of human existence can be defined in economic terms. Over the last decade or so there has been a worldwide rise in many different forms of fundamentalist belief.

Life today can be very confusing. The pace of change in this century has been amazing, with traditional habits, beliefs and cultures under constant pressure to adapt. In an increasingly materialistic world our individual worth is measured according to standards of how much money or power we have. We no longer seem to belong anywhere. Old communities are disappearing. Governments are increasingly large and remote. The traditional family is no longer, in many cases, a place of security. Our world is getting more violent. The global economy means that our livelihoods can be changed by the touch of a computer in Brussels or Tokyo. All this confusion provides fertile ground on which the seeds of fundamentalism can grow.

Fundamentalists can sell their ideas by referring back to the 'old ways': the intimate gathering around the family hearth; a clear sense of what is right (and will be rewarded) and what is wrong (and what will be punished). We have to ask, however, whether there was ever a time on Earth when people lived in total harmony with themselves and their neighbours? Fundamentalists often talk as if this time once existed. If it did and it was perfect, why does it not exist today? Why did it disappear? Why did we ever leave this 'Garden of Eden' where idyllic family life, hard work and god-fearing

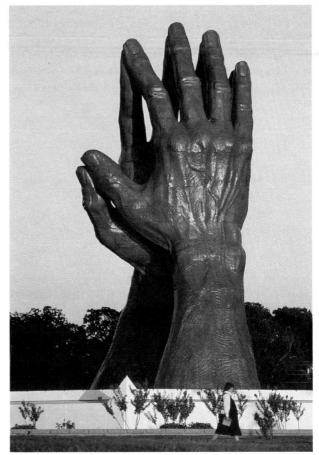

The sculpture outside Faith Hospital in Tulsa, USA

morality kept us all happy? The seeds of discontent that have grown and flowered in the modern world must have been planted in that garden.

Fundamentalists do not only hark back to a golden age. They are obsessed by the idea that we are heading towards an apocalyptic crisis if we don't mend our ways. Christian Fundamentalists talk about the 'second coming of Christ', known as 'endtimes'. Each different Fundamentalist movement aims to put things right with a programme of moral reform.

'When the Christian majority takes over this country, there will be no Satanic churches, no more free distribution of pornography, no more abortion on demand and no more talk of rights for homosexuals. After the Christian majority takes control our society will not put up with other religions, they will be seen as immoral and evil and the State will not permit anybody to practise them.'

(Pat Robertson, TV Evangelist and US Presidential candidate)

FUNDAMENTALIST BELIEFS

Christian Fundamentalists take the Bible quite literally, concentrating particularly on the Old Testament. They defend literal translations of controversial Biblical passages like the Garden of Eden interpretation of creation. They see God and the Devil as active forces in everyday life and often talk about divine intervention in the most ordinary events of life. Fundamentalists usually believe in the moral authority of the State and all its instruments, such as the police, and the armed forces.

Most of them believe society is not far from the final judgement where God will descend to Earth and take the side of the 'righteous' (their side) against all 'His enemies', e.g. Humanists (see Section 6), supporters of abortion (see Sections 48 and 49), Liberation Theologians (see Section 85), homosexuals (see Section 24), supporters of women's rights (see Section 68) and 'false Christians' who make the assumption that they know what Truth is.

Fundamentalists often support right-wing causes. During the last 12 years in the USA there have been 34 bombings and 47 arson attacks against abortion clinics, in which they have been suspected of involvement.

In America there are 3,000 or so fundamentalist cults, some of which are spreading into the Third World and Europe. Each cult tends to have its own holy book containing the 'revealed truth'; they usually have one authoritarian leader who demands absolute obedience; they believe in a coming apocalypse where the few will be saved and the many will be eternally damned; and they believe in the total explanation of the world provided by cult mythology.

'There is no question there is a hell. It's eternal torment, too, like being strapped into an electric chair forever but you never quite die.'

(Dr Jordan, American Evangelist)

CHRISTIAN FUNDAMENTALISM IN LATIN AMERICA

Some Protestant organizations in the USA send missionaries to try and convert peoples in Latin America. They push their own Christian views, which are often Fundamentalist views, and deliberately work to destroy the culture of these peoples. This is known as **ethnocide**. There are four steps to ethnocide:

1 **Contact** Missionaries leave gifts for indigenous peoples (see Section 90) or use 'tame' Indians to make initial contact.

2 **Dependency** Missionaries treat indigenous peoples as children. Dependency increases as the missionaries often provide some real improvements in health care and nutrition.

3 **Breakdown** Persuasion, bribery and force are used to make indigenous customs seem worthless. Customary behaviour is outlawed and children are separated from their parents so that they can learn to be 'civilized'.

4 **Indoctrination** The narrow norms of the missionaries are foisted on the demoralized Indians. They are taught to respect the Church, work for money, obey the boss, live in small family units and wear Western clothes.

FOR YOUR FOLDERS

▶ Why do you think Fundamentalism is on the increase? Give reasons for your answers.

▶ Explain in your own words what some of the main beliefs of Fundamentalism are.

▶ What do you think might be the dangers of Fundamentalist belief? Why do you think people feel the need for Fundamentalist belief on a personal level?

▶ Explain the meaning of the word 'ethnocide'. How do some Fundamentalist groups work towards forcing their belief-systems onto others?

In Latin America a movement called 'Liberation Theology' has emerged. It consists of Christians who believe the Gospels demand that people stand up and fight against poverty, exploitation and lack of human rights, inspired by the words of Jesus:

> *'He has sent me to bring good news to the poor, to proclaim liberty to the captives and to set free the oppressed.'*
>
> *(Luke 4: 18)*

In the past the Catholic Church in South America has done little to alleviate injustice. Many priests today, however, identify themselves with the poor as Jesus did. In the words of one leading theologian, Gustavo Gutiérrez,

> *'The poverty of the poor is not a summons to alleviate their plight with acts of generosity but rather a compelling obligation to fashion an entirely different social order.'*

Anti-poll tax protesters confront the police

One man whose leadership inspired millions of people in El Salvador was the Archbishop Oscar Romero. The Government in El Salvador consistently violates human rights. It is controlled by a small and violent clique of wealthy families known as *los catorce* – the fourteen. Since civil war broke out in 1980 many thousands of civilians have disappeared or been murdered. Most of the people there live in desperate poverty and in order to keep power the Government crushes all opposition. Despite many threats against his life, Oscar Romero spoke out against the Government in his sermons. In 1980, while celebrating mass in his cathedral, he was gunned down by four masked men who worked for the Government. Troops outside opened fire murdering women and children. Romero's last words were,

> *'May Christ's sacrifice give us the courage to offer our own bodies for justice and peace.'*

Latin America is a continent rich in natural resources. The vast majority of its people, however,

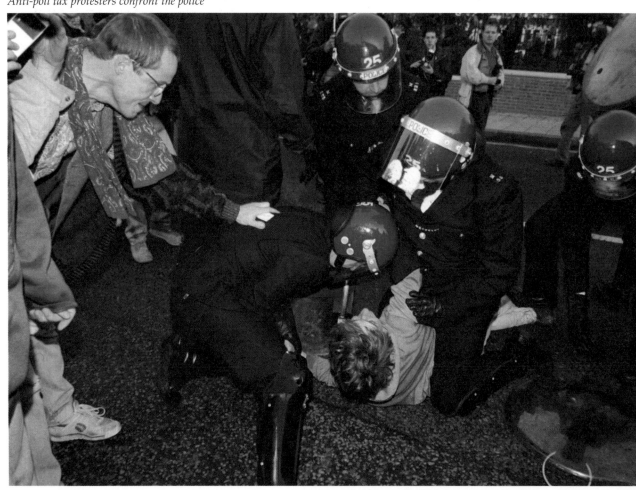

are trapped in poverty and squalor. Many of the countries, like El Salvador, are ruled by a wealthy and powerful elite. Millions of people suffer not only from poverty but also from the oppression of these governments. The few people at the top are determined to keep their power at all costs. Torture, assassination and 'death squads' are the harsh realities if anyone dares to oppose them. To many peasants living in Latin America the Roman Catholic Church is their only hope of creating a fairer, peaceful and more just system.

In 1968 a conference of bishops met in Medellin in Colombia. Concerned with the general situation in Latin America, they declared:

'In many places in Latin America there is a situation of injustice that must be recognized as institutionalized violence, because the existing structures violate people's basic rights; a situation which calls for far-reaching, daring and urgent action.'

The bishops recognized the temptation of resorting to revolutionary violence to change the system, and agreed that in some cases such action might be justified. But they also warned that such violence would not really improve things in the long term. They stressed the need for the people to be given 'liberation'. Many priests have courageously put their lives on the line by speaking out against their governments and some take an active part in movements which fight injustice and oppression.

TALKING POINTS

'People are always worried about the violence done with machine guns and machetes. But there is another kind of violence that you must be aware of too. To watch your children die of sickness and hunger while you can do nothing is a violence of the spirit. We have suffered silently for too many years.'

(El Salvadorean peasant)

'When I give food to the poor they call me a saint. When I ask why the poor have no food, they call me a communist.'

(Helder Camera)

'Revolution is necessary to free the hungry, give drink to the thirsty, clothe the naked and procure a life of well-being for the needy majority of our people. I believe that the revolutionary struggle is appropriate for the Christian and the priest. Only by revolution, by changing the concrete conditions of our country we can enable men to practise love for each other . . . The Catholic who is not a revolutionary is living in mortal sin.'

(Camilo Torres, Colombian priest who became a freedom fighter and died in 1966 at the hands of the Colombian Government.)

'In Central America a man of God can't turn his back on political struggle. At Mass we discussed the Gospels with the peasants and they began to understand the divine message: the coming of God's Kingdom which is the establishment on earth of a just society. At first we had preferred to make a non-violent revolution, but later came to understand that right now non-violent struggle is not possible.'

(Father Cardenal)

FOR YOUR FOLDERS

▶ Write a short article called 'Injustice in Latin America'.

▶ Explain in your own words what you understand by the phrase 'Liberation Theology'.

! ▶ 'Blessed are the peace-makers' *(Matthew 5: 9).* Do you think that in the light of this teaching by Jesus, Christians are still justified in resorting to revolutionary violence?

▶ 'Every person must submit to the supreme authorities.' *(Romans 13: 1).* How might some of the people quoted in this section respond to these words by St Paul?

DESMOND TUTU

In 1984 a black man, Desmond Mpilo Tutu, was awarded the Nobel Peace Prize. In September 1986 the same man became South Africa's first black archbishop. People from all over the world attended the ceremony and guests included Stevie Wonder, the Archbishop of Canterbury and Coretta King, wife of the late Dr Martin Luther King.

Born on 7 October 1931, Desmond Tutu became a priest at the age of 25. After working in Britain and in South Africa he became Bishop of Lesotho in 1976 and secretary of the South Africa Council of Churches (SACC) in 1978. The SACC represents some 13 million Christians in South Africa, mostly black. In the same year, the Dutch Reform Church which generally supports the Government's 'apartheid' system, withdrew from the Council.

During his ministry Archbishop Tutu has consistently spoken out against apartheid, believing it to be evil and totally unchristian. Even before he became Bishop of Johannesburg, he found himself increasingly in conflict with the authorities as he organized non-violent protests against apartheid. In 1976, for instance, he led a march through the slums of Soweto during the riots when more than 600 blacks were shot dead. In 1982 he saved the life of a black policeman by flinging himself across the man's body when a crowd tried to stone the man to death.

Archbishop Desmond Tutu in Cape Town

Archbishop Tutu believes that being a Christian means working for justice and equality in South Africa. For him the Bible is the 'most revolutionary book' ever written, demanding that people fight against injustice.

Some people argue that Christians should not become involved in politics. Archbishop Tutu, in a sermon called 'Divine Intervention' has argued otherwise:

> *'Christian worship can never let us be indifferent to the needs of others, to the cries of the hungry, of the naked and the homeless, of the sick and the prisoner, of the oppressed and the disadvantaged. Our Lord said, "As much as you have done this [i.e. fed the hungry, clothed the naked, visited the sick and the prisoners] to the least of my brethren, you have done it to me, and in as much as you have not done it to the least of these my brethren you have not done it to me. "'Matthew 25: 40 and 45]*
>
> *True Christian worship includes the love of God and the love of neighbour. The two must go together or your Christianity is false. St John asks, in his First Epistle, how you can say you love God who you have not*

seen if you hate your brother whom you have. Our love for God is tested and proved by our love for our neighbour.

*We are Christian not only in church on Sunday. Our Christianity is not something we put on, like our Sunday best, only for Sundays. It is for every day. We are Christians from Monday to Monday. We have no off day. We are Christians at play, at work and at prayer. They are all rolled into one. It is not **either** worship **or** trying to do all the good works in our community. It is both. The wise men came to the Child and worshipped. Then they gave him their gifts. We too must worship our God for ever and ever, and serve him by serving our neighbour today and always.'*

(Desmond Tutu, *Hope and Suffering*, 1984)

JESUS AND POLITICS

One of the most controversial issues in the Christian Church has been whether Christians should become directly involved in political action. Some Christians argue that Jesus' message is purely a 'spiritual' one, whilst other Christians argue that you cannot separate the 'spiritual' and the 'political'.

In the Gospels Jesus is portrayed as opting for a peaceful role, as can be seen in the Temptation (*Matthew chapter 4*) and his entry into Jerusalem on a donkey (a symbol of peace – *Mark 11: 1–10*). However, many events and sayings of Jesus point to the fact that he *was* concerned with improving peoples' lives. He was not afraid to challenge those in authority; he was on the side of the disadvantaged members of society; he tried to make people aware and concerned about each other's needs.

THE WORLD COUNCIL OF CHURCHES (WCC)

The Geneva-based WCC includes Christians of all traditions apart from Catholics and some Evangelical Churches. Its membership brings together Christians from many different backgrounds and its main concern is with making Christianity relevant in a modern world. Practical action includes funding emergency aid and long-term development programmes; research and study; conferences; dialogues with other faiths; and statements on some of the issues facing humankind today. It provides an essential platform for the churches of the world to talk and work together for a better future.

BLACK THEOLOGY

Over the last 30 years, particularly in the USA and South Africa, many black Christians have developed a new way of thinking about their faith. This is sometimes called 'Black Theology'.

'Black Theology arises in a context of black suffering at the hands of rampant white racism. It burns to awaken the white man to the degredation into which he has fallen by dehumanizing the black man and so is concerned with the liberation of the oppressor equally as with that of the oppressed. It tries to help people assert their humanity and to look the other chap in the eye and speak face to face without shuffling their feet and apologizing for their black existence.'

(Archbishop Desmond Tutu, *Hope and Suffering*, 1984)

FOR YOUR FOLDERS

▶ Write a short article about the life and work of Archbishop Desmond Tutu.

▶ Why does he believe that Christians have a duty to become involved in politics?

▶ Explain in your own words (a) the work of the World Council of Churches and (b) the ideas behind Black Theology.

▶ Using a Bible look up the following references: *Leviticus 19: 18*; *Amos 4:1–2*; *Isaiah 58: 9–10*; *Mark 12: 13–17*; *Luke 4: 18*; *Romans 13: 1*. Copy these quotes down. Write an essay on the arguments for and against a Christian being involved in politics using some of the quotes.

CAUSES FOR CONCERN

There are more than five billion people in the world today and the number could be double by the middle of the next century. The higher the population, the greater the strain on the environment; more people use more natural resources and produce more waste. It is not just the reality of life which should concern us. It is also the quality of life. As the countryside is choked by pollution, and disappears under concrete we are losing something of immense psychological value. Attractive and inspiring, the natural world is essential for human happiness.

Man is still dependent on the forces of nature, despite his knowledge of science

THE OCEANS

The seas and oceans cover more than 70% of our planet's surface. They provide homes for an incredible variety of wildlife, from seals and fish to seabirds, corals and turtles. There is even life in the permanently dark world of mountains, canyons, valleys and cliffs deep down on the ocean floor. But human activities underwater tend to be even more irresponsible than on the land. The sea is viewed by many people as nothing more than a huge dumping ground and pollution from oil spills, raw sewage and industrial waste is an ever-growing problem. Coral reef destruction, hunting, overfishing and coastal development are also taking their toll.

At the same time, efforts to care for marine life

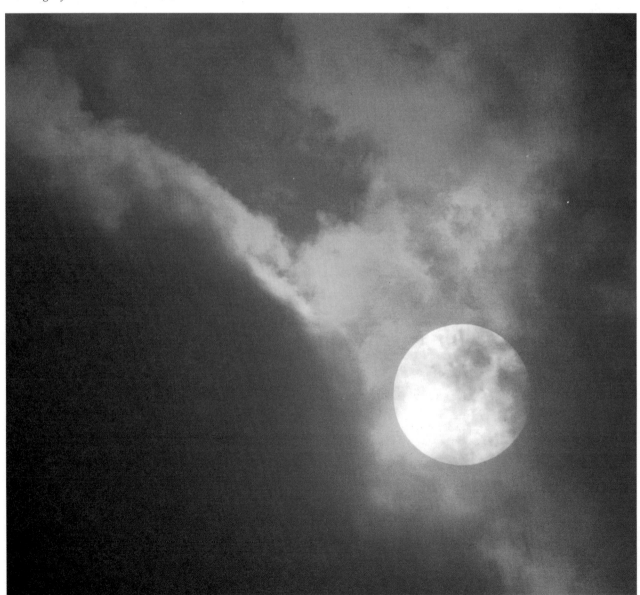

are complicated by the fact that seas and oceans belong to everyone. No single country has to take responsibility for their protection – or is accountable for their misuse.

LIFE ON EARTH

The world contains a staggering diversity of plants and animals. Centuries of study have so far revealed nearly one and a half million species. But although new ones are being found all the time we have discovered only a tiny proportion of all the living things with which we share the planet.

This kaleidoscope of unique species is known as biological diversity. it has been described as the 'Earth's life insurance' because it enables nature to fulfil different functions, and to meet different challenges, in a continually changing environment.

A rich biological diversity is important to our own survival. We rely, directly or indirectly, on the many different characteristics of plants and animals for our food, building materials, medicines and other necessities of life.

The fact that we know so little about which species we are plunging into extinction – and about their potential importance in our lives – makes it increasingly likely that we will eventually plunge all life on Earth into extinction.

TROPICAL RAIN FORESTS

Tropical forests cover only 7% of the Earth's surface, yet they contain more than half of the world's species. From the highest treetop to the darkest forest floor, they are alive with a teeming variety of animals and plants – jaguars, gorillas, tapirs, parrots, frogs, birdwing butterflies, orchids… But half the world's rainforests have been destroyed since the 1940s – cleared by commercial timber companies, farmers, ranchers and miners.

The forest cover that remains is roughly equal to the size of the United States. But the cutting, burning and bulldozing continues – an area half the size of California is being cleared or seriously degraded every year. This terrible destruction is already creating a spasm of extinction unequalled since the disappearance of the dinosaurs. We are losing species even before we have given them names. If current trends continue, most of the world's rainforests could be cleared completely within the next 50 years. The message is clear – drastic action needs to be taken immediately if they are to be saved.

OUR FUTURE

The universe was formed around 20,000 million years ago. If that were midnight on a 24 hour clock, our own planet would have been born around half past six the following evening. The earliest forms of life appeared at quarter past seven. On this timescale people have been around for no more than a few seconds – a mere blink in the history of the world.

The damage we have done in such a short space of time is so formidable that it strains our ability to believe; the world's rainforests reduced to fragmented patches; thousands of animals and plants plunged into extinction; hole in the ozone layer the size of the United States, and so on. We lull ourselves into a false sense of security by believing that, somehow, Nature will cope with the damage and cover up our mistakes. Yet the dangers of using natural resources wastefully and excessively, instead of carefully and sensibly, are obvious.

CHRISTIAN PERSPECTIVES

'The dignity of nature as creation needs to be bound up with our responsibility for the preservation of life.'

(World Council of Churches)

'You appointed him ruler over everything you made; you placed him over all creation.'

(Psalms 8: 6)

FOR YOUR FOLDERS

▶ Write an article entitled 'Planet in crisis – causes for concern'.

▶ Using the two quotes given, explain in your own words what the Christian response is to the crisis.

The average British household throws away about one tonne of rubbish a year, including around 132 kg of food. Nearly a third of this garbage is from packaging and the rest from bottles, cans and plastic containers.

If we walk along a seashore we will have to pick our way through all sorts of waste. Our streets are littered with polystyrene french-fry containers, parks with dog faeces, and our countryside with plastic fertilizer sacks and abandoned cars.

Pollution, however, is about more than individual behaviour. It breaks over us in great waves. Take acid rain. Half of West Germany's trees are dying from acid rain. Take nuclear power. The 'accidental' dumping of half a tonne of uranium in the Irish Sea helps ensure those waters are the most radioactive in the world. Cancer rates around the Sellafield/Windscale nuclear power station are six times the national average for children. So waste is not just a messy habit of individuals. It is a by-product of industrial growth. We are overburdening the planet with our rubbish the effluence of our affluence.

Little or no accounting is done, for instance, on the damage to clean air or water. If we argue that pollution means profits, then it follows that industry's worst offenders should be the biggest and wealthiest. And this is the case. Petro-chemical, car and electronic companies predominate. They are the most profitable precisely because they are getting something for nothing: use of never to be repeated finite resources, like oil and natural gas. Created millions of years ago, these fossil fuels are being fast used up. Nothing is put in their place. And a by-product of their use is waste.

The 400 million cars in the world today are the cause of the choking smog that covers so many of our cities (see Section 00). Their emissions contain lead and cause the build up of carbon dioxide (CO_2) in the atmosphere. At present rates of emission, CO_2 concentrations will have doubled in 60 years. This could trigger the destruction of the ozone layer which shields the Earth from the harmful effects of the Sun's ultra-violet rays. If this happens it could cause a 'hot house' effect, increasing temperatures by two or three degrees, enough to melt the Arctic and the Antarctic ice caps, raising sea levels and flooding all low-lying areas.

The industrial, capitalist world encourages us to consume more and more. We can see the effects of this if we pick up a current affairs magazine. Half the pages are concerned with violent crime, economic disaster and war; the other half shows carefree people behind packets of cigarettes, bottles of alcohol and shining new cars. Glossy advertising encourages greed and produces envy in a world where the consequences of such selfishness are all too obvious. Societies which produce satellite nuclear technology to make death rays in space when one billion people live in absolute poverty is irrational. A society which supports huge industries for petfoods or cosmetics while claiming it cannot afford to build hospitals or schools clearly needs to look at its values and morality.

FOULING THE NEST

NUCLEAR WASTE

After 30 years of trying nobody has yet come up with a way of safely disposing of nuclear waste. Plutonium from a nuclear reactor is still lethal after 240,000 years. Nuclear waste has polluted the seas to a terrifying degree. It contaminates the fish we eat and the water we swim in. Buried underground, no-one is certain that nuclear waste won't eventually seep into water reserves and so contaminate the water we drink and the food we eat.

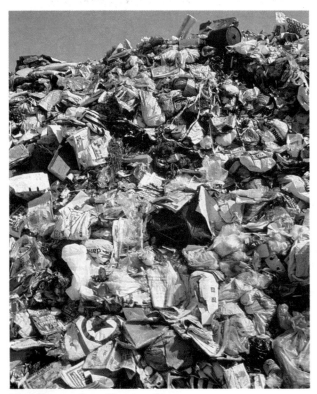

The effluence of an affluent society

ACID RAIN

The pollutant gases of industry pour into the Earth's atmosphere and dissolve in rain. They come down again as sulphuric and nitric acid, eat into trees and deaden our lakes.

PESTICIDES

According to the World Health Organization, every year half a million people are poisoned by pesticides. Killers like DDT can easi¹y enter the food chain. Pesticides are an $8 billion business in the USA and some of the most deadly are exported to the Third World.

HAZARDOUS WASTES

Developed countries manufacture over 70,000 chemicals every year, many untested. The USA alone produces some 250 million tonnes of toxic industrial waste – one tonne per person per year. The waste is not easy to get rid of. To overcome this problem some companies ship their waste to the Third World for disposal.

WHAT IS THE SOLUTION?

Obviously we cannot continue in this way for ever. The world is a delicate organism, and we are in the process of destroying it. On a personal level we can use bottle banks, recycled paper, 'environmentally friendly' products. We can try to save energy and reduce our use of cars. If the world is to be saved, however, we need to do more than this. We need to put pressure on companies and governments to become more responsible. At the moment profit, not environmental health, dictates the way that governments and huge multinational companies behave. This must change.

TALKING POINTS

'It is tragic that our technological mastery is greater than our wisdom about ourselves.'

(Pope John Paul II)

'The love of money is the root of all evil.'

(1 Timothy 6: 10)

'Continue to contaminate your bed, and you will one night suffocate in your own waste.'

(Chief Seattle, 1855)

FOR YOUR FOLDERS

▶ Design a poster on the theme, 'Our Throwaway World'.

▶ What are the main causes of pollution?

! ▶ 'We will either have to begin to accept a new lifestyle or perish.' What do you think this means? Would you be prepared to change your lifestyle?

▶ Why might Christians quote *1 Timothy 6: 10* in exploring the root causes of pollution?

▶ Explain what you think Pope John Paul II means in the Talking Point.

Planet Earth is in a state of crisis. We are at a crossroads. The next few years will be crucial. We will either succeed in saving the planet by changing our attitudes to life, or we will destroy it . . . and ourselves.

THE CHRISTIAN CHURCH HAS NOT BEEN BLAMELESS

In principle, the Christian religion has taught that God created the earth and that human beings are the responsible 'stewards', or managers, of creation. Human beings should work wisely to protect what has been given to them, to work with nature and not against it. However, people have, and still do, exploit nature for greedy economic gain. Today enormous multinational companies make vast sums of money by exploiting the Earth's natural resources and show little concern for the environmental damage that they themselves cause.

Many people feel that some of the ideas in the Christian religion have been deliberately abused by man in the pursuit of wealth and power. They argue that our present environmental crisis has a lot to do with Christian arrogance. In particular, they point to the idea that nature only exists to serve humanity, and that humanity, as recorded in the *Genesis* account of creation, has some sort of divine right to exploit nature. The Church has done very little to counter this destructive idea. It has done little, either, to warn of the risks to the environment; to lead by example and show that a simpler lifestyle is more in line with Jesus' teachings; or to speak up and challenge the lifestyles of our consumer-ridden, wasteful and unaware society.

THOUGHTS FOR OUR FUTURE

'We are faced with the need to make real present sacrifices in order to serve a future in which we may not even be alive. Not one person in 10,000 is capable of such self-denial . . . our own immediate welfare is bound up with the entire life of the Earth and its future.'

(J. G. Bennett)

'Remember the face of the Earth is similar to that of a human being. Don't forget that you are but a traveller on this planet and nothing belongs to you.'

(Ivan Lackovic Croata, Yugoslav painter)

The planet earth from the moon

'The most important step we can take is to tell our leaders that if they don't protect the environment, they won't get elected.'

(Robert Redford, American actor)

'When we look into the sky it seems to us to be endless . . . We think without consideration about the boundless ocean of air, and then you sit aboard a spacecraft, you tear away from Earth, and within ten minutes you have been carried straight through the layer of air, and beyond there is nothing! Beyond the air there is only emptiness, coldness, darkness. The "boundless" blue sky, the ocean which gives us breath and protects us from the endless black and death, is but an infinitesimally thin film. How dangerous it is to threaten even the smallest part of this gossamer covering, this conserver of life.'

(Vladimir Shatalov, Russian space explorer)

'We all moan and groan about the loss of the quality of life through the destruction of our ecology, and yet each one of us, in our own little comfortable ways, contributes daily to that destruction. It's time now to awaken in each of us the respect and attention our beloved mother deserves.'

(Ed Asner, American actor)

'If the Earth were only a few feet in diameter, floating a few feet above a field somewhere, people would come from everywhere to marvel at it. People would walk around it marvelling at its big pools of water, its little pools and the water flowing between. People would marvel at the bumps on it and the holes in it. They would marvel at the very thin layer of gas surrounding it and the water suspended in the gas. The people would marvel at all the creatures walking around the surface of the ball and at the creatures in the water. The people would declare it as sacred because it was the only one, and they would protect it so that it would not be hurt. The ball would be the greatest wonder known, and people would come to pray to it, to be healed, to gain knowledge, to know beauty and to wonder how

it could be. People would love it and defend it with their lives because they would somehow know that their lives could be nothing without it. If the Earth were only a few feet in diameter.'

(Joe Miller, an artist living in the State of Washington, USA)

'Hello, hello, do you know that you and I, each and every one of us, are members of the crew on the spaceship "Earth". It depends on no one else but us, it depends on every one of us that the planet "Earth" keeps turning, that the water stays pure, that the air gets cleaner so that the human flower may continue to blossom once we have turned the page of this century. We have just a few years to the year 2000 to roll up our sleeves and clean up our house to welcome the 21st century. On the ninth day of the ninth month of the year 1999 the world will be in the cradle or the grave. If all the televisions and all the radios of the world were ready to make the effort, with all the satellites that spin and relay the pictures and the voices, the Earth could become in the space of three months an earthly paradise.'

(Julos Beaucarne, Belgian singer and songwriter)

(All quotes taken from *Save the Planet* by Jonathan Porritt, © Dorling Kindersley 1991)

FOR YOUR FOLDERS

▶ Write a paragraph on the following:
- 'Earth – a unique haven for life'
- The Gaia Hypothesis

FOR DISCUSSION

▶ 'Life on earth is not the product of chance.'

▶ 'In the beginning God created the heavens and the earth.'

(Genesis 1: 1)

WHO ARE THE FIRST PEOPLES?

The first peoples were the original inhabitants of their lands which have since been colonized by foreigners. They are sometimes called 'indigenous', a term widely accepted by the peoples themselves and now adopted by the United Nations. The names indigenous people give themselves, e.g. Inuit, Maori, generally mean simply 'people' and the names they give their territories often can be translated as 'our land'. There are 250 million indigenous peoples worldwide – 4% of the global population – living in over 70 countries.

For first peoples the land is the source of life. The land is a gift from the Creator that nourishes, supports and teaches. Although these peoples vary widely in their customs and cultures, all consider the Earth like a parent and revere it accordingly. 'Mother Earth' is the centre of the universe, the core of their culture, the origin of their identity as people. They do not consider one creature superior to another but believe that all things are connected.

The first peoples have an understanding of nature. Wisdom is passed down orally from generation to generation. The people understand the spiritual power of the plants around them as well as their physical properties. The monuments of their civilizations are not found in cities or temples but in the natural environment itself.

Aborigines were the first people of Australia

'Now your way of life is no longer working, and so you are interested in our way. But if we tell you our way, then it will be polluted, we will have no medicine and we will be destroyed as well as you.'

(Buffalo Tiger, Miccasukee Indian)

Indigenous people, in recognizing their need for animals, whether it be for food, transport, clothing or shelter, develop a deep respect for living creatures. Seen as equals, animals and their animal spirits become part of their everyday lives.

'When we Indians kill meat we eat it all up . . . When we build houses we make little holes. When we burn grass for grasshoppers, we don't ruin things. We shake down acorns and pinenuts. We don't chop down the trees.'

(Wintu Indian, California)

Because many of these peoples live in small communities their social relationships depend on mutual support, cooperation and harmony. In many cultures men and women are treated equally. All decisions are arrived at by debate and discussion. The nuclear family is a rare concept. Most individuals in these communities are related to each other – a tradition that fosters a sense of belonging to

The family plays a vital supportive role

the group. Each of the stages of life are marked by rituals and each individual has a clear set of roles. The elderly are traditionally respected as 'elders' and the ill are cared for by the community. No one person is thought of as more important than another; all people are seen as being part of a greater whole.

We are conditioned in the West to believe that human beings are innately aggressive and often, in the past, we accepted the 'savage' stereotype of so-called 'primitive' peoples. These stereotypes were very useful for colonizers and were used to reinforce the economic exploitation of indigenous peoples all over the globe.

> '*Was it an awful war?*'
> '*It was a terrible war.*'
> '*Were many people killed?*'
> '*One man was killed.*'
> '*What did you do?*'
> '*We decided that those of us who had done the killing should never meet again because we were not fit to meet one another.*'
>
> (A member of the African San tribe, describing a war to Laurens van der Post)

The first peoples see existence as a living blend of spirits, nature and people. The word for 'religion' does not exist in many cultures, as spiritual beliefs and customs are so closely integrated into life itself. The way that early Christian missionaries tried to change these ancient belief systems is tragic. Great knowledge, passed from generation to generation for thousands of years, which had enabled people to live in harmony with nature was destroyed by the white man's vision of truth. It continues today (see Section 84).

TALKING POINT

> 'Indigenous knowledge is important, extremely important to humanity . . . It's an alternative model, which we can in fact learn from and must learn from if we're going to stop this senseless destruction of the Amazon.'
>
> (Darrell Posey, ethnobotanist)

FOR YOUR FOLDERS

▶ Who are the first peoples?

▶ Explain in your own words their attitudes to the land and to animals.

▶ What do you think they can teach us about social relationships, the old and warfare?

❗▶ Why do you think the introduction of Christianity had such a devastating effect on the cultures of the first peoples?

WHAT IS THE FOURTH WORLD?

The Fourth World is the name given to indigenous peoples descended from a country's original population and who today are completely or partly deprived of the right to their own territory and its land. Nothing has been so destructive to indigenous people as what we call 'progress'. Mines, dams, roads, colonization schemes, plantations, cattle ranches and other expressions of 'economic development' have forced indigenous peoples from lands they have occupied for centuries. Moreover this 'progress' has severely damaged the environment.

EUROPEAN COLONIALISM

European colonialism has been one of the most destructive processes in human history. 1492, the year Colombus arrived in the Americas, marked the beginning of a tragic adventure. Within 400 years continuous expansion had pushed most of the world's original peoples off their lands and decimated their numbers. In South America the number of indigenous people fell from 30 million to 5 million in just 50 years. At least 10 million Africans were shipped as slaves to the Americas.

The Europeans came bearing their civilization as if it were a gift. Yet, to the people they termed 'savage', whose well ordered societies and rich cultures stretched back thousands of years, the gift was lethal. Contact with Europeans brought not only murder, theft and enslavement but disease and the destruction of their ways of life.

The colonizers came with a sword in one hand and a Bible in the other. A Spanish soldier said: 'We come to bring light to those in darkness and also to get rich'. The Europeans took no account of the highly developed spiritual awareness of the people. They sought to convert them to their own misguided understandings of truth, to an alien religion – often on pain of death.

> 'In the long hundred years since the white man came, I have seen my freedom disappear like the salmon going mysteriously out to sea. The white man's strange customs which I could not understand pressed down on me until I could no longer breathe. And when I fought to protect my land and home, I was called a "savage". When I neither understood nor welcomed the white man's way of life I was called "lazy". When I tried to lead my people I was stripped of my authority.'
>
> (Chief Dan George, Vancouver)

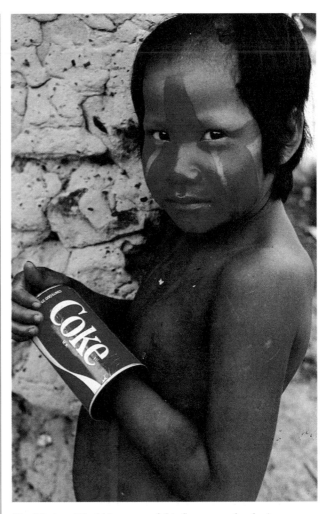

The Western World is a powerful influence on developing countries.

DEFORESTATION

This colonialism, which has been going on for 400 years, continues today with ever increasing tragic results.

The rainforests are home and source of life to 50 million indigenous people. Destruction of the forests alienates forest people from themselves and each other. The outsiders who do it also bring disease, conflict, displacement and death. The most vulnerable people are those who have previously had little contact with the outside world. For example, measles and whooping cough brought in by workers have wiped out more than 30% of the population among some groups of Venezuelan Yanomami. Between 1900 and 1970 one Amazonian tribe, on average, became extinct each year.

It is a sad fact that because of the profitable US market for beefburgers, millions upon millions of trees in South America are being cut down to make way for cattle ranches. By the year 2000, unless the rich world sees sense, virtually all primary forest in Guatemala, India, the Philippines, Malaysia and Thailand will have gone and about 8 million indigenous people will have lost their forest homes.

The desire for timber, land, oil and cattle ranches, and the damming of huge areas to provide electricity for cities, continue to destroy the living space of the first peoples. Mining is perhaps the greatest threat to their continued existence. It pollutes vital water supplies; it imposes an economy that doesn't work and alien social values; it destroys sacred sites, disfigures familiar landscapes, and separates people from their homes, their past and each other.

'We are on the one hand the most oppressed people on the globe. On the other hand, we are the hope for the future of people on the planet. The peoples that surround us now are beginning to experience in the 20th century . . . limitations to the kind of economic organizations that define their societies.'
(John Mohawk)

TALKING POINTS

'When a person dies we bury the body in the land and it turns into earth. So we can't leave our land; it would be like leaving our dead, our bodies. Because the earth is our mother. The liver of the earth is coal; the lung is uranium. Earthquakes and tornados are her breath. Now she is in pain. When the government takes her organs she dies. The government only wants money it doesn't think of her children.'
(Navajo woman)

'We need to start educating the West . . . teaching them some social alternatives which place priority on humankind — not profits, not political power, not bombs, but on humanity.'
(John Mohawk)

'We are global citizens with tribal souls.'
(Piep Hein, Danish poet)

FOR YOUR FOLDERS

▶ What is the Fourth World?

▶ Why is progress often so destructive?

▶ Why did 1492 mark the beginning of 'a tragic adventure'?

! ▶ How do you think racist attitudes have enabled European culture to dominate the world?

▶ Why is the Earth, according to the Navajo Indian, 'in pain'?

▶ We like to think that we are civilized. After reading this section and Section 90 write an article entitled 'The Savages from the West'.

▶ The Christian Church has played its part in the destruction of the first peoples. How can it redeem itself today and work towards helping those people who are struggling for survival?

SURVIVAL INTERNATIONAL

Survival International is a worldwide movement to support tribal peoples. It stands for their right to decide their own future and helps them protect their lands, environment and way of life. The principles behind their action are outlined below.

'We all know what the outside world is trying to do to tribal peoples. Having exhausted its own resources the so-called 'developed' world is now running over the globe tearing the minerals, oil and wood from areas which were once remote and thought to be useless, or governments are pushing poor people to colonize these places to avoid fair land distribution elsewhere. They are carting the poor off to areas the rich do not want. And more often than not these are the lands of the world's remaining 200 million tribal people . . . Put a mine on an Australian sacred site and you put a knife straight into the heart of an Aboriginal people's heritage.

Tribal peoples are the victims of our greed for resources, coupled with a deep and extraordinary racism which says that they are backward and primitive and must catch up with the 20th Century or perish. How short sighted this is. Apart from our own technological strength, which in any case may be short lived, there is clearly nothing superior about our own way of life.

Survival's work deliberately maintains a specific focus: the campaign for land. We stress continually that tribal peoples have rights to the lands they live on and use. it is their land.'

(Survival International)

MILITARIZATION

'The scientists, generals and leaders – recognized, paid, honored and treated as learned and knowledgeable men in this society, though obviously not necessarily wise men – are playing little boys' games with our lives and the lives of unborn generations of human, plant and animal life. These big boys are members of a special club based on power.

They think in terms of moves and counter moves, attack and retreat, winning and losing.'

(Marie-Helen Laraque)

A Chinese army convoy enters Tibet

Monks of Tibet offer light to Buddha

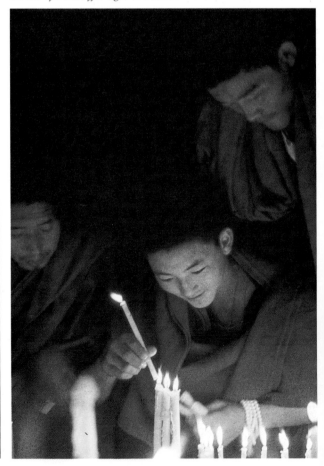

Today the rich nations see the indigenous peoples' homelands as 'empty territory', i.e. testing grounds for nuclear and chemical weapons, bases for military installations, or a source of uranium, the raw material for nuclear weapons.

Since 1963 the USA has exploded over 650 nuclear weapons in the Nevada Desert, the home of the Shoshone Indians. Early warning systems, prime targets in case of war, are situated on Inuit lands in the Arctic. Cruise missiles are tested on the traditional hunting grounds of the Cree Indians.

Russia has established military bases on indigenous land in eastern Siberia and the Soviet far-east.The Chinese have invaded Tibet and destroyed its ancient culture. They now keep one quarter of China's nuclear force in this once peace-loving nation. They have destroyed nearly all the 6,000 monasteries and holy shrines, and thousands of Tibetans (including the Dalai Lama, Tibet's political and spiritual leader) have fled to India.

The human cost is immense. Almost all nuclear tests have taken place on indigenous lands and waters. The radiation released during these tests damages the environment, contaminates the peoples' staple foods, and increases the risk of birth defects, miscarriages, sterility, cancer and other diseases. After the atomic explosions on the Polynesian island of Bikini in the 1950s, 70 out of 1093 people died of cancer within three years. Britain and France have exploded over 215 nuclear bombs in the South Pacific.

MISSIONARY ZEAL

Over the past 400 years the Christian Church has sent out missionaries to the Fourth World to convert the people to Christianity. This missionary zeal continues today (see Section 84).

It raises many questions about the whole idea of 'conversion', the arrogant assumption that one religion is superior to another. There can be no justification, for example, for the activities of the New Tribes Mission (NTM), based in Florida. This organisation believes that the way of life of indigenous people is worthless, that they are merely heathens, awaiting conversion to the missionaries' god.

FOR YOUR FOLDERS

▶ Explain in your own words the principles that guide the work of Survival International.

▶ With examples illustrate how the USA, China and Russia use so-called 'empty territory' for military purposes. What are the consequences of this?

▶ How do you think a Christian or a Humanist should respond to such militarization?

▶ Write a paragraph about the two photographs taken in Tibet. How do they illustrate the contrast between peaceful living and modern militarization?

TALKING POINT

'The mere continuance of nuclear tests, undertaken with war in mind, will have fatal consequences for life on earth.'

(*Pacem in Terris*, Roman Catholic statement, 1965)

THINGS TO DO

Write to Survival International Ltd (see Addresses). Send on s.a.e. and ask for information about their work.

OUR EXTERNAL WORLD

The 1990s have become the decade of decision. There is no hiding place. The age of communication is making us all aware of the enormous problems that face the human race. We live in what has been called 'the global village'. We are beginning to realize that much of what we do in Britain affects the welfare of millions of people living thousands of miles away. We all belong to **one world**.

Humankind is the only species that has been able to leave its planet and study it from the outside. We have acquired great power. We have increased violence, but have also raised hope of organization, order and interdependence in global society. We have acquired the power of life and death for our planet and most of its inhabitants.

Slowly we are becoming aware of what we have done. The time is right not to sink into the pit of hopelessness and despair but rather to make the decision to do something. We must work for our own survival and the survival of other living things.

Never before have you, the young generation, had so much access to information. It is up to you to use this information in a positive way. This book has tried to make you think about many issues that face you on a personal, a social and a global level. All things are connected.

We can no longer afford to think of progress as being simply a matter of creating further wealth. That road, as we are learning, leads to pollution and over-exploitation of the Earth's resources. The worst problems are to be found in developing countries with rapidly rising populations, dismal standards of health care and minimal education. But all too often it is the rush for quick profits in the industrialized North which lies behind their problems. We, the wealthy countries of the world, are the biggest consumers of energy, minerals and food. We are also the biggest polluters. It is our wasteful way of living that produces most of the gases which threaten the ozone layer, the climate and humanity's chances of surviving in a healthy world.

We are the lucky ones. As well as living in relative comfort we have the ability and **the power** to change things. Here are a few ideas:

1   Support some of the organizations listed in the Address section. Remember, always send a stamped, addressed envelope.

2   Join a local group.

3   Air your views by writing to your elected representatives (councillors and MPs) and newspapers.

4   Encourage your school to link with a Third World community.

5   Buy recycled paper products.

6   Start recycling glass bottles, aluminium drinks cans and paper.

7   Re-use your plastic bags.

8   Use pump sprays or CFC-free aerosols.

Sting meets an Amazonian chieftain.

9 Try to eat organic fruit and vegetables to reduce the use of pesticides.

10 Encourage your parents to cycle, use low phosphate detergents and have the car converted to lead-free petrol.

OUR INNER WORLD

Thomas Merton, one of the greatest Christian thinkers of the 20th century, said:

'He who attempts to act and do things for others without deepening his own self understanding will not have anything to give others.'

In this book you will have been exposed to many different issues. If you didn't know it before, you'll certainly know it now — we all face many enormous challenges.

It has been said that we can't really change the world until we learn how to change ourselves. What does this mean? Well, what happens in the outer, visible external world is caused by what's going on in our inner, invisible, internal worlds. A war may break out in the external world but if we look honestly into our *internal* world we will find that *we* are often at war. We have nasty thoughts about other people. Sometimes we even wish others dead. We have violent thoughts. We sometimes tell lies. We are sometimes intolerant. We even hate other people.

Now we might want to change these things in ourselves, but it's not that easy. We are not always able to control our thoughts, or our feelings. They come flooding in.

Thoughts and feelings take us over. During the course of a day we may experience amazingly different emotions — hatred and love; happiness and despair; contentment and frustration; embarrassment and confidence; peace and violence. We are like little corks, tossed about by the sea of life. What happens in the external world deeply affects our internal world. However, it is in this internal world that the important things that really matter to us exist.

These things are true of all human beings. Have you ever thought about murder? We live in an enormous universe and a potentially beautiful world. Yet every few minutes in this world, somebody, somewhere gets so caught up in his own personal anger and violence that he takes somebody else's life away. This is known as being in a *state of sleep*. If he was a little more awake he would see that his victim was once a child; his victim had people who loved him; his victim once had the gift of life

and had a right to be here. What a terrible thing violence is, yet it is something that we all have inside us!

So, if we are going to try to make the world a better place, what can we do?

We can begin with ourselves. We can begin by trying to find peace within ourselves. It is only when we search for an inner peace that we can begin to understand our inner world, and our relationship to the outer world.

Your life is a journey. It is an adventure, both in the external world and in your internal world. If you can begin to grasp the idea that you are here to learn, not only about the external world, but also about what is going on inside you (your internal world), then your life will begin to have *meaning*.

PEACE MEDITATION

Close your eyes and sit comfortably. Concentrate on the sensation of your breath as it passes in and out of your nostrils. Imagine that the air is light — very pure and healing, like a miracle medicine. As you breathe in, visualize the light entering your body through your nostrils. Imagine it gradually filling your body, from your toes upwards, to the top of your head. As you breathe out, visualize the tension and pain leaving your body through your nostrils, in the form of smoke, which disappears into the depths of the earth. Eventually, you can imagine that the light is pouring out of every opening and pore of your body, as if you are radiating light. Enjoy the feeling of being calm, peaceful and relaxed.

THINKING POINT

'Peace is a state in which the whole being is filled with an uncritical tolerance, so that whatever one sees it does not strike inwardly unpleasantly, even when it previously did, so that there goes with this state a surprising freedom, as if escaping from prison.'

(Dr Maurice Nicholl, *The Mark*)

SOME IMPORTANT ADDRESSES

Action by Christians Against Torture
32 Wentworth Hills
Wembley, Middlesex HA9 9SG

Amnesty International (British Section)
99–119 Rosebery Avenue
London EC1R 4RE

Animal Aid
7 Castle Street
Tonbridge, Kent TN9 1BH

Anti-Apartheid Movement
13 Mandela Street
London NW1 0DW

British Humanist Association
14 Lambs Conduit Passage
London WC1R 4RH

Campaign Against the Arms Trade
(CAAT)
11 Goodwin Street
London N4 3HO

Campaign Against Pornography
Wesley House, 4 Wild Court
London WC2B 5AU

Campaign for Homosexual Equality
PO BOX 342
London WX1X 0DU

Campaign for Nuclear Disarmament
(CND)
162 Holloway Road
London N7 8DQ

Catholic Agency for Overseas Development (CAFOD)
21a Soho Square
London W1V 6NR

Catholic Truth Society
38/40 Eccleston Square
London SW1Y 1PD

Central American Information Service
1 Amwell Street
London EC1R 1UL

Christian Aid
35 Lower Marsh
London SE1 7RT

Church of England Board of Social Responsibility
Church House
Dean's Yard
London SW1P 2NZ (*Information for teaching staff only.*)

Church of England Children's Society
Old Town Hall
Kennington Road
London SE11

Commission for Racial Equality
10/12 Allington House
London SW1E 5EH

El Salvador Committee for Human Rights
83 Margaret Street
London W1N 7HB

EXIT (Voluntary Euthanasia Society)
13 Prince of Wales Terrace
London W8 5PG

Friends of the Earth (FOE)
26–28 Underwood Street
London N1 7JQ

Gay Christian Movement
BM 6914
London WC1N 3XX

Gingerbread Association for One Parent Families
35 Wellington Street
London WC2 7BN

Greenpeace
30–31 Islington Green
London N1 8XE

Health Education Authority
Hamilton House, Mabledon Place
London WC1H 9TX

Help the Aged
St James Walk
London EC1R 0BE

Information on Ireland
PO Box 189
Ivor Place
London

Institute for the Study of Drug Dependency
(ISDD)
1/4 Hatton Place
Hatton Gardens
London EC1N 8ND

LIFE Organization
Life House, Newbold Terrace
Royal Leamington Spa CV32 4EA

Martin Luther King Memorial Trust
1/3 Hildreth Street
London SW12 9RQ

Minority Rights Group
29 Craven Street
London WC2N 5NT

National Abortion Campaign
70 Great Queen Street
London WC2

New Internationalist
42 Hythe Bridge Street
Oxford OX1 2EP

Nicaraguan Solidarity Campaign
23 Beverden Street
London N1 6BH

Oxfam
274 Banbury Road
Oxford OX2 7D2

Pax Christi
St Francis of Assisi Centre
Pottery Lane
London W11 4NQ

Peace Pledge Union
Dick Sheppard House
6 Endsleigh Street
London WC1H 0DX

Quakers (The Religious Society of Friends)
Friends House

Euston Road
London NW1 2BJ

Radical Alternatives to Prison
BMC Box 4842
London WC1N 3XX

Refugee Council
3 Bond Way
London SW8 1SJ

Relate
76a New Cavendish Street
London W1M 7LB

Royal Association for Disability and Rehabilitation
25 Mortimer Street
London W1N 8AD

Samaritans
17 Uxbridge Road
Slough SL1 1SN

Save the Children Fund
17 Grove Lane
London SE5 8RD

SHELTER
157 Waterloo Road
London SE1 8XF

Survival International Ltd
310 Edgware Road
London W2 1DY

Tear Fund
11 Station Road
Teddington
Middlesex TW11 9AA

Terence Higgins Trust
52–54 Grays Inn Road
London W1X 8JU

Tibet Support Group
43 New Oxford Street
London WC1A 1BH

United Nations Association
3 Whitehall Court
London SW1A 2EL

World Development Movement
Beford Chambers
Covent Garden
London WC2

Worldwide Fund for Nature
11/13 Ockford Road
Godalming
Surrey GU7 1QU

As many of the organizations rely on donations to survive it is very important that you:

1 State clearly what information you require and why you require it;

2 Always enclose an SAE.

For local organizations use your telephone directory or reference library. It may be helpful for your class to write *one* letter to an organization to cut down on the administrative work required by them.

SUBJECT INDEX

NAME INDEX

Adams, Gerry   149
Age Concern   15, 87
Amnesty International   15, 112
Animal Liberation League   142, 143
Anti-Apartheid Movement   174, 175
Aquinas, Thomas 146
Arthur, Chris   83, 85

Bach, Richard   9
Bentham, Jeremy   20
Brandt, Willy   156
Buddha, The   14
Buffalo Tiger   182

Camera, Helder   173
Campaign Against Pornography (CAP)   40, 41, 102, 103
Campaign Against the Arms Trade (CAAT)   163
Campaign for Nuclear Disarmament (CND)   15
Catholic Housing Aid Society   67
Chief Seattle   125, 157, 178
Children's Society   67
Christian Aid   67
Churchill, Winston   151
Coleridge, Samuel Taylor   86
Conservation Society   15
Cuellar, Javier Perez de   145

Dala Lama   187
De Beauvoir, Simone   89
Dominion, Jack   36, 37
Donne, John   30
Dylan, Bob   10

Einstein, Albert   10, 147, 153
Epicurus   20
EXIT   47, 48, 64

Feild, Reshad   7
Fletcher, Joseph   20
Friends of the Earth   15
Fowles, John   7

Galeano, Eduardo   159
Gandhi, Mahatma   145, 154
Geldof, Bob   158
Gibran, Kahlil   33, 55
Gutiérrez, Gustavo   172

Help the Aged   87
Hemming, James   27, 39, 57
Horace   65
Hospice Movement   96
Howard League for Penal Reform   115, 151
Humanist Housing Association 15

Independent Adoption Agency   15

Jesus   10, 14, 16, 25, 27, 30, 34, 39, 50, 54, 56, 64, 79, 85, 96, 104, 122, 123, 155, 157, 160, 172, 173, 174, 175, 178, 189

Kennedy, J F   9
Kierkegaard, Soren   104
King, John   28, 29
King, Martin Luther   67, 74, 75, 79, 153, 154, 169

Koestler, Arthur   112, 153
Kolbe, Maximilian   78, 79

L'Arche Community   91
Laraque, Marie Helen   186
Laurens Van der Post   183
Leech, Daniel   91, 92
LIFE Organisation   99, 101
Luther, Martin   104

Maitland, Sara   105
Mill, John Stuart   20
Mountbatten, Earl   151, 153
Muggeridge, Malcolm   83

National Abortion Campaign   98, 101
National Council for Civil Liberties   15
National Society for Prevention of Cruelty to Children   126, 127
Navajo, The   185
Nicholl, Dr Maurice   9

Oxfam   164, 165

Papanek, Victor   85
Phaedrus   30
Picasso   86
Pilger, John   71
Plato   27
Pope John Paul II   54, 141, 145, 153, 179
Porritt, Jonathan   83

Russell, Betrand   8

St Augustine   9
St Jerome   104
Salvation Army   67
Samaritans   31
Sappho   24
Shelter   15, 119
Short, Clare   41, 103
Sting   134, 135, 188
Survival International   186, 187

Temple, William   120
Terrence Higgins Trust 45
Tertullian   104
Tibetans   186, 187
Tom and Jerry   25
Torres, Camilo   173
Trotsky, Leon   86
Tutu, Desmond   143, 159, 174, 175

United Nations   130, 131, 132, 145

Van Gogh, Vincent   10
Vanier, Jean   91
Voltaire   10, 65

World Council of Churches   42, 43, 69, 133, 175, 177
World Development Campaign   15
World Health Organization   44, 131

Yanomami Indians   184